NEW POETS
OF ENGLAND
AND AMERICA

SECOND SELECTION

NEW POETS
OF ENGLAND
AND AMERICA

SECOND SELECTION

ENGLISH POETS EDITED BY Donald Hall

AMERICAN POETS EDITED BY Robert Pack

A MERIDIAN BOOK

NEW AMERICAN LIBRARY

TIMES MIRROR

MERIDIAN TRADEMARK REG. U.S. PAT. OFF. AND FOREIGN COUNTRIES
REGISTERED TRADEMARK—MARCA REGISTRADA
HECHO EN CHICAGO, U.S.A.

SIGNET, SIGNET CLASSICS, MENTOR, PLUME and MERIDIAN BOOKS
*are published by The New American Library, Inc.,
1301 Avenue of the Americas, New York, New York 10019*

FIRST PRINTING, 1962

9 10 11 12 13 14 15 16 17

PRINTED IN THE UNITED STATES OF AMERICA

ACKNOWLEDGMENTS

AMIS, KINGSLEY: "Autobiographical Fragment," from *A Case of Samples,* copyright 1956 by Kingsley Amis, reprinted by permission of the author and Harcourt, Brace & World, Inc. Published in Great Britain by Victor Gollancz, Ltd. "Sight Unseen," "Terrible Beauty," and "Science Fiction" (all three first published in *Encounter*), "A Tribute to the Founder" (first published in *The Spectator*), "On a Portrait of Mme. Rimsky-Korsakov" (first published in *The Observer*), and "After Goliath" (first published by The Marvell Press), reprinted by permission of the author. BARO, GENE: The following poems are reprinted by permission of Charles Scribner's Sons from *Poets of Today VI, Northwind and Other Poems:* "The Ladder" (first published in *The New Yorker*), copyright 1958 by The New Yorker Magazine, Inc.; "Lament for Better or Worse," "The Horsemen," and "Northwind" (first published in *Discovery,* Sept. 1955), copyright 1955 by Pocket Books, Inc.; "Judges, Judges," copyright 1959 by Gene Baro. "A Northern Spring" printed by permission of the author. BOOTH, PHILIP: "The Tower," copyright 1960 by Philip Booth, and "Was a Man," copyright 1958 by Philip Booth, from *The Islanders,* reprinted by permission of The Viking Press, Inc. BOYARS, ARTHUR: "Initial," reprinted by permission of the author. BROWN, GEORGE MacKAY: "The Old Women" and "The Death of Peter Esson," from *Loaves and Fishes,* reprinted by permission of The Hogarth Press, Ltd. "The Five Voyages of Arnor," "Unlucky Boat," "Our Lady of the Waves," and "Harald, the Agnostic Ale-Loving Old Shepherd Enemy of the Whisky-Drinking Ploughmen and Harvesters, Walks over the Sabbath Hill to the Shearing," reprinted by permission of the author. COOPER, JANE: "For a Very Old Man, on the Death of His Wife," "Obligations," and "The Graveyard," printed by permission of the author. "The Faithful" (first published in *New World Writing* #11), reprinted by permission of the author. COULETTE, HENRI: "The War of the Secret Agents" and "The Attic," reprinted by permission of the author. DAVIE,

DONALD: "A Winter Talent," "Gardens No Emblems," "Hearing Russian Spoken," "The Wind at Penistone," "Time Passing, Beloved," "The Mushroom Gatherers," and "Heigh-ho on a Winter Afternoon," from *A Winter Talent*, reprinted by permission of Routledge & Kegan Paul, Ltd. "For an Age of Plastics. Plymouth," from *New and Selected Poems*, copyright 1961 by Donald Davie, reprinted by permission of Wesleyan University Press. DICKEY, JAMES: The following poems are reprinted by permission of Charles Scribner's Sons from *Poets of Today VI, Into the Stone and Other Poems:* "The Call," copyright 1959 by The Hudson Review, Inc.; "The Performance" and "On the Hill below the Lighthouse," copyright 1959 by Poetry Magazine; "Trees and Cattle" and "Walking on Water" both first published in *The New Yorker*), copyright 1960 by The New Yorker Magazine, Inc. FINKEL, DONALD: The following poems are reprinted by permission of Charles Scribner's Sons from *Poets of Today VI, The Clothing's New Emperor and Other Poems:* "The Imbecile," copyright 1958 by Poetry Magazine; "Target Practice," "King Midas Has Asses' Ears," and "Solo for Bent Spoon," copyright 1959 by Donald Finkel; "Give Way," copyright 1953 by Epoch Associates. FULLER, JOHN: "Snapshot," "Band Music," "The Statue," "In a Railway Compartment," "White Queen," and "Morvin," reprinted by permission of the author. GARDONS, S. S.: "The Mother," copyright 1958 by The Hudson Review, Inc., and "To a Child," copyright 1961 by The Hudson Review, Inc., reprinted by permission of the author. GUNN, THOM: "Innocence," "My Sad Captains," "Considering the Snail," "Loot," "The Annihilation of Nothing," "The Byrnies," and "In Santa Maria del Popolo," reprinted by permission of the author. "On the Move," "The Unsettled Motorcyclist's Vision of His Death," and "Vox Humana," from *A Sense of Movement*, published by The University of Chicago Press, reprinted by permission of the author. HALL, DONALD: "The Snow," "The Long River," "In the Old House," "The Child," and "New Hampshire," printed by permission of the author. "The Three Movements," from *The Dark Houses*, copyright 1957 by Donald Hall, reprinted by permission of The Viking Press, Inc. HAMBURGER, MICHAEL: "The Dual Site," "Mathematics of Love," and "Epitaph for a Horseman," from *The Dual Site*, copyright 1958 by Michael Hamburger, reprinted by permission of Routledge & Kegan Paul, Ltd. "Man of the World" and "Blind Man," reprinted by permission of the author. HECHT, ANTHONY: "The End of the Weekend," "Third Avenue in Sunlight," and "Behold the Lilies of the Field" (all three first published in *The Hudson Review*), "More Light! More Light!" (first published in *The Nation*), and "The Dover Bitch" (first published in *Transatlantic Review*), reprinted by permission of the author. HILL, GEOFFREY: "The Guardians," "Of Commerce and Society," "Doctor Faustus," "A Pastoral," "Orpheus and Eurydice," "In Piam Memoriam," and "To the (Supposed) Patron," from *For the Unfallen*, published by André Deutsch, Ltd., reprinted by permission of the publisher. "Annunciations" (first published in *X*), reprinted by permission of the author. HOLBROOK, DAVID: "Living? Our Supervisors Will Do That for Us!," "Delivering Children," "Fingers in the Door," and "Poor Old Horse," from *Imaginings*, reprinted by permission of Putnam & Co., Ltd., London. HOLLANDER, JOHN: "The Great Bear," from *A Crackling of Thorns*, copyright 1958 by Yale University Press, Inc., reprinted by permission of the publisher ("The Great Bear" was first published in *The New Yorker* magazine). "A Lion Named Passion," reprinted by permission of the author. HUFF, ROBERT: "Rainbow," "The Smoker," and "Traditional Red," from *Colonel Johnson's Ride*, copyright 1959, reprinted by permission of the Wayne State University Press. "Getting Drunk with Daughter" (first published in *Poetry*), copyright 1961 by Robert Huff, reprinted by permission of the author. HUGHES, TED: Reprinted by permission of Harper & Brothers from *The Hawk in the Rain:* "The

6 ACKNOWLEDGMENTS

Thought-Fox" first published in *The New Yorker*), copyright 1957 by Ted Hughes, and "Roarers in a Ring," copyright 1956 by Ted Hughes. Reprinted by permission of Harper & Brothers from *Lupercal:* "A Dream of Horses," copyright 1957 by Ted Hughes; "Hawk Roosting," "Thrushes," and "Pike," copyright 1959 by Ted Hughes; and "The Retired Colonel," "An Otter," and "November," copyright 1960 by Ted Hughes. "Pibroch," reprinted by permission of the author. JENNINGS, ELIZABETH: "Old Man," "The Child and the Shadow," "Disguises," "The Parting," "Ghosts," "The Storm," and "Teresa of Avila," from *A Sense of the World*, copyright 1958 by Elizabeth Jennings, reprinted by permission of Holt, Rinehart and Winston, Inc. "The Room," "A World of Light," and "Harvest and Consecration," from *Song for a Birth or a Death*, published by André Deutsch, Ltd., copyright 1961 by Elizabeth Jennings, reprinted by permission of Harold Ober Associates, Inc. JUSTICE, DONALD: Reprinted by permission of Wesleyan University Press from *The Summer Anniversaries:* "The Snowfall," copyright © 1959 by Donald Justice; "On a Painting by Patient B of the Independence State Hospital for the Insane" and "Another Song," copyright 1954 by Donald Justice ("Another Song" was first published in *The New Yorker* magazine); and "Tales from a Family Album," copyright 1957 by Donald Justice. "Anonymous Drawing" (first published in *The Carleton Miscellany*) and "But That Is Another Story" (first published in *Harper's Magazine*), reprinted by permission of the author. KENNEDY, X. J.: "Nude Descending a Staircase," "Solitary Confinement," and "B Negative," copyright 1960 by X. J. Kennedy; "First Confession," copyright 1961 by X. J. Kennedy; "Faces from a Bestiary," from *Nude Descending a Staircase*, reprinted by permission of Doubleday and Company, Inc. KINNELL, GALWAY: "The Wolves" and "The Avenue Bearing the Initial of Christ into the New World," from *What a Kingdom It Was*, copyright 1960 by Galway Kinnell, reprinted by permission of Houghton Mifflin Company. KIZER, CAROLYN: "The Intruder," "The Ungrateful Garden," and "The Great Blue Heron," from *The Ungrateful Garden*, copyright 1961 by Indiana University Press, reprinted by permission of the publisher. LA FOLLETTE, MELVIN WALKER: "Love for a Hare" and "Spring Landscape," printed by permission of the author. "I Knew a Boy with Hair Like Gold," copyright 1959 by Melvin Walker La Follette, from *The Clever Body*, published by the Spenserian Press, reprinted by permission of the author. LARKIN, PHILIP: "An Arundel Tomb," "Mr. Bleaney," and "The Whitsun Weddings," reprinted by permission of the author. LERNER, LAURENCE: "The Way to the Sea," "What's Hard," and "A Meditation upon the Toothache," from *Domestic Interior*, reprinted by permission of The Hutchinson Publishing Group. "In a Shoreham Garden," reprinted by permission of the author. LEVERTOV, DENISE: "The Charge," "The Offender," "Seems Like We Must Be Somewhere Else," "Obsessions," and "The Vigil," from *With Eyes at the Back of Our Heads*, copyright 1958, 1959 by Denise Levertov Goodman, reprinted by permission of New Directions. "To the Snake," "A Solitude," "The Presence," and "The Rainwalkers," from *The Jacob's Ladder*, copyright 1961 by Denise Levertov, reprinted by permission of New Directions. LEVI, PETER: "L'Aurore Grelottante," "He Met Her at the Green Horse," and "In a Corner of Eden," from *The Gravel Ponds*, copyright 1960 by Peter Levi, reprinted by permission of The Macmillan Company. "To My Friends" and "Ship-Building Emperors Commanded," reprinted by permission of the author. LEVINE, PHILIP: "Night Thoughts over a Sick Child," "The Negatives," and "The Drunkard," reprinted by permission of the author. LOGAN, JOHN: "Concert Scene," "The Picnic," and "Lines to His Son on Reaching Adolescence," from *Ghosts of the Heart*, copyright 1960 by The University of Chicago, reprinted by permission of The University of Chicago Press. LUCIE-SMITH, EDWARD: "At the Roman Baths, Bath," "On Looking at Stubbs's *Anatomy of the*

Horse," "Meeting Myself," "Rabbit Cry," and "The Fault," reprinted by permission of the author. MacBETH, GEORGE: "The Drawer," "The Compasses," and "Bedtime Story," reprinted by permission of the author. MERRILL, JAMES: Reprinted by permission of Alfred A. Knopf, Inc., from *The Country of a Thousand Years of Peace*: "A Timepiece," copyright 1953, 1958 by James Merrill; "Some Negatives: X at the Chateau," copyright 1958 by James Merrill; "Hotel de l'Univers et Portugal," copyright 1951, 1958 by James Merrill; "Mirror," copyright 1958 by James Merrill; "Laboratory Poem," copyright 1958 by James Merrill; and "A View of the Burning," copyright 1958 by James Merrill. MERWIN, W. S.: reprinted from *The Drunk in the Furnace*, published by The Macmillan Company and Hart-Davies, by permission of Harold Ober Associates, Inc., and David Higham Associates, Ltd.: "The Drunk in the Furnace" and "Grandmother and Grandson," copyright 1958 by W. S. Merwin; "The Bones" and "The Native," copyright 1959 by W. S. Merwin; "Blind Girl" and "Plea for a Captive" (both first published in *The New Yorker*), copyright 1960 by W. S. Merwin. MEZEY, ROBERT: "The Lovemaker" and "The Wandering Jew" from *The Lovemaker*, reprinted by permission of the publisher, The Cummington Press. MICHIE, JAMES: "Dooley Is a Traitor," "Three Dreams," and "Closing Time," from *Possible Laughter*, copyright 1959 by James Michie, reprinted by permission of The Macmillan Company. MIDDLETON, CHRISTOPHER: "The Thousand Things," "News from Norwood," "Thinking of Hölderlin," "Male Torso," "Alba after Six Years," and six poems from *Herman Moon's Hourbook* ("Abasis," "The Ant Sun," "The Forenoon," "Ode on Contemplating Clapham Junction," "Waterloo Bridge," and "Pointed Boots"), reprinted by permission of the author. MILLER, VASSAR: Reprinted by permission of Wesleyan University Press from *Wage War on Silence*: "Receiving Communion," "The Worshiper," "The Tree of Silence," and "Though He Slay Me," copyright 1960 by Vassar Miller; "A Lesson in Detachment," copyright 1957 by Vassar Miller; and "The Quarry," copyright 1958 by Vassar Miller. "Fulfillment," reprinted by permission of the author. MORAES, DOM: "Song," from *Beginning*, published by Parton Press, reprinted by permission of Curtis Brown, Ltd., London. "Girl," "Lullaby," "The Final Word," and "Queen," from *Poems*, published by Eyre & Spottiswoode, Ltd., reprinted by permission of the publisher and Curtis Brown, Ltd., London. MOSS, HOWARD: Reprinted by permission of Charles Scribner's Sons from *A Swimmer in the Air*: "Horror Movie," copyright 1949 by Hearst Magazines, Inc.; "Local Places," copyright 1956 by Howard Moss, and "Underwood," copyright 1954 by Howard Moss (both first published in *The New Yorker*). "Water Island," copyright 1960 by Howard Moss, and "Movies for the Home," copyright 1960 by Howard Moss (both first published in *The New Yorker*), reprinted by permission of the author. PACK, ROBERT: "Descending" (first published in *The Sewanee Review*), copyright 1961 by Robert Pack, "Resurrection," and "Chopping Fire-Wood," reprinted by permission of the author. "The Boat" (first published in *Forum*), copyright 1962 by Robert Pack. "In a Field," copyright 1961 by Robert Pack (first published in *The New Yorker*), reprinted by permission of the author. "Parable" (first published in *A Stranger's Privilege* by The Macmillan Company), reprinted by permission of the author. PERRY, RONALD: "Still-Life," "The Shellpicker," and "Prologue for a Bestiary," from *The Rock Harbor*, copyright 1959 by Ronald Perry, reprinted by permission of the publisher, Alan Swallow. PETERSEN, DONALD: "True to a Dream" (first published in *The Western Review* under the title "In a Child's Bedroom"), "Narcissus" (first published in *Poetry* under the title "The Stages of Narcissus"), and "Sonnet in Autumn," printed by permission of the author. PLATH, SYLVIA: "Black Rook in Rainy Weather," from *The Colossus*, reprinted by permission of William Heinemann, Ltd. Reprinted from *The Colossus and Other Poems* by permission of Alfred A. Knopf, Inc.: "The

Colossus," copyright 1961, 1962 by Sylvia Plath; "Lorelei," copyright 1959, 1962 by Sylvia Plath; "Mushrooms," copyright 1960, 1962 by Sylvia Plath; "The Ghost's Leavetaking," copyright 1959, 1962 by Sylvia Plath; and "Snakecharmer," copyright 1959, 1962 by Sylvia Plath. RAY, DAVID: "X-Ray" (first published in *Accent*), "On a Fifteenth-Century Flemish Angel," "On the Poet's Leer," and "The Problems of a Writing Teacher," reprinted by permission of the author. REDGROVE, PETER: "On Catching a Dog Daisy in the Mower," "Shearing Grass," and "Bedtime Story for My Son," from *The Collector*, reprinted by permission of Routledge & Kegan Paul, Ltd. "I Stroll," "Corposant," "Story from Russian Author," and "The Ghostly Father," from *The Nature of Cold Weather*, reprinted by permission of Routledge & Kegan Paul, Ltd. REID, ALASTAIR: "In Memory of My Uncle Timothy," "Ghosts' Stories," and "The Tale the Hermit Told," from *Oddments, Inklings, Omens, Moments*, copyright 1958 by Alastair Reid, reprinted by permission of Little, Brown & Company. "Outlook Uncertain," reprinted by permission of the author and *The Atlantic Monthly*. RICH, ADRIENNE: Reprinted from *The Diamond Cutters* by permission of Harper & Brothers: "The Tourist and the Town," copyright 1955 by Adrienne Rich Conrad; "Lucifer in the Train," copyright 1952 by Adrienne Rich Conrad; and "The Middle-Aged," copyright 1955 by Adrienne Rich Conrad. "At Majority" (first published in *The New Yorker*), copyright 1956 by Adrienne Rich Conrad, reprinted by permission of the author. "The Raven" (first published in *The Nation*), copyright 1961 by Adrienne Rich Conrad, reprinted by permission of the author. "Double Monologue" and "New Year's Eve in Troy," published by permission of the author. SEXTON, ANNE: "The Farmer's Wife" and "The Division of Parts," from *To Bedlam and Part Way Back*, copyright 1960 by Anne Sexton, reprinted by permission of Houghton Mifflin Company. "The Truth the Dead Know" (first published in *The Hudson Review*), copyright 1961 by Anne Sexton, reprinted by permission of the author. "For God While Sleeping" (first published in *Partisan Review*), copyright 1961 by Anne Sexton, reprinted by permission of the author. SILKIN, JON: "Furnished Lives" and "The Return," from *The Two Freedoms*, copyright 1958 by Jon Silkin, reprinted by permission of The Macmillan Company. "Respectabilities" (first published in *Stand*), reprinted by permission of the author. SIMPSON, LOUIS: Reprinted from *A Dream of Governors* by permission of Wesleyan University Press: "To the Western World," copyright 1957 by Louis Simpson; "The Bird," copyright 1957 by Louis Simpson; and "Against the Age," copyright 1959 by Louis Simpson. "My Father in the Night Commanding No" (first published in *The New Yorker*), copyright 1961 by Louis Simpson, reprinted by permission of the author. "Walt Whitman at Bear Mountain" (first published in *The Paris Review*), copyright 1960 by Louis Simpson, reprinted by permission of the author. SINGER, BURNS: "Still and All," "Words Made of Water," and sonnets XV, XXX, XXXIII, XXXIX, and XLVIII from "Sonnets for a Dying Man," from *Still and All*, reprinted by permission of Martin Secker & Warburg, Ltd. SMITH, IAIN CRICHTON: "The Window" and "End of the Season on a Stormy Day—Oban," from *New Poets 1959;* and "Old Woman," "A Young Highland Girl Studying Poetry," and "Schoolgirl on Speech-Day in the Open Air," from *Thistles and Roses*, reprinted by permission of Eyre & Spottiswoode, Ltd. SNODGRASS, W. D.: "Mementos, i" and "Mementos, ii," copyright 1960 by The Hudson Review, Inc., reprinted by permission of the author. "A Flat One" (first published in *Quarterly Review of Literature*), reprinted by permission of the author. STARBUCK, GEORGE: "Poems from a First Year in Boston," from *Bone Thoughts*, copyright 1960 by George Starbuck, reprinted by permission of Yale University Press. THWAITE, ANTHONY: "Rites for a Demagogue" and "Child Crying," from *Home Truths*, copyright by The

Marvell Press, reprinted by permission of The Marvell Press. "Looking On" and "At Birth," reprinted by permission of the author. TOMLINSON, CHARLES: "Paring the Apple," "More Foreign Cities," "Meditation on John Constable," and "The Ruin," from *Seeing Is Believing*, copyright 1950, 1955, 1956, 1957, 1958 by Charles Tomlinson, reprinted by permission of Ivan Obolensky, Inc. "Observation of Facts," "Ode to Arnold Schoenberg," "The Hand at Callow Hill Farm," and "Le Musée Imaginaire," reprinted by permission of the author. WAGONER, DAVID: "The Man from the Top of the Mind," "A Warning to My Love," "The Feast," and "News from the Court," from *A Place to Stand*, copyright 1958 by Indiana University Press, reprinted by permission of the publisher. "The Emergency-Maker," reprinted by permission of the author. WAIN, JOHN: "Poem without a Main Verb," "Au Jardin des Plantes," "Apology for Understatement," "The New Sun," and "Anniversary," from *Weep before God*, reprinted by permission of Macmillan & Company, Ltd., and St. Martin's Press, Inc.

CONTENTS

New Poets of America

EDITORS' PREFACE

New Poets of England and America: Second Selection is a completely new book. Poets included in the earlier volume who are now over forty have been omitted; poets appearing for a second time here are represented by more recent work; and many new poets have been added. We have retained the age limit in order to continue an emphasis on the new and the relatively unknown poets.

This book is edited in two separate sections: Robert Pack has selected the American poets, and Donald Hall the English. We have not tried to represent everything that is being done in poetry, but to choose the best that was available to us.

We wish to record here our thanks to Mary Louise Vincent, whose industry and skill were indispensable in assembling this book.

We should like to thank Louis Simpson, whose help, by virtue of his work on the first anthology, and his suggestions for the second, was invaluable.

And once again, with gratitude, we dedicate this anthology to Mr. Thomas Langbert.

D. H.
R. P.

February 1962

NEW POETS
OF ENGLAND

Edited by Donald Hall

INTRODUCTION BY DONALD HALL

One might as well start with some dialogue. *The scene is the office of a magazine in London, where the* PROTAGONIST, *who is an American poet, is calling on an English acquaintance who has become a literary editor. The* EDITOR *is a young, intelligent Oxford man who likes novels very much.*

PROTAGONIST: You don't seem to review poetry very much in your magazine. In fact you don't seem to *print* poetry very much.

EDITOR: Oh, it's hard to fit it in. The people who run this magazine don't care for literature.

PROTAGONIST: Can't you wedge open a little more space for poems, at least? Not mine, of course! Somebody's.

EDITOR: I suppose we print enough, really. Not much is going on over here, do you think? Things are better in your country, I suppose. At least that's what everybody assumes. I print a lot of poems I don't like.

PROTAGONIST: *I* think there are some good people writing. Of course the magazines are full of ghastly poems by E. D. Fennis and people like that, but there are others.

EDITOR: Oh. I think Fennis is one of the best, really. (*A competent dramatist might end his scene here, and let the silence swell with implication, but really the* EDITOR *continues.*) He isn't pretentious. I like his irony and his tone.

PROTAGONIST (*too shocked to make points*): But—he can't write! He doesn't know what a metaphor is! He starts out with one meter and abandons it as soon as it gets difficult! He has compassion for everything—trees, dogs, natives— for everything except his poems!

EDITOR (*cool*): Do you think so? Perhaps you're right. I don't suppose Edwin takes his poems very seriously, actually.

Drama escapes us. Curtain. The PROTAGONIST *emerges dressed as an essay, and provides a moment of transition by remarking that it is strange but true that most poets, most of the time, seem to have taken poetry seriously. Then he implies that the* EDITOR *thinks that "not much is going on" because he prefers bad poems to good ones. Good poems, the* PROTAGONIST *says, are often ambitious ("pretentious") and they are not always ironical. Sometimes they are solemn and sometimes they are jolly. They are always well written.*

People are writing some very good poems in England these days. Not many American critics will admit it, partly because they are ignorant and partly because they substitute an uncritical Anglophobia for the uncritical Anglophilia of their great-grandfathers. But then, not many Englishmen will admit it either. The one-act play above is imitated from life, and is accurate except that E. D. Fennis is not *quite* the name of the poet; it would be unfair to attack only one of the overpraised and incompetent.

Of course *some* of the best poems are being written by men who are generally praised, or at least accepted. Robert Conquest's anthology *New Lines*, which gave form to the Movement of the fifties, printed Philip Larkin, Thom Gunn, and Donald Davie, among others. I suspect that if Ted Hughes had published a book by that time he would have found himself included. He is another good poet who is widely known to be one.

But others of the best contemporary English poets find themselves largely without critical notice. Christopher Middleton is publishing his first book while this anthology is in press. It is obvious that publication has been delayed because of the difficulty, possibly even the originality of his poems. In a time when terms like common sense, consolidation, and conservatism are terms of poetical praise, Middleton has been silly enough to learn from Continental masters. It won't do. Neither will it do to learn from the Americans, as the career of Charles Tomlinson indicates, for his poetry derives from Pound and Stevens as well as from native sources, from his own work as a painter, and from the ideas of perception which were current in the Cambridge he attended. Geoffrey Hill is another; his poems are intense and highly wrought, with a subtle use of syntax. For comparison one looks in vain, though he has been compared to a number of people he does not resemble. His first book, *For the Unfallen*, was well reviewed by A. Alvarez in *The Observer*, but otherwise caused little more than consternation.

Obscurity, Europeanism, and even intensity have come to be regarded as phony in themselves. When one sees the beginnings of this attitude in Kingsley Amis's novels, or in Philip Larkin's poems, one sees something that works in its context. One sees opinions which have causes and which are truly held; and one recognizes that a type of English literary phony is accurately enough described. But the feelings and observations of the originators become the critical clichés of the followers, and English literary opinion is beset by false standards derived from true prejudices. Really the source of this prejudice is class: to be obscure in your poems can be a form of social climbing. Possibly it has something to do with the Sitwells.

Such limiting standards cannot last. I suspect that when the revolution of the sixties takes place, it will come in the name of Europe, and the Common Market will extend to poetry. When it comes, it will find that an excellent body of cosmopolitan poetry has already been written. Of course, it will probably manage at that time to dispose of the good poetry which was written from the contrary position. Perhaps only a total outsider can realize that the poetry of Larkin and Tomlinson, Hughes and Hill, will all survive.

The selection of Philip Larkin's poetry here is not as substantial as I would like. Mr. Larkin felt it necessary to limit the number of poems printed, lest we assemble here too great a proportion of his next book. One understands, and is grateful for the three poems here collected.

I have printed only English poets born in 1922 and later. This omits a number of poets I would like to have, but allows me to print selections of many of the youngest English poets. We have also chosen, as in our last edition, to print only poets of whom we could choose at least three or four pages of poetry. Thus I have omitted a number of poets who have written poems I admire, but not enough of them.

I have decided as well to omit Irish poets, like Thomas Kinsella, and poets from the Commonwealth. It would be unfair to print only those poets I have come across, and I could not attempt at this time a complete survey of what is written in English all over the world. I regret the omission of some admirable poets from Ireland, Canada, Australia, New Zealand, the West Indies, Africa, and India. This volume does include the poems of Dom Moraes, who is Indian, and Laurence Lerner, who is South African—but in both cases the reputation and the publication, as well as the current residence, of the poets is English.

Kingsley Amis

AUTOBIOGRAPHICAL FRAGMENT

When I lived down in Devonshire
   The callers at my cottage
Were Constant Angst, the art critic,
   And old Major Courage.

Angst always brought me something nice
   To get in my good graces:
A quilt, a roll of cotton-wool,
   A pair of dark glasses.

He tore up all my unpaid bills,
   Went and got my slippers,
Took the telephone off its hook
   And bolted up the shutters.

We smoked and chatted by the fire,
   Sometimes just nodding;
His charming presence made it right
   To sit and do nothing.

But then—those awful afternoons
   I walked out with the Major!
I ran up hills, down streams, through briars;
   It was sheer blue murder.

Trim in his boots, riding-breeches
   And threadbare Norfolk jacket,
He watched me, frowning, bawled commands
   To work hard and enjoy it.

I asked him once why I was there,
   Except to get all dirty;

He tugged his grey moustache and snapped:
  "Young man, it's your duty."

What duty's served by pointless, mad
    Climbing and crawling?
I tell you, I was thankful when
    The old bore stopped calling.

SIGHT UNSEEN

As I was waiting for the bus
    A girl came up the street,
Detectable as double-plus
    At seven hundred feet.

Her head was high, her step was free,
    Her face a lyric blur,
Her waist was narrow, I could see,
    But not the rest of her.

At fifty feet I watched her stop,
    Bite at a glove, then veer
Aside into some pointless shop,
    Never to reappear.

This happens every bloody day:
    They about-turn, they duck
Into their car and belt away,
    They hide behind a truck.

Look, if they knew me—understood,
    There might be cause to run;
Or if they saw me, well and good;
    And yet they don't, not one.

Love at first sight: by this we mean
    A stellar entrant thrown
Clear on the psyche's radar-screen,
    Recognised before known.

All right—things work the opposite
 Way with the poles reversed;
It's galling, though, when girls omit
 To switch the set on first.

TERRIBLE BEAUTY

Hearing how tourists, dazed with reverence,
Look through sun-glasses at the Parthenon,
I thought of that cold night outside the Gents
When Dai touched Gwyneth up with his gloves on.

A TRIBUTE TO THE FOUNDER

By bluster, graft, and doing people down
Sam Baines got rich, but mellowing at last,
Felt that by giving something to the town
He might undo the evils of his past.

His hope was to prevent the local youth
From making the mistakes that he had made:
Choosing expediency instead of truth,
And quitting what was honest for what paid.

A university seemed just the thing,
And that old stately home the very place.
Sam wept with pleasure at its opening.
He died too soon to weep at its disgrace.

Graft is refined among the tea and scones,
Bluster (new style) invokes the public good,
And doing-down gets done in pious tones
That Sam tried to put on, but never could.

SCIENCE FICTION

What makes us rove that starlit corridor
May be the impulse to meet face to face
Our vice and folly shaped into a thing,
And so at last ourselves; what lures us there
Is simpler versions of disaster:
A web confounding time and space,
A world of ocean without shore,
A sentence to perpetual journeying,
And simplest, flapping down the poisoned air,
A ten-clawed monster.

In him, perhaps, we see the general ogre
Who rode our ancestors to nightmare,
And in his habitat their maps of hell;
But climates and geographies soon change,
Spawning mutations none can quell
With silver sword or necromancer's ring,
Worse than their sires, of wider range,
And much more durable.

ON A PORTRAIT OF
MME. RIMSKY-KORSAKOV

Serene, not as a prize for conflict won,
But mark of never having had to fight,
And beautiful enough to need no mind,
She sat embodying her unconcern
For all charades of love or symbolism.
    Nicholas was inspecting a brass band,
    Driving to lunch with Cui and Borodin,
    Checking the full score of *The Snow Maiden.*

That dateless look, impersonal beyond
The coarse placing of the heart's Hollywood,
Writes off poor Janey Morris as a paddler

In joy and agony, a pop-eyed clown
Skinny and thick-lipped with her pomegranate.
  The Snow Maiden and the rest of the stuff
  Attain the permanence of print, wax, and
  Footnotes in treatises on orchestration.

AFTER GOLIATH

> *What shall be done to the man that killeth this
> Philistine?—I Sam. xvii, 27*

The first shot out of that sling
Was enough to finish the thing:
The champion laid out cold
Before half the programmes were sold
And then, what howls of dismay
From his fans in their dense array:
From aldermen, adjutants, aunts,
Administrators of grants,
Assurance-men, auctioneers,
Advisers about careers,
And advertisers, of course,
Plus the obvious b----s in force—
The whole reprehensible throng
Ten times an alphabet strong.
But such an auspicious debut
Was a little too good to be true,
Our victor sensed; the applause
From those who supported his cause
Sounded shrill and excessive now,
And who were they, anyhow?
Academics, actors who lecture,
Apostles of architecture,
Ancient-gods-of-the-abdomen men,
Angst-pushers, adherents of Zen,
Alastors, Austenites, A-test
Abolishers—even the straightest
Of issues looks pretty oblique
When a movement turns into a clique,
The conqueror mused, as he stopped
By the sword his opponent had dropped:

Trophy, or means of attack
On the rapturous crowd at his back?
He shrugged and left it, resigned
To a new battle, fought in the mind,
For faith that his quarrel was just,
That the right man lay in the dust.

Arthur Boyars

INITIAL

for Eugenio Montale

I

Passing out of a great city
A flower in confusion,
I, the speaker, and you, the listener;
You, who would never listen except through words,
Learning with your clay implement,
Moving to change even in daylight,
And I, holding neither the middle way
Of this direction nor any part
Valid for measurement, will lead
Dead Virgil through my private world.

Finding that the wood has not altered,
The Leopard, the Lion
They remain constant, and through them is forward,
And they as unshaken as stone beasts
On the walls, laughing at enemies;
Mating with their bodies after death,
Fruit of a human craftsman;
But He knowing the Hound
From outside, and he with me
Walking equal, the Knowledge and Discord.

How he would come retrieving
Hostages from night,

The way still periculous, overstarred
By new refinements of space: buildings
Settle their grand lumber near incurious skies,
Night blows setting the card
Face downwards, the hand of daylight
Gropes for rescuing fingers,
Finds none, and relapsing slides
Beneath view by its ultimate candle.

The river an eye of bad mirrors
Drawing her face,
A distributed mask on their breaking;
And she, not so much present
As remembered where there is separation
Of whole things: a moment of incaution
And the face gives its relic,
Waits for surprise at the move
Waits for its equal, knows none.
Eyes above it. Knowledge and Discord.

I will watch here for the movement,
Not as the ghost
Appears once under lamplight, seen clearly
And then dissolves, a pattern of houses
His backcloth, dwarfed by comparison
Of wires in a no-man's-land: web
On the word as a face stranded
Between spidered branches,
Framed weakly—extending
Without edge. The focus is altered.

Now the somewhere is plain, the rhymes
Run to refuse,
In spite coherence is lost, the names
Of anonymous trees which make this now
Are recalled, the word goes to barter:
Bodies and wheat are ploughed up, the Willow
Remains asserting its sadness;
The last husk of the pearl droops
To dust, her body before me
Emerges a spire to the sun.

This place, this time: all other
Exhausted through love.
Quicksands graze at your harbours,
Shaft at the breakers, tidal, temporary
Report you, too tall for their depth;
On this inner day of the year, fall
Of the meteor cargoed with red veins
Flows branches between, overcoming
Heat, slows the pulse, the Pole-
Star held as a shield.

This time, and the manic dance
Starting differently,
New rhythm of feet, it is You,
New wings to the eye, cone to the heart,
Precipice of lips to the next spending,
And then again. It is not the lights
Of a city, one by one weakening
The roots of feet growing dark, these threads
Cannot bear them: outwards the sand
Wrinkles in the same folds,
And yet differently.

Matching the foot to the furrow,
Unvenomed in Eden,
The short measure divides, music flattens,
A moment, the Queen flashes to cardboard, situations
Flung out wild, paper-decks for a generation.
Silver the serpent uncoils from his tree, silver
Bad mirrors look back; the Lion laying proud paw
On their surface uncovers a head,
It was that dancer they told of,
Water the last valley.

Dead by his own rib. Beatrice
Is Eve with a human
Example: for short pleasure, long displeasure;
It was that dancer, Fantastick, tripping lightly,
Missing the shore he stumbled to deep stones,
Joined with the beast, unexpected
Mingling; bellowed from the maze
To the rampart: "Is there no sound

Thing that I may devour?" But He with me
Treading equal. Knowledge and Discord.

II

There was a bed prepared and avoided
Smoke faces
Too great a distraction
In space

Others lay heavy
Where I was not
A sigh where a face had been
So then was space droning
With scissors of legs
And prelude of breath

Alliance matured
Gone into disrepute
And she desirous

I change the tune of her

Two pits in cheeks
Of her smiles
And feet forcing
The ultimate world
Of her sheets
These holding her
For me virginal
In frame represented
A profile
Against her walking

Night
And the bed I avoided
Confusion
Of faces I repeat
Forerunners
Less worthy
And she
In need of an agony

I change the tune of her

A density of feet ranging and the earth a tabor
Moist night falls from the sky Troy wakens in me
Queen do I need to make a beginning? Say only
There was a woman as you are now
Where she touched there are ashes where she loved
Bones crunched into filigree Hector and Priam
This disconnection of stones her doing
Who will say surely caprice or intention
In her mind rotted the mortar but all in private
Agreed her voyage a search for an agony
Such as comes in movement of feet a tiptoed
Boldness and the face holding what is
Not there if the moment were split into motives

A bed prepared I avoided it
Were you a fool at her court
And rumoured the flight of her night-times?
Had you fashioned a flower of mythologies
An abstract of all faces
So that attempting all cities
One compass-leg slipped and really
You had not moved? Always in night
The one place? Had you?

I change the tune of her

Now my bridge moves
I have thrown one point to another
And strengthen the fastening

Consider which men
In the myths have triumphed
I see remorse in all heroes
A grief of Odysseus
Three times attempting
To hold his dead mother
(She stood as in life)
Three times his hands
Caught the air
This is the manner

Of men
Gone from under the sky

(Later Penelope
Wondered that he passed
His hands three times over her face
Before touching her eyes)

A remorse untouched
By return there is none
A journey of ready death

My bridge moves
The boards hunger
And groan as I twine them
Trees have been cut
To one length
Thoughts fitted
Hollowed the mould of ambition

The tooth of the wheel
The business on other shores
My banks
Myself the explorer

A bed prepared
A motive in history
Many such in the rubble
Of Pergamon or Helen
Had crazed the world with a promise
I avoided it

Leave this road

I change the tune of her

Now like lovers stumbling because of their locked fingers
And their gaze

George Mackay Brown

THE OLD WOMEN

Go sad or sweet or riotous with beer
Past the old women gossiping by the hour,
They'll fix on you from every close and pier
An acid look to make your veins run sour.

"No help," they say, "his grandfather that's dead
Was troubled with the same dry-throated curse,
And many a night he made the ditch his bed.
This blood comes welling from the same cracked source."

On every kind of merriment they frown.
But I have known a gray-eyed sober boy
Sail to the lobsters in a storm, and drown.
Over his body dripping on the stones
Those same old hags would weave into their moans
An undersong of terrible holy joy.

THE DEATH OF PETER ESSON

TAILOR, TOWN LIBRARIAN, FREE KIRK ELDER

Peter at some immortal cloth, it seemed,
Fashioned and stitched, for so long had he sat
Heraldic on his bench. We never dreamed
It was his shroud that he was busy at.

Well Peter knew, his thousand books would pass
Gray into dust, that still a tinker's tale
As hard as granite and as sweet as grass,
Told over reeking pipes, outlasts them all.

The Free Kirk cleaves gray houses—Peter's ark
Freighted for heaven, galeblown with psalm and prayer.
The predestined needle quivered on the mark.
The wheel spun true. The seventieth rock was near.

Peter, I mourned. Early on Monday last
There came a wave and stood above your mast.

THE FIVE VOYAGES OF ARNOR

I, Arnor the red poet, made
Four voyages out of Orkney.

The first was to Ireland.
That was a viking cruise.
Thorlief came home with one leg.
We left Guthorm in Ulster,
His blood growing cold by the saint's well.
Rounding Cape Wrath, I made my first poem.

Norway threw fogs about me.
I won the girl Ragnhild
From Paul her brother, after
I beat him at draughts, three games to two.
Out of Bergen, the waves made her sick.
She was uglier than I expected, still
I made five poems about her
That men sing round the bench at Yule.
She filled my quiet house with words.

A white wave threw me on Iceland.
Rolf there, in a field under Rangower
Had killed Wistan, the skald, whom Sigurd
Loved for his curly head.
Sigurd put the axe in my hand, pointing north.
Lilies and snow on the hill above Broadfirth.
Rolf had sailed to the islands.
We stayed in Unst two nights, coming home.
We drank ale and discussed new metres.
For Sigurd, I reddened the axe at a dog's throat.

I went the blue road to Jerusalem,
With fifteen ships in a brawling company
Of poets, warriors, and holy men.
A hundred swords were broken that voyage.
Prayer on a hundred white wings
Rose every morning. The Mediterranean
Was richer by a hundred love songs.
We saw the hills where God walked
And that last hill, where his feet were broken.
At Rome, the earl left us. His hooves beat north.

Three Fridays sick of the black cough,
Tomorrow I make my last voyage.
I would have chosen to loose the cable
Heaving the axe, with Sweyn, in the Dublin trap,
But here, at Hamnavoe, a pillow is under my head.
May all things be done in order.
The priest has given me oil and bread, a sweet cargo.
Ragnhild my daughter will cross my hands.
The boy Ljot must ring the bell.
I have said to Erling Saltfingers: *Drop my harp*
Through a green wave, off Yesnaby,
Next time you row to the lobsters.

UNLUCKY BOAT

That boat has killed three people. Building her
Sib drove a nail through his thumb, and died up by
Bunged to the eyes with rust and penicillin.
One evening when the Bring was a bar of silver
Under the moon, and Mansie and Tom with wands
Were putting a spell on cuithes, she dipped a bow
And invited Mansie, his pipe still in his teeth,
To meet the cold green angels. They hauled her up
Among the rocks, right in the path of Angus,
Whose neck, rigid with pints from the Dounby market,
Snapped like a barley stalk. . . . There she lies,
A leprous unlucky bitch, in the quarry of Moan.

Tinkers, going past, make the sign of the cross.

HARALD, THE AGNOSTIC
ALE-LOVING OLD SHEPHERD
ENEMY OF THE WHISKY-DRINKING
PLOUGHMEN AND HARVESTERS,
WALKS OVER THE SABBATH
HILL TO THE SHEARING

Two bells go pealing through my age,
Two mad majestic criers,
One celebrates the pastured saints,
One thunders of hell fires.
They storm at me with trembling mouths
And both of them are liars.

The barman had a little bell
That swayed my soul to peace
At ten last night. When the mad horns
Raged in the barley lees,
From up to bottom of my glass
Clung a shining fleece.

OUR LADY OF THE WAVES

The twenty brothers of Eynhallow
Have made a figure of Our Lady.
From red stone they carved her
And set her on the headland.
There is spindrift about her feet.
At dawn the brothers sang this

　　Blessed Lady, since midnight
　　We have done three things.
　　We have bent hooks.
　　We have patched a sail.
　　We have sharpened knives.
　　Yet the little silver brothers are afraid.

Bid them come to our net.
Show them our fire, our fine round plates.
Look mildly on our hungers.

The codling hang in a row by the wall.
At noon the brothers sang this

Holy mother, Una the cow
Gives thin blue milk.
Put the golden thread of butter in it.
The stone in the middle of our glebe
Has deep black roots.
We have broken three ploughs on it.
Save Una from the axe,
Our dappled cow with large eyes.

The girls go by with pails to the byre.
At sunset the brothers sang this

Sweet virgin, the woman of Garth
Is forever winking at Brother Paul.
She puts an egg in his palm.
She lays peats in his cowl.
Her neck is long as spilt milk.
Brother Paul is a good lad,
His mass is sweetly sung,
But three midnights running
His tongue has run loose among dreams.

Brother Paul's back is white and red.
At midnight the brothers sang this

Queen of heaven, this good day
There is a new cradle at Quoys.
He rocks on the blue floor.
And there is a new coffin at Hamnavoe.
Arnor the poet lies there,
Tired of words and wounds.
In between, what is man?
A head inclined over fish and bread and ale.
Outside, the long furrow.
Through a door, a board with a shape on it.

Guard the ploughs and the nets.

Star of the Sea, shine for us.

Donald Davie

A WINTER TALENT

Lighting a spill late in the afternoon,
I am that coal whose heat it should unfix;
Winter is come again, and none too soon
For meditation on its raft of sticks.

Some quick bright talents can dispense with coals
And burn their boats continually, command
An unreflecting brightness that unrolls
Out of whatever firings come to hand.

What though less sunny spirits never turn
The dry detritus of an August hill
To dangerous glory? Better still to burn
Upon that gloom where all have felt a chill.

GARDENS NO EMBLEMS

Man with a scythe: the torrent of his swing
Finds its own level; and is not hauled back
But gathers fluently, like water rising
Behind the watergates that close a lock.

The gardener eased his foot into a boot;
Which action like the mower's had its mould,
Being itself a sort of taking root,
Feeling for lodgment in the leather's fold.

But forms of thought move in another plane
Whose matrices no natural forms afford
Unless subjected to prodigious strain:
Say, light proceeding edgewise, like a sword.

HEARING RUSSIAN SPOKEN

Unsettled again and hearing Russian spoken
I think of brokenness perversely planned
By Dostoievsky's debauchees; recall
The "visible brokenness" that is the token
Of the true believer; and connect it all
With speaking a language I cannot command.

If broken means unmusical I speak
Even in English brokenly, a man
Wretched enough, yet one who cannot borrow
Their hunger for indignity nor, weak,
Abet my weakness, drink to drown a sorrow
Or write in metres that I cannot scan.

Unsettled again at hearing Russian spoken,
"Abjure politic brokenness for good,"
I tell myself. "Recall what menaces,
What self-loathings must be re-awoken:
This girl and that, and all your promises
Your pidgin that they too well understood."

Not just in Russian but in any tongue
Abandonment, morality's soubrette
Of lyrical surrender and excess,
Knows the weak endings equal to the strong;
She trades on broken English with success
And, disenchanted, I'm enamoured yet.

THE WIND AT PENISTONE

The wind meets me at Penistone.
                    A hill
Curves empty through the township, on a slope
Not cruel, and yet steep enough to be,
Were it protracted, cruel.
                    In the street,
A plain-ness rather meagre than severe,
Affords, though quite unclassical, a vista
So bald as to be monumental.
                    Here
A lean young housewife meets me with the glance
I like to think that I can recognize
As dour, not cross.
                    And all the while the wind,
A royal catspaw, toying easily,
Flicks out of shadows from a tufted wrist,
Its mane, perhaps, this lemon-coloured sun.

The wind reserves, the hill reserves, the style
Of building houses on the hill reserves
A latent edge;
                    which we can do without
In Pennine gradients and the Pennine wind,
And never miss or, missing it, applaud
The absence of the aquiline;
                    which in her
Whose style of living in the wind reserves
An edge to meet the wind's edge, we may miss
But without prejudice.
                    And yet in art
Where all is patent, and a latency
Is manifest or nothing, even I,
Liking to think I feel these sympathies,
Can hardly praise this clenched and muffled style.

For architecture asks a cleaner edge,
Is open-handed.

And close-fisted people
Are mostly vulgar; only in the best,
Who draw, inflexible, upon reserves,
Is there a stern game that they play with life,
In which the rule is not to show one's hand
Until compelled.
And then the lion's paw!
Art that is dour and leonine in the Alps
Grows kittenish, makes curios and clocks,
Giant at play.
Here, nothing. So the wind
Meets me at Penistone, and, coming home,
The poet falls to special pleading, chilled
To find in Art no fellow but the wind.

TIME PASSING, BELOVED

Time passing, and the memories of love
Coming back to me, carissima, no more mockingly
Than ever before; time passing, unslackening,
Unhastening, steadily; and no more
Bitterly, beloved, the memories of love
Coming into the shore.

How will it end? Time passing, and our passages of love
As ever, beloved, blind
As ever before; time binding, unbinding
About us; and yet to remember
Never less chastening, nor the flame of love
Less like an ember.

What will become of us? Time
Passing, beloved, and we in a sealed
Assurance unassailed
By memory. How can it end,
This siege of a shore that no misgivings have steeled,
No doubts defend?

THE MUSHROOM GATHERERS
after Mickiewicz

Strange walkers! See their processional
Perambulations under low boughs,
The birches white, and the green turf under.
These should be ghosts by moonlight wandering.

Their attitudes strange: the human tree
Slowly revolves on its bole. All around
Downcast looks; and the direct dreamer
Treads out in trance his lane, unwavering.

Strange decorum: so prodigal of bows,
Yet lost in thought and self-absorbed, they meet
Impassively, without acknowledgment.
A courteous nation, but unsociable.

Field full of folk, in their immunity
From human ills, crestfallen and serene.
Who would have thought these shades our lively friends?
Surely these acres are Elysian Fields.

HEIGH-HO ON A WINTER
AFTERNOON

There is a heigh-ho in these glowing coals
By which I sit wrapped in my overcoat
As if for a portrait by Whistler. And there is
A heigh-ho in the bird that noiselessly
Flew just now past my window, to alight
On winter's moulding, snow; and an alas,
A heigh-ho and a desultory chip,
Chip, chip on stone from somewhere down below.

Yes I have "mellowed," as you said I would,
And that's a heigh-ho too for any man;

Heigh-ho that means we fall short of alas
Which sprigs the grave of higher hopes than ours.
Yet heigh-ho too has its own luxuries,
And salts with courage to be jocular
Disreputable sweets of wistfulness,
By deprecation made presentable.

What should we do to rate the long alas
But skeeter down a steeper gradient?
And then some falls are still more fortunate,
The meteors spent, the tragic heroes stunned
Who go out like a light. But here the chip,
Chip, chip will flake the stone by slow degrees,
For hour on hour the fire will gutter down,
The bird will call at longer intervals.

FOR AN AGE OF PLASTICS.
PLYMOUTH

With the effect as of carving, almost, the hillside
    They climb in their stiff terraces, these houses
Feed the returning eye with national pride
    In the "built to last." Approving elegance
Where there is only decency, the eye
    Applauds the air of nothing left to chance
Or brilliantly provisional. Not the fact
    But the air of it, the illusion, we observe;
Chance in the bomb-sight kept these streets intact
    And razed whole districts. Nor was the lesson lost
On the rebuilt city, how an age of chance
    Is an age of plastics. In a style pre-cast
Pre-fabricated, and as if its site
    Were the canyon's lip, it rises out of rubble
Sketchily massive, moulded in bakelite.

Annoyed to take a gloomy sort of pride
    In numbering our losses, I suppose
The ploughman ceased his carving of the hillside
    And all the coulters and the chisels broke

When he was young whom we come home to bury,
    A man like clay in the hands of his womenfolk.

A ploughman carved three harvests, each a son,
    Upon the flesh of Wales. And all were carried
Long since from those hillsides, yet this one
    Comes first to threshing. Nutriment and grain
For all the mashing of the interim
    Lives in the load of him. Living again
His shipwright's years, the countryman's walks in the park,
    The scrape of a mattock in his too small garden,
The marriage to the able matriarch,
    What would he change? Perhaps a stubbornness
That bristled sometimes, for the capable hands
    To circumvent and gentle, would be less
Amenable to their shaping. But all told,
    His edged tools still would lie in the garden shed,
Still he would flow, himself, from mould to mould.

Whatever he showed of something in the rough,
    Sluggish in flow and unadaptable,
I liked him for; affecting to be gruff,
    An awkward customer—so much was due,
He seemed to think, to what a man was, once:
    Something to build with, take a chisel to.

John Fuller

IN A RAILWAY COMPARTMENT

Oxford to London, 1884:
Against the crimson arm-rest leant a girl
Of ten, holding a muff, twisting a curl,
Drumming her heels in boredom on the floor
Until a white-haired gentleman, who saw
She hated travelling, produced a case
Of puzzles: "Seven Germans run a race . . .

Unwind this maze, escape the lion's paw . . .
The princess must be lowered by her hair . . ."
The train entered a tunnel, shrieking, all
The lights went out and when he took her hand
She was the princess in the tower and
A lion faced her on the moonlit wall
Who roared and reached and caught and held her there.

THE STATUE

Your buttonholes for eyes, your solemn face,
The golden hair against your sleeping back:
This is no other time, no other place,
A moment certain as the almanac,
Vivid as weather, quiet as the deep,
As innocent as hands that curl in sleep.

For dreams disguise our wish to be awake
With bells, lagoons and squalls of tinsel trees.
In dreams you are not cruel, yet can't fake
An understanding of your cruelties.
Later, we're on the road: our object is
To judge a dead art's possibilities.

The radiator choked with butterflies,
We reach the city in a thumbed-down car
And I discover that the staring eyes
And cool lips of the promised statue are
Though fabulous, immortalised in stone,
Less rare and calm and perfect than your own.

For, in the camera's illusion, he
Preserved a moment from a laughing past,
A consolation for inconstancy,
Carefree, amorous, dynamic, vast,
Making a message on a mantelpiece,
A famous face sent by a friend from Greece.

But when we view the postcard subject fresh,
Gazing from curls to reconstructed toes,

Gone is the gentle and the human flesh,
Slyly dramatic in a talking pose:
Instead I see, and think I understand
The broken smile, whips in the missing hand.

BAND MUSIC

Cows! Cows! With ears like mouths of telephones!
They creak towards him with their heads thrust out,
So baby wauls among the cabbages
Till Betty runs to kiss his quivering pout
And lumping Ernest takes a stick and stones
To drive them off, cursing their ravages.

"Hush, child," she whispers, rocking. "There, there then!
Watch Ernest. Clever Ernest. Nasty cows."
Inside the cottage from a dusty box
Thumps martial music. Flowers on Betty's blouse
Grow out in lines like cabbages while men
In gold braid blow among the hollyhocks.

SNAPSHOT

A girl is twirling a parasol.
A dog is worrying a doll.

Postcards and lace shawls
Are sold by garden waterfalls.

Chopin spins from wax and horn.
The terrier bounds across the lawn,

Aching for rivers while the doll
Gets prodded by the parasol.

Roger, fresh from soap and razor,
Approaches in his candy blazer

And strokes his Maupassant moustache:
"This July sun is really *harsh!*"

Soft and quiet as a panda
She follows him to the verandah

Where the cool pebble lemonade
Burns and burns in a green shade.

Upon a chair of mother-of-pearl
He pulls his smiling panda girl

Into the crook of his striped arm,
His thumb upon her closing palm.

The girl puts down her parasol.
The dog swallows the doll.

MORVIN

Serpents exploded, open balconies
Offered their gazers to the bursting stars
And sparks like worlds fell slowly down
Upon the statues and the waiting cars.

My limbs moved tightly underneath the lights
And I remembered awe, excitement, shots,
Lanterns were ikons, rockets streaming blood,
The royal crest upon the chamber pots.

My nerves were better the next day, but as
I strolled in rain along the promenade
I caught my breath again, chancing to glimpse
A tram-race in the wet, a red-haired guard.

"Morvin!" I murmured, and the smell of fruit
Rose warmly to my nostrils, but I knew
That this was but a token of my state
Of feebleness, making imagined true.

Before the blood I had a solemn role
In the land, a statesman useful to the king
For striding on the great stairhead to cry
"Back with the greasy mob!" or keep a ring

For squeezing at the bottom of a writ
To get a burgher killed. In better days
(Ah, it was fresh in the North!) I walked abroad
Unrecognised, guilty, but proud always

To glimpse the workings of my "famous" laws.
(Out of his kitchen peeped the smirking cook
To see his clients satisfied. Behind,
Insidiously, where he did not look,

Flames crept.) The Crown was gutted in its bed.
More blood was got . . . Now I am stripped of robes
And strangely, too, of self. I scratch and wheeze,
Fingers which lopped, now sadly tug at, lobes,

And in this warmer land to which I flew,
Lucky to live, I sip aperitifs,
Chat with the guests, write in my attic room
Inventions for my loss of place, my grief.

Now it is dark again. I feel some stir
Within me. Is it over? Am I dead
Indeed? Perhaps *I* should have been that stabber,
Been that revolution's brilliant head,

Whom I see in whiteness, whom I hold
As gangling, filthy, vital, like a wink
Regrettably ignored, haunting: Morvin!
(Whom perhaps I only think I think),

O Morvin! As the silent puffs of cannon
Move like thistleseed across the hill,
I sit and ponder at the end of day
Upon your complex smiling presence still.

If, after one illuminating phrase,
I smash a pane, admitting the night air,

Shall I arise to stormy deeds of nothing,
Or in a mirror see *your* glowing hair?

You thrill with your suggestions like a child.
Prompting my arm you ruin the gathered page.
You are the fumbling conscience of us all,
The poking finger to a nervous age.

WHITE QUEEN

Who has a feeling she will come one day,
Not as a silly girl, nor beautiful
Like Marlowe's Spirit, unapproachable,
But gray, gray, gray from being shut away?

For this is what the poets will not say:
"Helen grew paler and was old, I fear,
(Sixty at Troy's loud fall) and for a year
Was seen by no one, wandering fat and gray."

In her appearance all will have their say.
Movements of flesh about eternal needs
Promote the spectacle of Helen's deeds
In the mind's eye at least, but in what way?

What figure scampers as this verse begins,
Ashen and wailing, scattering veils and pins?

Thom Gunn

ON THE MOVE

"Man, you gotta Go."

The blue jay scuffling in the bushes follows
Some hidden purpose, and the gust of birds

That spurts across the field, the wheeling swallows,
Have nested in the trees and undergrowth.
Seeking their instinct, or their poise, or both,
One moves with an uncertain violence
Under the dust thrown by a baffled sense
Or the dull thunder of approximate words.

On motorcycles, up the road, they come:
Small, black, as flies hanging in heat, the Boys,
Until the distance throws them forth, their hum
Bulges to thunder held by calf and thigh.
In goggles, donned impersonality,
In gleaming jackets trophied with the dust,
They strap in doubt—by hiding it, robust—
And almost hear a meaning in their noise.

Exact conclusion of their hardiness
Has no shape yet, but from known whereabouts
They ride, direction where the tires press.
They scare a flight of birds across the field:
Much that is natural, to the will must yield.
Men manufacture both machine and soul,
And use what they imperfectly control
To dare a future from the taken routes.

It is a part solution, after all.
One is not necessarily discord
On earth; or damned because, half animal,
One lacks direct instinct, because one wakes
Afloat on movement that divides and breaks.
One joins the movement in a valueless world,
Choosing it, till, both hurler and the hurled,
One moves as well, always toward, toward.

A minute holds them, who have come to go:
The self-defined, astride the created will
They burst away; the towns they travel through
Are home for neither bird nor holiness,
For birds and saints complete their purposes.
At worst, one is in motion; and at best,
Reaching no absolute, in which to rest,
One is always nearer by not keeping still.

THE UNSETTLED MOTORCYCLIST'S
VISION OF HIS DEATH

Across the open countryside,
Into the walls of rain I ride.
It beats my cheek, drenches my knees,
But I am being what I please.

The firm heath stops, and marsh begins.
Now we're at war: whichever wins
My human will cannot submit
To nature, though brought out of it.
The wheels sink deep; the clear sound blurs:
Still, bent on the handle-bars,
I urge my chosen instrument
Against the mere embodiment.
The front wheel wedges fast between
Two shrubs of glazed insensate green
—Gigantic order in the rim
Of each flat leaf. Black eddies brim
Around my heel which, pressing deep,
Accelerates the waiting sleep.

I used to live in sound, and lacked
Knowledge of still or creeping fact,
But now the stagnant strips my breath,
Leant on my cheek in weight of death.
Though so oppressed I find I may
Through substance move. I pick my way,
Where death and life in one combine,
Through the dark earth that is not mine,
Crowded with fragments, blunt, unformed;
While past my ear where noises swarmed
The marsh plant's white extremities,
Slow without patience, spread at ease
Invulnerable and soft, extend
With a quiet grasping toward their end.

And though the tubers, once I rot,
Reflesh my bones with pallid knot,
Till swelling out my clothes they feign
This dummy is a man again,
It is as servants they insist,
Without volition that they twist;
An habit does not leave them tired,
By men laboriously acquired.
Cell after cell the plants convert
My special richness in the dirt:
All that they get, they get by chance.

And multiply in ignorance.

VOX HUMANA

Being without quality
I appear to you at first
as an unkempt smudge, a blur,
an indefinite haze, mere-
ly pricking the eyes, almost
nothing. Yet you perceive me.

I have been always most close
when you had least resistance,
falling asleep, or in bars;
during the unscheduled hours,
though strangely without substance,
I hang, there and ominous.

Aha, sooner or later
you will have to name me, and,
as you name, I shall focus,
I shall become more precise.
O Master (for you command
in naming me, you prefer)!

I was, for Alexander,
the certain victory; I
was hemlock for Socrates;

and, in the dry night, Brutus
waking before Philippi
stopped me, crying out "Caesar!"

Or if you call me the blur
that in fact I am, you shall
yourself remain blurred, hanging
like smoke indoors. For you bring,
to what you define now, all
there is, ever, of future.

IN SANTA MARIA DEL POPOLO

Waiting for when the sun an hour or less
Conveniently oblique makes visible
The painting on one wall of this recess
By Caravaggio, of the Roman School,
I see how shadow in the painting brims
With a real shadow, drowning all shapes out
But a dim horse's haunch and various limbs,
Until the very subject is in doubt.

But evening gives the act, beneath the horse
And one indifferent groom, I see him sprawl,
Foreshortened from the head, with hidden face,
Where he has fallen, Saul becoming Paul.
O wily painter, limiting the scene
From a cacophony of dusty forms
To the one convulsion, what is it you mean
In that wide gesture of the lifting arms?

No Ananias croons a mystery yet,
Casting the pain out under name of sin.
The painter saw what was, an alternate
Candor and secrecy inside the skin.
He painted, elsewhere, that firm insolent
Young whore in Venus' clothes, those pudgy cheats,
Those sharpers; and was strangled, as things went,
For money, by one such picked off the streets.

I turn, hardly enlightened, from the chapel
To the dim interior of the church instead,
In which there kneel already several people,
Mostly old women: each head closeted
In tiny fists holds comfort as it can.
Their poor arms are too tired for more than this
—For the large gesture of solitary man,
Resisting, by embracing, nothingness.

THE ANNIHILATION OF NOTHING

Nothing remained: Nothing, the wanton name
That nightly I rehearsed till led away
To a dark sleep, or sleep that held one dream.

In this a huge contagious absence lay,
More space than space, over the cloud and slime,
Defined but by the encroachments of its sway.

Stripped to indifference at the turns of time,
Whose end I knew, I woke without desire,
And welcomed zero as a paradigm.

But now it breaks—images burst with fire
Into the quiet sphere where I have bided,
Showing the landscape holding yet entire:

The power that I envisaged, that presided
Ultimate in its abstract devastations,
Is merely change, the atoms it divided

Complete, in ignorance, new combinations.
Only an infinite finitude I see
In those peculiar lovely variations.

It is despair that nothing cannot be
Flares in the mind and leaves a smoky mark
Of dread.
          Look upward. Neither firm nor free,

Purposeless matter hovers in the dark.

INNOCENCE

to Tony White

He ran the course and as he ran he grew,
And smelt his fragrance in the field. Already,
Running he knew the most he ever knew,
The egotism of a healthy body.

Ran into manhood, ignorant of the past:
Culture of guilt and guilt's vague heritage,
Self-pity and the soul; what he possessed
Was rich, potential, like the bud's tipped rage.

The Corps developed, it was plain to see,
Courage, endurance, loyalty and skill
To a morale firm as morality,
Hardening him to an instrument, until

The finitude of virtues that were there
Bodied within the swarthy uniform
A compact innocence, child-like and clear,
No doubt could penetrate, no act could harm.

When he stood near the Russian partisan
Being burned alive, he therefore could behold
The ribs wear gently through the darkening skin
And sicken only at the Northern cold,

Could watch the fat burn with a violet flame
And feel disgusted only at the smell,
And judge that all pain finishes the same
As melting quietly by his boots it fell.

CONSIDERING THE SNAIL

The snail pushes through a green
night, for the grass is heavy
with water and meets over

the bright path he makes, where rain
has darkened the earth's dark. He
moves in a wood of desire,

pale antlers barely stirring
as he hunts. I cannot tell
what power is at work, drenched there
with purpose, knowing nothing.
What is a snail's fury? All
I think is that if later

I parted the blades above
the tunnel and saw the thin
trail of broken white across
litter, I would never have
imagined the slow passion
to that deliberate progress.

LOOT

I

I am approaching. Past dry
towers softly seeding from mere
delicacy of age, I
penetrate, through thickets, or

over warm herbs my feet press
to brief potency. Now with
the green quickness of grasses
mingles the smell of the earth,

raw and black. I am about
to raid the earth and open
again those low chambers that
wary fathers stand guard in.

II

Poised on hot walls I try to
imagine them caught beneath

in the village, in shadow:
I can almost hear them breathe.

This time what shall I take? Powers
hidden and agile, yield now
value: here, uniquely yours.
Direct me. But dark below

in the boneworks, you only
move in time with my pulse, and
observe without passion the
veer of my impassioned mind.

III

This. Hands numb from sifting soil
I find at last a trinket
carved whole from some mineral:
nameless and useless thing that

is for me to name and use.
But even as I relax my
fingers round its cool surface,
I am herald to tawny

warriors, woken from sleep, who
ride precipitantly down
with the blood toward my hands, through
me to retain possession.

THE BYRNIES

　　The heroes paused upon the plain.
When one of them but swayed, ring mashed on ring:
　　Sound of the byrnie's knitted chain,
Vague evocations of the constant Thing.

　　They viewed beyond a salty hill
Barbaric forest, mesh of branch and root
　　—A huge obstruction growing still,
Darkening the land, in quietness absolute.

That dark was fearful—lack of presence—
Unless some man could chance upon or win
   Magical signs to stay the essence
Of the broad light that they adventured in.

   Elusive light of light that went
Flashing on water, edging round a mass,
   Inching across fat stems, or spent
Lay thin and shrunk among the bristling grass.

   Creeping from sense to craftier sense,
Acquisitive, and loss their only fear,
   These men had fashioned a defence
Against the nicker's snap, and hostile spear.

   Byrnie on byrnie! as they turned
They saw light trapped between the man-made joints,
   Central in every link it burned,
Reduced and steadied to a thousand points.

   Thus for each blunt-faced ignorant one
The great grey rigid uniform combined
   Safety with virtue of the sun.
Thus concepts linked like chainmail in the mind.

   Reminded, by the grinding sound,
Of what they sought, and partly understood,
   They paused upon that open ground,
A little group above the foreign wood.

MY SAD CAPTAINS

One by one they appear in
the darkness: a few friends, and
a few with historical
names. How late they start to shine!
but before they fade they stand
perfectly embodied, all

the past lapping them like a
cloak of chaos. They were men
who, I thought, lived only to
renew the wasteful force they
spent with each hot convulsion.
They remind me, distant now.

True, they are not at rest yet,
but now that they are indeed
apart, winnowed from failures,
they withdraw to an orbit
and turn with disinterested
hard energy, like the stars.

Michael Hamburger

THE DUAL SITE

To my twin who lives in a cruel country
   I wrote a letter at last;
For my bones creaked out in our long silence
   That seven years had passed,

Seven whole years since he and I
   By word or token exchanged
The message I dare not do without:
   That still we are not estranged,

Though I watch figures in a city office
   And he the waves of the sea,
Keeping no count since he hardly cares
   What happens to him or to me;

Since to names and numbers he closed his head
   When, children still, we were parted,
Chose birth and death for his calendar,
   But leaves the dates uncharted,

Being one who forgets what I remember,
　Who knows what I do not,
Who has learnt the ways of otter and raven
　While I've grown polyglot.

Lately I found a cactus in flower
　And feared for his apple-trees,
Dozed in the club and saw his cattle
　Drag with a foul disease,

And my bones grown stiff with leaning and lying
　Cried out that I'll labour in vain
Till I help my twin to rebuild his hovel
　That's open to wind and rain.

So I sent him a note, expecting no answer,
　And a cheque he'd never cash,
For I knew he was one who'd smile if he heard
　His own roof come down with a crash,

But above the porpoise-leaping bay
　Where ploughshare fin and tail
Cut furrows the foam-flecked sea fills up
　He'd stand in the swishing gale,

Calm as the jackdaws that nest in crannies
　And no more prone to doubt,
With gull and cormorant perched on the rocks
　Would wait the weather out.

Yet he wrote by return: "Have no fear for your dwelling
　Though dry-rot gnaws at the floors;
Only lighten their load of marble and metal,
　Keep clear the corridors,

Move out the clocks that clutter your study,
　And the years will leave you alone:
Every frame I know of lasts long enough,
　Though but cardboard, wood or bone.

And spare me your nightmares, brother, I beg you,
　They make my daemons laugh,

They scare the spirits that rarely will visit
   A man with no wand or staff,

With no symbol, no book and no formula,
   No lore to aid him at all,
Who wherever he walks must find the image
   That holds his mentors in thrall.

But your waking cares put down on paper
   For me to give to the wind,
That the seed may fall and the dry leaf crumble,
   Not a wisp be left behind

Of the tangle that hides the dual site
   Where even you and I
Still may meet again and together build
   One house before we die."

MATHEMATICS OF LOVE

The links are chance, the chain is fate,
Constricting as Hephaistos' net
Which to the smiles of gods betrayed
Two bodies on a single bed,
So tightly knit, the truth was plain:
One multiplied by one is one.

Subtracting lovers who retort
That what chance coupled, choice can part
(As if mere effort could relax
The clutches of a paradox)
At last to their amazement find
Themselves the dwindled dividend,

Deep in that hell where Don Juan
Knows he has added names in vain
Since all the aggregate is lost
To him, not widowed but a ghost,
While those bereaved of one possess
A minus greater than his plus.

True love begins with algebra,
Those casual actors x and y,
Nonentities whose magic role
Is to turn nothing into all,
To be and not to be, to mate:
The links are chance, the chain is fate.

EPITAPH FOR A HORSEMAN

Let no one mourn his mount, upholstered bone
He rode so cruelly over bog and stone,
Log, fence and ditch in every kind of weather;
Nor glibly hint those two came down together:
A horse fell dead and cast his master down,
But by that fall their union was undone.
A broken jade we found, the rider gone,
Leaving no token but his cold clean gear,
Bit, reins and riding-crop for friends to gather.
None but a beast's remains lie buried here.

BLIND MAN

He can hear the owl's flight in daylight
When, surprised, on silky wings it shoots
From a low perch; and by the open window at night
The stag-beetles blundering in the hedges
On the far side of the meadow. Geese half a mile away
Honk near as hooters of swerving cars
And do not alarm him. Indifferently he awaits
Dogs that he feared when they slunk or bounded
Visible at him, as if in his carapace
Of darkness for ever secure from harm,
Wombed and housed and coffined within a wound
That has hardened to armour. The screech and the hum
Blend and subside in a resonant quiet,
Shapes he has fumbled to feel fall back
Into unbroken space when his hands forget them,
And still are present in his no man's land,

Above the nightmare tamed by light's extinction
The apple that hangs unplucked, grown fabulous.

MAN OF THE WORLD

Strange, but he cheats his master
Who without fail or stint pays in good notes and coinage,
For ever seeking to convert that currency
Into the sleep of metals and of stone.
Malachite, agate, lapis lazuli
Weigh down his papers; his eyelids are heavy with sleep.
Not bonds, nor journals line his inmost walls
But rows of books, his graveyard of choice minds,
Asleep until he rouses them,
Images fixed on paper, canvas, wood,
The disc engraved with voices of the dead,
Not flesh or leaf, time's pasture, but porcelain, ivory, bone.

Sleep is his wages; hatred of sleep
And fear of what might break it,
Sickness or slump,
The clumsy servant's duster,
Instruments of the retribution that will shatter
All that belies his means, outlasts his ends—
His master's ends, not his:
Though on a nightmare's back, he gallops into truth,
Though but to crash or stumble, rid of the glazed disasters
That were his juggler's toys,
Fell the raw grain and jagged crust of earth
And wake to serve his master loyally.

Geoffrey Hill

THE GUARDIANS

The young, having risen early, had gone,
Some with excursions beyond the bay-mouth,

Some toward lakes, a fragile reflected sun.
Thunder-heads drift, awkwardly, from the south;

The old watch them. They have watched the safe
Packed harbours topple under sudden gales,
Great tides irrupt, yachts burn at the wharf
That on clean seas pitched their effective sails.

There are silences. These, too, they endure:
Soft comings-on; soft after-shocks of calm.
Quietly they wade the disturbed shore;
Gather the dead as the first dead scrape home.

OF COMMERCE AND SOCIETY

VARIATIONS ON A THEME

> *Then hang this picture for a calendar,*
> *As sheep for goat, and pray most fixedly*
> *For the cold martial progress of your star,*
> *With thoughts of commerce and society,*
> *Well-milked Chinese, Negroes who cannot sing,*
> *The Huns gelded and feeding in a ring.*
> —ALLEN TATE: More Sonnets at Christmas, 1942

I THE APOSTLES: VERSAILLES, 1919

They sat. They stood about.
They were estranged. The air,
As water curdles from clear,
Fleshed the silence. They sat.

They were appalled. The bells
In hollowed Europe spilt
To the gods of coin and salt.
The sea creaked with worked vessels.

II THE LOWLANDS OF HOLLAND

Europe, the much-scarred, much-scoured terrain,
Its attested liberties, home-produce,

Labelled and looking up, invites use,
Stuffed with artistry and substantial gain:

Shrunken, magnified—(nest, holocaust)—
Not half innocent and not half undone;
Profiting from custom: its replete strewn
Cities such ample monuments to lost

Nations and generations: its cultural
Or trade skeletons such hand-picked bone:
Flaws in the best, revised science marks down:
Witness many devices; the few natural

Corruptions, graftings; witness classic falls;
(The dead subtracted; the greatest resigned;)
Witness earth fertilised, decently drained,
The sea decent again behind walls.

III THE DEATH OF SHELLEY

i

Slime; the residues of refined tears;
And, salt-bristled, blown on a drying sea,
The sunned and risen faces.
                              There's Andromeda
Depicted in relief, after the fashion.

"His guarded eyes under his shielded brow"
Through poisonous baked sea-things Perseus
Goes—clogged sword, clear, aimless mirror—
With nothing to strike at or blind
                              in the frothed shallows.

ii

Rivers bring down. The sea
Brings away;
Voids, sucks back, its pearls and auguries.
Eagles or vultures churn the fresh-made skies.

Over the statues, unchanging features
Of commerce and quaint love, soot lies.

Earth steams. The bull and the great mute swan
Strain into life with their notorious cries.

IV

Statesmen have known visions. And, not alone,
Artistic men prod dead men from their stone:
Some of us have heard the dead speak:
The dead are my obsession this week

But may be lifted away. In summer
Thunder may strike, or, as a tremor
Of remote adjustment, pass on the far side
From us: however deified and defied

By those it does strike. Many have died. Auschwitz,
Its furnace chambers and lime pits
Half-erased, is half-dead; a fable
Unbelievable in fatted marble.

There is, at times, some need to demonstrate
Jehovah's touchy methods, that create
The connoisseur of blood, the smitten man.
At times it seems not common to explain.

V ODE ON THE LOSS OF THE "TITANIC"

Thriving against façades the ignorant sea
Souses our public baths, statues, waste ground:
Archaic earth-shaker, fresh enemy:
("The tables of exchange being overturned");

Drowns Babel in upheaval and display;
Unswerving, as were the admired multitudes
Silenced from time to time under its sway.
By all means let us appease the terse gods.

VI THE MARTYRDOM OF SAINT SEBASTIAN

Homage to Henry James

"But then face to face"

Naked, as if for swimming, the martyr
Catches his death in a little flutter
Of plain arrows. A grotesque situation,
But priceless, and harmless to the nation.

Consider such pains "crystalline": then fine art
Persists where most crystals accumulate.
History can be scraped clean of its old price.
Engrossed in the cold blood of sacrifice,

The provident and self-healing gods
Destroy only to save. Well-stocked with foods,
Enlarged and deep-oiled, America
Detects music, apprehends the day-star

Where, sensitive and half-under a cloud,
Europe muddles her dreaming, is loud
And critical beneath the varied domes
Resonant with tribute and with commerce.

DOCTOR FAUSTUS

*For it must needs be that offences come; but woe
to that man by whom the offence cometh.*

I THE EMPEROR'S CLOTHES

A way of many ways: a god
Spirals in the pure steam of blood.
And gods—as men—rise from shut tombs
To a disturbance of small drums;

Immaculate plumage of the swan
The common wear. There is no-one

Afraid or overheard, no loud
Voice (though innocently loud).

II THE HARPIES

Having stood hungrily apart
From the gods' politic banquet,
Of all possible false gods
I fall to these gristled shades

That show everything, without lust;
And stumble upon their dead feast
By the torn *Warning To Bathers*
By the torn waters.

III ANOTHER PART OF THE FABLE

The Innocents have not flown;
Too legendary, they laugh;
The lewd uproarious wolf
Brings their house down.

A beast is slain, a beast thrives.
Fat blood squeaks on the sand.
A blinded god believes
That he is not blind.

A PASTORAL

Mobile, immaculate and austere,
The Pities, their fingers in every wound,
Assess the injured on the obscured frontier;
Cleanse with a kind of artistry the ground
Shared by War. Consultants in new tongues
Prove synonymous our separated wrongs.

We celebrate, fluently and at ease.
Traditional Furies, having thrust, hovered,

Now decently enough sustain Peace.
The unedifying nude dead are soon covered.
Survivors, still given to wandering, find
Their old loves, painted and re-aligned—

Queer, familiar, fostered by superb graft
On treasured foundations, these ideal features!
Men can move with purpose again, or drift,
According to direction. Here are statues
Darkened by laurel; and evergreen names;
Evidently-veiled griefs; impervious tombs.

ORPHEUS AND EURYDICE

Though there are wild dogs
    Infesting the roads
We have recitals, catalogues
    Of protected birds;

And the rare pale sun
    To water our days.
Men turn to savagery now or turn
    To the laws'

Immutable black and red.
    To be judged for his song,
Traversing the still-moist dead,
    The newly-stung,

Love goes, carrying compassion
    To the rawly-difficult;
His countenance, his hands' motion,
    Serene even to a fault.

IN PIAM MEMORIAM

I

Created purely from glass the saint stands,
Exposing his gifted quite empty hands
Like a conjurer about to begin,
A righteous man begging of righteous men.

II

In the sun lily-and-gold-coloured,
Filtering the cruder light, he has endured,
A feature for our regard; and will keep;
Of worldly purity the stained archetype.

III

The scummed pond twitches. The great holly-tree,
Emptied and shut, blows clear of wasting snow,
The common, puddled substance; beneath,
Like a revealed mineral, a new earth.

TO THE (SUPPOSED) PATRON

Prodigal of loves and barbecues,
Expert in the strangest faunas, at home
He considers the lilies, the rewards.
There is no substitute for a rich man.
At his first entering a new province
With new coin, music, the barest glancing
Of steel or gold suffices. There are many
Tremulous dreams secured under that head.
For his delight and his capacity
To absorb, freshly, the inside-succulence
Of untoughened sacrifice, his bronze agents
Speculate among convertible stones
And drink desert sand. That no mirage
Irritate his mild gaze, the lewd noonday
Is housed in cool places, and fountains

Salt the sparse haze. His flesh is made clean.
For the unfallen—the firstborn, or wise
Councillor—prepared vistas extend
As far as harvest; and idyllic death
Where fish at dawn ignite the powdery lake.

ANNUNCIATIONS

I

The Word has been abroad; is back, with a tanned look
From its subsistence in the stiffening-mire.
Cleansing has become killing, the reward
More touchable, overt, clean to the touch.
Now at a distance from the steam of beasts
The loathly neckings and fat shook spawn
(Each specimen-jar fed with delicate spawn)
The searchers with the curers sit at meat
And are satisfied. Such precious things put down
And the flesh eased through turbulence the soul
Purples itself; each eye squats full and mild
While all who attend to fiddle or to harp
For betterment, flavour their decent mouths
With gobbets of the sweetest sacrifice.

II

O Love, subject of the mere diurnal grind,
Forever being pledged to be redeemed,
Expose yourself for charity; be assured
The body is but husk and excrement.
Enter these deaths according to the law,
O visited women, possessed sons! Foreign lusts
Infringe our restraints; the changeable
Soldiery have their goings-out and comings-in
Dying in abundance. Choicest beasts
Suffuse the gutters with their colourful blood.
Our God scatters corruption. Priests, martyrs,
Parade to this imperious theme: "O Love,
You know what pains succeed; be vigilant; strive
To recognise the damned among your friends."

David Holbrook

LIVING? OUR SUPERVISORS WILL DO THAT FOR US!

Dankwerts, scholarship boy from the slums,
One of many, studied three years for the Tripos,
Honours, English; grew a beard, imitated the gesture
And the insistent deliberate (but not dogmatic)
"There!" of his supervisor. For a time
The mimesis was startling. Dankwerts knew
Uncannily what was good, what bad.
Life and earning a living, *extra muros*, for a time after-
      wards,
Left him hard up: people in *their* ambiguity
Nuisances. A bracing need for self-justification
(And spot cash) drove some of the nonsense out of him:
He found a foothold in films, the evening papers,
With his photograph, up to the ears in steaks, or ivy,
In "art" magazines. Passing over the Metropolis
He ejaculates like a satellite, evaporates, and falls,
Albeit on to a fat bank balance of amoral earnings.

Whereas his supervisor can be seen any Friday
Walking up Trumpington Street with an odd movement
      of the feet,
Still looking like an old corm, lissom, and knowing
Uncannily what's good, what's bad,
And probably rather hard up out of the bargain.

DELIVERING CHILDREN

AFTER A PARTY

Down the lane by the Butts in the headlights
Wind danced the dead grass, while the young one

Clambered home on the path. One of those Christmas
    nights
When every window's alit and muffles shrieks of chil-
    dren's fun,
Carols are sung, and packing paper
Stamped underfoot as the adults caper
And the children, pale and weary
Clutch their slippers and fragile gear. Hey!
How the pink straw danced like the hair of one in the
    night, carried away . . .

Before she was born, my dark child by the piano,
Abstracted, angelfaced? Once we stopped in sadness the
    car,
The grass danced so in the silent light? Ah, yes, we're now
Five: might have been six, one was never born; when we
    are
Back at her school, I recall this, singing around the tree
In the dark, at the fancy-dress party,
The disguise stuff coming apart, after they
Have worn themselves out with laughter Hey!
How the pink straw danced again tonight in that dead-
    remembering way!

And will dance so, too, when the child I unload
Is woman, we gone—cheerlessly lifted
Like hair in the unremitting wind on the road,
When the stars have sufficiently swung; drifted
The kind teachers; dead the father at door
Now cheerfully thanking; balloon-strewn floor
Worn, stripped and burnt; another yawn-at-end-of-day
Generation of children followed and followed on this. Hey!
How the dead grass dances on under the passing lamps,
    under the large star Way!

FINGERS IN THE DOOR

for Kate

Careless for an instant I closed my child's fingers in the
    jamb. She

Held her breath, contorted the whole of her being, foetus-
    wise, against the
Burning fact of the pain. And for a moment
I wished myself dispersed in a hundred thousand pieces
Among the dead bright stars. The child's cry broke,
She clung to me, and it crowded in to me how she and I
    were
Light-years from any mutual help or comfort. For her I
    cast seed
Into her mother's womb; cells grew and launched itself as
    a being:
Nothing restores her to my being, or ours, even to the
    mother who within her
Carried and quickened, bore, and sobbed at her separa-
    tion, despite all my envy,
Nothing can restore. She, I, mother, sister, dwell dis-
    persed among dead bright stars:
We are there in our hundred thousand pieces!

POOR OLD HORSE

A child skipping jump on the quay at the Mill,
With parted legs jump, soft-footed in April,
And the lovers on the bridge, sweet soft women's mouths
Pressing jowls of men, in jeans or loose trousers, youths
Packed in punts. And the masons on the bridge
Pause as they lift white stone to dress the face of the ridge
Of the balustrade, to imagine an actorish man
(Uxorious to a self-possessed blonde) as well as they can,
Back in the hotel room, making love; they laugh,
Turn back to the mortar. Ducks rise over trees, the chaff
Of mixed men and women floats over. A boy with a shiny
    red face
Attentively wipes some beer from his sweetheart's sleeve.
    The place
I remember assignments of old at, by moon and water,
The same acts of living, the same weir-splashed happiness
    after.
But today I sit here alone—with my daughter rather,

Who critically watches the child skipping jump on the
  waterfall quay,
And we after go back to the car. I am dumb, and silent
  she.
I see the spring love on the bridge for her: for me decay,
Or at most the wry pretension, "Well, we have had our
  day!"
I do not want to have had my day: I do not accept my
  jade,
Any more than the grey old horse we meet in the street,
His shaggy stiff dragged aside for a smart sports blade
And his smart sports car; yet that's no doubt my fate
As the water flows by here each year, April to April,
With a soft-footed child skipping jump on the quay at the
  Mill.

Ted Hughes

THE THOUGHT-FOX

I imagine the midnight moment's forest:
Something else is alive
Beside the clock's loneliness
And this blank page where my fingers move.

Through the window I see no star:
Something more near
Though deeper within darkness
Is entering the loneliness:

Cold, delicately as the dark snow,
A fox's nose touches twig, leaf;
Two eyes serve a movement, that now
And again now, and now, and now

Sets neat prints into the snow
Between trees, and warily a lame

Shadow lags by stump and in hollow
Of a body that is bold to come

Across clearings, an eye,
A widening deepening greenness,
Brilliantly, concentratedly,
Coming about its own business

Till, with a sudden sharp hot stink of fox
It enters the dark hole of the head.
The window is starless still; the clock ticks,
The page is printed.

ROARERS IN A RING

Snow fell as for Wenceslas.
   The moor foamed like a white
Running sea. A starved fox
   Stared at the inn light.

In the red gridded glare of peat,
   Faces sweating like hams,
Farmers roared their Christmas Eve
   Out of the low beams.

Good company kept a laugh in the air
   As if they tossed a ball
To top the skip of a devil that
   Struck at it with his tail,

Or struck at the man who held it long.
   They so tossed laughter up
You would have thought that if they did not
   Laugh, they must weep.

Therefore the ale went round and round.
   Their mouths flung wide
The cataract of a laugh, lest
   Silence drink blood.

And their eyes were screwed so tight,
  While their grand bellies shook—
O their flesh would drop to dust
  At the first sober look.

The air was new as a razor,
  The moor looked like the moon,
When they all went roaring homewards
  An hour before dawn.

Those living images of their deaths
  Better than with skill
Blindly and rowdily balanced
  Gently took their fall

While the world under their footsoles
  Went whirling still
Gay and forever, in the bottomless black
  Silence through which it fell.

A DREAM OF HORSES

We were born grooms, in stable-straw we sleep still,
All our wealth horse-dung and the combings of horses,
And all we can talk about is what horses ail.

Out of the night that gulfed beyond the palace-gate
There shook hooves and hooves and hooves of horses:
Our horses battered their stalls; their eyes jerked white.

And we ran out, mice in our pockets and straw in our hair,
Into darkness that was avalanching to horses
And a quake of hooves. Our lantern's little orange flare

Made a round mask of our each sleep-dazed face,
Bodiless, or else bodied by horses
That whinnied and bit and cannoned the world from its
    place.

The tall palace was so white, the moon was so round,
Everything else this plunging of horses
To the rim of our eyes that strove for the shapes of the
    sound.

We crouched at our lantern, our bodies drank the din,
And we longed for a death trampled by such horses
As every grain of the earth had hooves and mane.

We must have fallen like drunkards into a dream
Of listening, lulled by the thunder of the horses.
We awoke stiff; broad day had come.

Out through the gate the unprinted desert stretched
To stone and scorpion; our stable-horses
Lay in their straw, in a hag-sweat, listless and wretched.

Now let us, tied, be quartered by these poor horses,
If but doomsday's flames be great horses,
The forever itself a circling of the hooves of horses.

HAWK ROOSTING

I sit in the top of the wood, my eyes closed.
Inaction, no falsifying dream
Between my hooked head and hooked feet:
Or in sleep rehearse perfect kills and eat.

The convenience of the high trees!
The air's buoyancy and the sun's ray
Are of advantage to me;
And the earth's face upward for my inspection.

My feet are locked upon the rough bark.
It took the whole of Creation
To produce my foot, my each feather:
Now I hold Creation in my foot

Or fly up, and revolve it all slowly—
I kill where I please because it is all mine.

There is no sophistry in my body:
My manners are tearing off heads—

The allotment of death.
For the one path of my flight is direct
Through the bones of the living.
No arguments assert my right:

The sun is behind me.
Nothing has changed since I began.
My eye has permitted no change.
I am going to keep things like this.

THE RETIRED COLONEL

Who lived at the top end of our street
Was a Mafeking stereotype, ageing.
Came, face pulped scarlet with kept rage,
For air past our gate.
Barked at his dog knout and whipcrack
And cowerings of India: five or six wars
Stiffened in his reddened neck;
Brow bull-down for the stroke.

Wife dead, daughters gone, lived on
Honouring his own caricature.
Shot through the heart with whisky wore
The lurch like ancient courage, would not go down
While posterity's trash stood, held
His habits like a last stand, even
As if he had Victoria rolled
In a Union Jack in that stronghold.

And what if his sort should vanish?
The rabble starlings roar upon
Trafalgar. The man-eating British lion
By a pimply age brought down.
Here's his head mounted, though only in rhymes,
Beside the head of the last English

Wolf (those starved gloomy times!)
And the last sturgeon of Thames.

AN OTTER

I

Underwater eyes, an eel's
Oil of water body, neither fish nor beast is the otter:
Four-legged yet water-gifted, to outfish fish;
With webbed feet and a long ruddering tail
And a round head like an old tomcat.

Brings the legend of himself
From before wars or burials, in spite of hounds and
vermin-poles;
Does not take root like the badger. Wanders, cries;
Gallops along land he no longer belongs to;
Re-enters the water by melting.

Of neither water nor land. Seeking
Some world lost when first he dived, that he cannot come
at since,
Takes his changed body into the holes of lakes;
As if blind, cleaves the stream's push till he licks
The pebbles of the source; from sea

To sea crosses in three nights
Like a king in hiding. Crying to the old shape of the star-
lit land,
Over sunken farms where the bats go round,
Without answer. Till light and birdsong come
Walloping up roads with the milk wagon.

II

The hunt's lost him. Pads on mud,
Among sedges, nostrils a surface bead,
The otter remains, hours. The air,
Circling the globe, tainted and necessary,

Mingling tobacco-smoke, hounds and parsley,
Comes carefully to the sunk lungs.
So the self under the eye lies,
Attendant and withdrawn. The otter belongs

In double robbery and concealment—
From water that nourishes and drowns, and from land
That gave him his length and the mouth of the hound.
He keeps fat in the limpid integument

Reflections live on. The heart beats thick,
Big trout muscle out of the dead cold;
Blood is the belly of logic; he will lick
The fishbone bare. And can take stolen hold

On a bitch otter in a field full
Of nervous horses, but linger nowhere.
Yanked above hounds, reverts to nothing at all,
To this long pelt over the back of a chair.

NOVEMBER

The month of the drowned dog. After long rain the land
Was sodden as the bed of an ancient lake,
Treed with iron and birdless. In the sunk lane
The ditch—a seep silent all summer—

Made brown foam with a big voice: that, and my boots
On the lane's scrubbed stones, in the gulleyed leaves,
Against the hill's hanging silence;
Mist silvering the droplets on the bare thorns

Slower than the change of daylight.
In a let of the ditch a tramp was bundled asleep:
Face tucked down into beard, drawn in
Under its hair like a hedgehog's. I took him for dead,

But his stillness separated from the death
Of the rotting grass and the ground. A wind chilled,

And a fresh comfort tightened through him,
Each hand stuffed deeper into the other sleeve.

His ankles, bound with sacking and hairy band,
Rubbed each other, resettling. The wind hardened;
A puff shook a glittering from the thorns,
And again the rains' dragging grey columns

Smudged the farms. In a moment
The fields were jumping and smoking; the thorns
Quivered, riddled with the glassy verticals.
I stayed on under the welding cold

Watching the tramp's face glisten and the drops on his coat
Flash and darken. I thought what strong trust
Slept in him—as the trickling furrows slept,
And the thorn-roots in their grip on darkness;

And the buried stones, taking the weight of winter;
The hill where the hare crouched with clenched teeth.
Rain plastered the land till it was shining
Like hammered lead, and I ran, and in the rushing wood

Shuttered by a black oak leaned.
The keeper's gibbet had owls and hawks
By the neck, weasels, a gang of cats, crows:
Some, stiff, weightless, twirled like dry bark bits

In the drilling rain. Some still had their shape,
Had their pride with it; hung, chins on chests,
Patient to outwait these worst days that beat
Their crowns bare and dripped from their feet.

THRUSHES

Terrifying are the attent sleek thrushes on the lawn,
More coiled steel than living—a poised
Dark deadly eye, those delicate legs
Triggered to stirrings beyond sense—with a start, a bounce,
    a stab

Overtake the instant and drag out some writhing thing.
No indolent procrastinations and no yawning stares,
No sighs or head-scratchings. Nothing but bounce and stab
And a ravening second.

Is it their single-mind-sized skulls, or a trained
Body, or genius, or a nestful of brats
Gives their days this bullet and automatic
Purpose? Mozart's brain had it, and the shark's mouth
That hungers down the blood-smell even to a leak of its
     own
Side and devouring of itself: efficiency which
Strikes too streamlined for any doubt to pluck at it
Or obstruction deflect.

With a man it is otherwise. Heroisms on horseback,
Outstripping his desk-diary at a broad desk,
Carving at a tiny ivory ornament
For years: his act worships itself—while for him,
Though he bends to be blent in the prayer, how loud and
     above what
Furious spaces of fire do the distracting devils
Orgy and hosannah, under what wilderness
Of black silent waters weep.

PIKE

Pike, three inches long, perfect
Pike in all parts, green tigering the gold.
Killers from the egg: the malevolent aged grin.
They dance on the surface among the flies.

Or move, stunned by their own grandeur,
Over a bed of emerald, silhouette
Of submarine delicacy and horror.
A hundred feet long in their world.

In ponds, under the heat-struck lily pads—
Gloom of their stillness:

Logged on last year's black leaves, watching upwards.
Or hung in an amber cavern of weeds

The jaws' hooked clamp and fangs
Not to be changed at this date;
A life subdued to its instrument;
The gills kneading quietly, and the pectorals.

Three we kept behind glass,
Jungled in weed: three inches, four,
And four and a half: fed fry to them—
Suddenly there were two. Finally one

With a sag belly and the grin it was born with.
And indeed they spare nobody.
Two, six pounds each, over two feet long,
High and dry and dead in the willow-herb—

One jammed past its gills down the other's gullet:
The outside eye stared: as a vice locks—
The same iron in this eye
Though its film shrank in death.

A pond I fished, fifty yards across,
Whose lilies and muscular tench
Had outlasted every visible stone
Of the monastery that planted them—

Stilled legendary depth:
It was as deep as England. It held
Pike too immense to stir, so immense and old
That past nightfall I dared not cast

But silently cast and fished
With the hair frozen on my head
For what might move, for what eye might move.
The still splashes on the dark pond,

Owls hushing the floating woods
Frail on my ear against the dream
Darkness beneath night's darkness had freed,
That rose slowly towards me, watching.

PIBROCH

The sea cries with its meaningless voice,
Treating alike its dead and its living,
Probably bored with the appearance of heaven
After so many millions of nights without sleep,
Without purpose, without self-deception.

Stone likewise. A pebble is imprisoned
Like nothing in the Universe.
Created for black sleep. Or growing
Conscious of the sun's red spot occasionally,
Then dreaming it is the foetus of God.

Over the stone rushes the wind,
Able to mingle with nothing,
Like the hearing of the blind stone itself.
Or turns, as if the stone's mind came feeling
A fantasy of directions.

Drinking the sea and eating the rock
A tree struggles to make leaves—
An old woman fallen from space
Unprepared for these conditions.
She hangs on, because her mind's gone completely.

Minute after minute, aeon after aeon,
Nothing lets up or develops.
And this is neither a bad variant nor a tryout.
This is where the staring angels go through.
This is where all the stars bow down.

Elizabeth Jennings

OLD MAN

His age drawn out behind him to be watched:
It is his shadow you may say. That dark
He paints upon the wall is his past self,
A mark he only leaves when he is still
    And he is still now always,
At ease and watching all his life assemble.

And he intends nothing but watching. What
His life has made of him his shadow shows—
Fine graces gone but dignity remaining,
While all he shuffled after is composed
    Into a curve of dark, of silences:
An old man tranquil in his silences.

And we move round him, are his own world turning,
Spinning it seems to him, leaving no shadow
To blaze our trail. We are our actions only:
He is himself, abundant and assured,
    All action thrown away,
And time is slowing where his shadow stands.

THE CHILD AND THE SHADOW

Your shadow I have seen you play with often.
O and it seems a shadow light before you,
Glittering behind you. You can see what lies
Beneath its marking dappled on the water
    Or on the earth a footprint merely;
No total darkness is cast by your body.

Say that it is a game of identities this—
You chasing yourself not caring whatever you find.
You have not sought a use for mirrors yet,
It is not your own shadow that you watch,
   Only our world which you learn slowly:
Our shadows strive to mingle with your own,

Chase them, then, as you chase the leaves or a bird,
Disturb us, disturb us, still let the light lie gently
Under the place that you carve for yourself in air;
Look, the fish are darting beneath your reflection
   But you see deep beyond your glance:
It is our shadow that slides in between.

DISGUISES

Always we have believed
We can change overnight,
Put a different look on the face,
Old passions out of sight:
And find new days relieved
Of all that we regretted
But something always stays
And will not be outwitted.

Say we put on dark glasses,
Wear different clothes and walk
With a new unpractised stride—
Always somebody passes
Undeceived by disguises
Or the different way we talk.
And we who could have defied
Anything if it was strange
Have nowhere we can hide
From those who refuse to change.

THE PARTING

Though there was nothing final then,
No word or look or sign,
I felt some ending in the air
As when a sensed design
Draws back from the completing touch
And dies along a line.

For through the words that seemed to show
That we were learning each
Trick of the other's thought and sense,
A shyness seemed to reach
As if such talk continuing
Would make the hour too rich.

Maybe this strangeness only was
The safe place all men make
To hide themselves from happiness;
I only know I lack
The strangeness our last meeting had
And try to force it back.

GHOSTS

Those houses haunt in which we leave
Something undone. It is not those
Great words or silences of love

That spread their echoes through a place
And fill the locked-up unbreathed gloom.
Ghosts do not haunt with any face

That we have known; they only come
With arrogance to thrust at us
Our own omissions in a room.

The words we would not speak they use,
The deeds we dared not act they flaunt,
Our nervous silences they bruise;

It is our helplessness they choose
And our refusals that they haunt.

THE STORM

Right in the middle of the storm it was.
So many winds were blowing none could tell
Which was the fiercest or if trees that bent
So smoothly to each impulse had been waiting
All of their growing-time for just that impulse
To prove how pliable they were. Beneath,
Beasts fled away through fern, and stiffest grasses,
Which bent like fluid things, made tidal motion.

These who had never met before but in
Calmest surroundings, found all shadows mingling;
No stance could be struck here, no peace attained,
And words blew round in broken syllables,
Half-meanings sounded out like trumpet blasts,
Decisive words were driven into hiding.
Yet some hilarity united them
And faces, carved and cleared by rain and lightning,
Stared out as if they never had been seen.

And children now, lost in the wood together,
Becoming the behaviour of the wind,
The way the light fell, learnt each other newly
And sudden gentleness was apprehended
Till the abating winds, the whole storm swerving
Into another quarter, left them standing
Unwild and watching in bewilderment
Their own delusive shadows slow and part.

TERESA OF AVILA

Spain. The wild dust, the whipped corn, earth easy for footsteps, shallow to starving seeds. High sky at night like walls. Silences surrounding Avila.

She, teased by questions, aching for reassurance. Calm in confession before incredulous priests. Then back—to the pure illumination, the profound personal prayer, the four waters.

Water from the well first, drawn up painfully. Clinking of pails. Dry lips at the well-head. Parched grass bending. And the dry heart too—waiting for prayer.

Then the water-wheel, turning smoothly. Somebody helping unseen. A keen hand put out, gently sliding the wheel. Then water and the aghast spirit refreshed and quenched.

Not this only. Other waters also, clear from a spring or a pool. Pouring from a fountain like child's play—but the child is elsewhere. And she, kneeling, cooling her spirit at the water, comes nearer, nearer.

Then the entire cleansing, utterly from nowhere. No wind ruffled it, no shadows slid across it. Her mind met it, her will approved. And all beyonds, backwaters, dry words of old prayers were lost in it. The water was only itself.

And she knelt there, waited for shadows to cross the light which the water made, waited for familiar childhood illuminations (the lamp by the bed, the candle in church, sun beckoned by horizons)—but this light was none of these, was only how the water looked, how the will turned and was still. Even the image of light itself withdrew, and the dry dust on the winds of Spain outside her halted. Moments spread not into hours but stood still. No dove brought the tokens of peace. She was the peace that her prayer had promised. And the silences suffered no shadows.

THE ROOM

This room I know so well becomes
A way to keep proportion near.
In other houses, other rooms
Only anomalies appear.

I chose these books, the pictures too,
Thinking that I would often look
Upon a canvas like a view
Or find a world within a book.

They lie or hang, each laden now
With my own past, yet there's no sign
For anyone who does not know
Me, that these attributes are mine.

Strange paradox—that I collect
Objects to liberate myself.
This room so heavy now, so decked
Has put my past upon a shelf.

And this is freedom—not to need
To choose those things again. I thus
Preside upon the present, cede
The ornaments to usefulness.

And yet I know that while I clear
The ground and win back liberty,
Tomorrow's debris settles here
To make my art, to alter me.

A WORLD OF LIGHT

Yes when the dark withdrew I suffered light
And saw the candles heave beneath their wax,
I watched the shadow of my old self dwindle

As softly on my recollection stole
A mood the senses could not touch or damage,
A sense of peace beyond the breathing word.

Day dawned at my elbow. It was night
Within. I saw my hands, their soft dark backs
Keeping me from the noise outside. The candle
Seemed snuffed into a deep and silent pool:
It drew no shadow round my constant image
For in a dazzling dark my spirit stirred.

But still I questioned it. My inward sight
Still knew the senses and the senses' tracks,
I felt my flesh and clothes, a rubbing sandal,
And distant voices wishing to console.
My mind was keen to understand and rummage
To find assurance in the sounds I heard.

Then senses ceased and thoughts were driven quite
Away (no act of mine). I could relax
And feel a fire no earnest prayer can kindle;
Old parts of peace dissolved into a whole
And like a bright thing proud in its new plumage
My mind was keen as an attentive bird.

Yes, fire, light, air, birds, wax, the sun's own height
I draw from now, but every image breaks.
Only a child's simplicity can handle
Such moments when the hottest fire feels cool,
And every breath is like a sudden homage
To peace that penetrates and is not feared.

HARVEST AND CONSECRATION

After the heaped piles and the cornsheaves waiting
To be collected, gathered into barns,
After all fruits have burst their skins, the sating
    Season cools and turns,
And then I think of something that you said
Of when you held the chalice and the bread.

I spoke of Mass and thought of it as close
To how a season feels which stirs and brings
Fire to the hearth, food to the hungry house
    And strange, uncovered things—
God in a garden then in sheaves of corn
And the white bread a way to be reborn.

I thought of priest as midwife and as mother
Feeling the pain, feeling the pleasure too,
    All opposites together,
Until you said no one could feel such passion
And still preserve the power of consecration.

And it is true. How cool the gold sheaves lie,
Rich without need to ask for any more
Richness. The seed, the simple thing must die
    If only to restore
Our faith in fruitful, hidden things. I see
The wine and bread protect our ecstasy.

Philip Larkin

MR. BLEANEY

"This was Mr. Bleaney's room. He stayed
The whole time he was at the Bodies, till
They moved him." Flowered curtains, thin and frayed,
Fall to within five inches of the sill,

Whose window shows a strip of building land,
Tussocky, littered. "Mr. Bleaney took
My bit of garden properly in hand."
Bed, upright chair, sixty-watt bulb, no hook

Behind the door, no room for books or bags—
"I'll take it." So it happens that I lie

Where Mr. Bleaney lay, and stub my fags
On the same saucer-souvenir, and try

Stuffing my ears with cotton-wool, to drown
The jabbering set he egged her on to buy.
I know his habits—what time he came down,
His preference for sauce to gravy, why

He kept on plugging at the four aways—
Likewise their yearly frame: the Frinton folk
Who put him up for summer holidays,
And Christmas at his sister's house in Stoke.

But if he stood and watched the frigid wind
Tousling the clouds, lay on the fusty bed
Telling himself that this was home, and grinned,
And shivered, without shaking off the dread

That how we live measures our own nature,
And at his age having no more to show
Than one hired box should make him pretty sure
He warranted no better, I don't know.

AN ARUNDEL TOMB

Side by side, their faces blurred,
The earl and countess lie in stone
Their proper habits vaguely shown
As jointed armour, stiffened pleat,
And that faint hint of the absurd—
The little dogs under their feet.

Such plainness of the pre-baroque
Hardly involves the eye, until
It meets his left-hand gauntlet, still
Clasped empty in the other; and
One sees, with a sharp tender shock,
His hand withdrawn, holding her hand.

They would not think to lie so long.
Such faithfulness in effigy
Was just a detail friends would see:
A sculptor's sweet commissioned grace
Thrown off in helping to prolong
The Latin names around the base.

They would not guess how early in
Their supine stationary voyage
The air would change to soundless damage,
Turn the old tenantry away;
How soon succeeding eyes begin
To look, not read. Rigidly they

Persisted, linked, through lengths and breadths
Of time. Snow fell, undated. Light
Each summer thronged the glass. A bright
Litter of birdcalls strewed the same
Bone-riddled ground. And up the paths
The endless altered people came,

Washing at their identity.
Now, helpless in the hollow of
An unarmorial age, a trough
Of smoke in slow suspended skeins
Above their scrap of history,
Only their attitude remains.

Time has transfigured them into
Untruth. The stone fidelity
They hardly meant has come to be
Their final blazon, and to prove
Our almost-instinct almost true:
What will survive of us is love.

THE WHITSUN WEDDINGS

That Whitsun, I was late getting away:
    Not till about
One-twenty on the sunlit Saturday
Did my three-quarters-empty train pull out,

All windows down, all cushions hot, all sense
Of being in a hurry gone. We ran
Behind the backs of houses, crossed a street
Of blinding windscreens, smelt the fish-dock; thence
The river's level drifting breadth began,
Where sky and Lincolnshire and water meet.

All afternoon, through the tall heat that slept
    For miles inland,
A slow and stopping curve southwards we kept.
Wide farms went by, short-shadowed cattle, and
Canals with floatings of industrial froth;
A hothouse flashed, uniquely; hedges dipped
And rose; and now and then a smell of grass
Displaced the reek of buttoned carriage-cloth
Until the next town, new and nondescript,
Approached with acres of dismantled cars.

At first, I didn't notice what a noise
    The weddings made
Each station that we stopped at: sun destroys
The interest of what's happening in the shade,
And down the long cool platforms whoops and skirls
I took for porters larking with the mails
And went on reading. Once we started, though,
We passed them, grinning and pomaded, girls
In parodies of fashion, heels and veils,
All posed irresolutely, watching us go,

As if out on the end of an event
    Waving goodbye
To something that survived it. Struck, I leant
More promptly out next time, more curiously,
And saw it all again in different terms:
The fathers with broad belts under their suits
And seamy foreheads; mothers loud and fat;
An uncle shouting smut; and then the perms,
The nylon gloves and jewellery-substitutes,
The lemons, mauves, and olive-ochres that

Marked off the girls unreally from the rest.
    Yes, from cafés

And banquet-halls up yards, and bunting-dressed
Coach-party annexes, the wedding-days
Were coming to an end. All down the line
Fresh couples climbed aboard; the rest stood round;
The last confetti and advice were thrown,
And, as we moved, each face seemed to define
Just what it saw departing: children frowned
At something dull; fathers had never known

Success so huge and wholly farcical;
 The women shared
The secret like a happy funeral;
While girls, gripping their handbags tighter, stared
At a religious wounding. Free at last,
And loaded with the sum of all they saw,
We hurried towards London, shuffling gouts of steam.
Now fields were building-plots, and poplars cast
Long shadows over major roads, and for
Some fifty minutes, that in time would seem

Just long enough to settle hats and say
 I nearly died
A dozen marriages got under way.
They watched the landscape, sitting side by side
—An Odeon went past, a cooling tower,
And someone running up to bowl—and none
Thought of the others they would never meet
Or how their lives would all contain this hour.
I thought of London spread out in the sun,
Its postal districts packed like squares of wheat:

There we were aimed. And as we raced across
 Bright knots of rail
Past standing Pullmans, walls of blackened moss
Came close, and it was nearly done, this frail
Travelling coincidence; and what it held
Stood ready to be loosed with all the power
That being changed can give. We slowed again,
And as the tightened brakes took hold, there swelled
A sense of falling, like an arrow-shower
Sent out of sight, somewhere becoming rain.

Laurence Lerner

THE WAY TO THE SEA

The young men leave the country for the town,
And in the oozing rain they walk the street,
Feeling the stones resentful of their feet.
Like beaked giraffes the agile cranes look down,
Hover above the agitated docks,
Bend, lift and beckon through the busy air.
Beneath them on the uncompleted hulls
Workmen like seeds are scattered everywhere,
Spray paint, fling rivets, call to the swinging crane,
Ignoring the distant ocean and the gulls.
Slowly the ships grow, in the endless rain.

ii

Under the beeches as the leaves swing down
Onto the unmoved water where they lie,
In the mauve air among the smooth-barked trees
Whose branches chase a pattern on the sky,
The watchhouse has outlived its families:
Stares with starred windows as the children climb
Unhindered now upon the obstinate gates
(They would not open if you tried) to mock
The seep and patience of the stream that waits
To act its stately and frustrated mime.
Weeds film the water in the silent lock.

iii

The river rounds the lock and makes its way
Unhindered through the darkening fields. The light
Seeks its chased surface. If a dead leaf drops
It floats upon the mirrored sky in which
Beyond the hawthorn and the naked beech

The rooks returning mark the hastening day.
The brindled waters redden in the gleam
As the sun sinks behind the autumn copse
And round the darkness curves the fading stream.

iv

The Lagan leaves the country for the town.
Its unambitious waters slide between
Grey buildings bulking on the urban scene.
A smoky drizzle makes the city smart,
Damps the drab swans, and fills the powdered air.
The river empties at the wharfs and quays,
And spreads around the oily dockyard where
Crowded with passengers for overseas
The finished ships disturb it, and depart.

WHAT'S HARD

"I hate successful people," you declare,
And pause for the approving murmur. While
Ensuing conversation fills the air
"You're a success," you fling at me, and smile.

What was it in your tone or look that jarred?
I fumble through my feelings, and find this:
"Failure is easy. It's success that's hard.
I know so many who achieve success

Only at being failures; play that role
With such aplomb (of course I don't mean you)
All gaze in awe at their aspiring soul,
And shake their heads at what they've fallen to."

I do not say this; but you watch my face.
Again you try an epigram: "What's hard
Is to succeed, and yet to keep the grace
Of failure." You sit back, and all applaud.

(Of course you don't mean me.) And now what's hard
Is to restrain the nervous smile of spite,

Not speak the words our friendship can't afford,
Because I love you, and I know you're right.

A MEDITATION UPON THE TOOTHACHE

It brims in the white cistern; flows
Over and floods the floor of the mouth; it beats
Over the closed and echoing chamber, like speech.
All day among
The silent ridges and around the tongue
The fluent toothache goes.

Every inquiry prompts me to a ruse;
I bite it into every phrase I use:
"As bad as ever, thanks." Or "Nothing to mention."
These are my quiet bids for the room's attention.

I meditate upon the well-known view
That pain's imaginary. Is it true?
The ache seeps upward to the brain, distorts
Like a half-mastered language all my thoughts.

I meditate. Where does a war exist?
You hold a newspaper coolly in your fist.
The words take meaning in your fear. You move
Through Odysseys of dread before you prove
The feel of endurance; before you hear the syrens
Lure you to suffer what your fear imagines.

For after a while the infected gum will heal,
The maudlin matter be washed from our words; the tide
Of feeling in the flooded mouth subside.
And is it real, the memory of a pain
That now exists in the newspapers only? Still
We shall meditate, and find it about as real
As this knowledge seeping into the aching brain:

The imagination hurts, like fear: or toothache.

"IN A SHOREHAM GARDEN"

Samuel, Samuel Palmer,
Tell me (if you know)
Where (and not in Shoreham)
Does that garden grow?

What is the great tree made of
That blooms in such a flurry,
Tossing up in bundles
Its white and bursting cherry?

Why is the crimson lady
Standing stately there,
Leaning on the silence
In the waiting air?

Tell me, Samuel Palmer,
Shall I get there one day?
Is it far from London?
Who showed you the way?

It was William showed me.
Some do, some don't get there.
It's as far from London
As wish is far from care.

The tree is made of longings;
Despair is at its root;
The hand must grow in sorrow
That plucks its perfect fruit.

And should you find the garden
Go up the garden path:
Learn of the stately lady
(For what the learning's worth)

That none can give directions,
No mortal breathes that air;

The sunshine of achievement
Ripens nothing there.

Peter Levi, S.J.

L'AURORE GRELOTTANTE

Three counties blacken and vanish,
rivers run unlighted and silent,
lamp by lamp of the city came, went,
into the utter dark, which was my wish.

In my scarred thought this city
burns to a ruin under the visiting air,
among the ashes of whose luxury
the young barbarians shake their scented hair.

Bitterer, deeper, in my desolate thought,
a lonely and a self-murdering love,
uninhabitable ashes, every dove
murdered, every winged buzzard caught.

The wind rises. At this time of night
condemned men lie quiet on their beds.
Birds start. Vagueness clears to light.
The wakeful old can let fall their heads.

The wind rises. A workman coughs in the cold.
It rises. Volleys and lines of mist
push from river to river and find no hold.
Leaves fall. Blood runs cold in the wrist.

"HE MET HER AT THE GREEN HORSE . . ."

He met her
at the Green Horse
by the Surrey Docks;
Saturday
was the colour of his socks.

So they loved,
but loving
made nothing better—
drowning cats
in an ocean of water.

What more,
what more could there be,
days or nights?
nothing
to hear or see but dances and sights.

So they loved,
like the aimless air
or like walking
past shut doors
in a never quiet street and talking.

"IN A CORNER OF EDEN . . ."

In a corner of Eden
the one-horned black
rare rhinoceros slept in the shade,
water among the reeds softly swam
yellow and green the ripening melons hang
softly slept.
In the hot light once
he went, stinking shade drops

dark over his head,
in Eden once
easy-bellied he lay
and breathed a gentle breath such as yellow
fruit or any sleeping beast may.

TO MY FRIENDS

for Dom

We took no notes of contemplated light
   or of delight
though (each one writing in his room alone)
   we could have done,

we were confused from treason by the exact
   spark of a fact,
touch of a self by salt and bone surrounded
   or self-compounded,

each one by love and season friend or fool
   of the beautiful,
wrote personal poems read by everyone,
   naming no one.

"SHIP-BUILDING EMPERORS COMMANDED . . ."

Ship-building emperors commanded
these night-obscuring giant beams,
with open-work like ribs defended
what is from what merely seems,
among those timbers old
the young sea-captains sailed.

Storms of a classical illusion
broke open, bit by bit, the mind
in oceans where a bleak confusion
on a ruined shore has left behind

dead Plato, litter of broken wood,
redefining moral good.

Some broken stone, sublimely quiet
poses against an open sky,
(the subject populations riot,
the discipline of the troops is high),
now in the officers' mess
they mention happiness.

And young men in romantic places
curbing an adolescent rage
reform the lines of their cold faces
in a dead father's still image,
whose mental life is now
this service which they owe:

by a nervous trick of rhetoricians,
judgement, language for events,
to deny all images, all visions,
to choose gay-coloured ornaments,
self-mirroring man and woman
in a lost image as human.

But when these mental forces break
no natural anguish can uncover
the lost ship in the draining lake
which a savage hermit brooded over,
who is now defined again
in a quiet craze of pain;

and those first virtuous professions
haunt angels and their whisering throats,
while the sad wise in grave processions
(deep-coloured gems, light-coloured coats)
let fall their heavy tears
gaunt music for lost ears.

Edward Lucie-Smith

AT THE ROMAN BATHS, BATH

Between trains, on this day of snow,
I kill an hour here. The old man
Who swabs the pavement makes us two—
I'm solitary, not alone.
In the bleak water goldfish swallow
As if they gulped the snowflakes down.
What do I feel? I wish I knew—
To-day thoughts swim, but feelings drown.

I see the snow twist back from steam
Above one pool; this other lies
Dragging the willing whiteness home,
Coldness to coldness. Back I gaze
At Sul-Minerva, chipped and grim—
The carving stares through centuries,
Celtic but Roman, *her* but *him*,
Reason's image with mad eyes.

The eyes are stone, and yet they weep—
Slow drops of water form and fall
(Steam mixed with snow in every drop),
I catch one running down the wall
And taste it from my fingertip—
It shocks the tongue with salt and chill:
This sign of a god's ownership
Can make me feel uneasy still.

ON LOOKING AT STUBBS'S ANATOMY OF THE HORSE

In Lincolnshire, a village full of tongues
Not tired by a year's wagging, and a man
Shut in a room where a wrecked carcass hangs,
His calm knife peeling putrid flesh from bone;
He whistles softly, as an ostler would;
The dead horse moves, as if it understood.

That night a yokel holds the taproom still
With tales new-hatched; he's peeped, and seen a mare
Stand there alive with naked rib and skull—
The creature neighed, and stamped upon the floor;
The warlock asked her questions, and she spoke;
He wrote her answers down in a huge book . . .

Two centuries gone, I have the folio here,
And turn the pages, find them pitiless.
These charts of sinew, vein and bone require
A glance more expert, more detached than this—
Fingering the margins, I think of the old
Sway-backed and broken nags the pictures killed.

Yet, standing in that room, I watch the knife;
Light dances on it as it maps a joint
Or scribes a muscle; I am blank and stiff,
The blade cuts so directly to my want;
I gape for anecdote, absurd detail,
Like any yokel with his pint of ale.

MEETING MYSELF

A scent of beeswax, dust; the empty rooms
Echo my footfalls; I am on the stair,
Have brushed my arm against the vase of roses,
When suddenly I see him standing there

Amid the petals shaken from the blooms,
Wearing my clothes. I see the look he chooses.

"You're trespassing," it says. "Who let you in?
You should have got no nearer than the gate—
How did you come so softly up the gravel?"
My outstretched fingers stub against the plate
Of the long glass, our touch barred by the thin
Clearness between: our nod is barely civil.

RABBIT CRY

The season? Not yet spring. The place? Beside
A knot of sapling birches, under sky
Silver as birchbark. Here were gaping wide
A warren's crumbling mouths to catch our feet.
We stooped, the nets were staked, the bag untied,
And into day's eye glared a blood-red eye—
The ferret trembled, with a sudden slide
Plunged white to darkness. Hearts resumed their beat.

Yet memory's fixed by what I did not see.
It was as if I heard the birches creak
Under a troubling gust, as if each tree
Now drew up from its roots those shreds of words
That in the windless day surrounded me.
It was the warren's mouths began to shriek;
I saw their breathless immobility
Ajar to the still sky stripped bare of birds.

THE FAULT

Frescoes that crumble, marbles bullet-scarred,
And Signorelli's *Pan* burnt in Berlin—
Meaning betrayed by matter, smudged and blurred,
Or altogether lost through shapes it took.
And yet it's hard to blame the paint or stone;
Even words crumble, buried in a book;

Rochester's puns seem almost innocent,
And schoolboys puzzle out what Chaucer meant.

"Blame Time," we say, though through it we exist;
To live's to alter, be from day to day,
From month to month, from one year to the next
A part of motion. Pictures, statues, words
Are part of us, and therefore will decay;
Bronzes will melt, pots smash themselves to sherds,
Musicians lose the knack of mind and ear
Which finds in certain noises something clear.

Goodbye, then, you who're gone or almost gone—
Zeuxis (no birds are tempted by your fruit),
Sappho (grammarians' rags), even you with one
Smiling statue to show, Praxiteles;
Nameless musicians left without a note
Who blindly finger harps upon a frieze
Swaying from the wall in an Egyptian tomb—
To fill each place you leave, let others come.

And farewell this, which lives for days or weeks,
For ten years or a thousand—let it go.
As the ink dries, the work already seeks
Its own oblivion, starts at once to change
From what I meant to say, or be, or do;
Already, as I look, the poem's strange,
No longer fluid, molten. See it lie
Apart—a cold moon, barren entity.

George MacBeth

THE DRAWER

Their belongings were buried side by side
In a shallow bureau drawer. There was her
Crocodile handbag, letters, a brooch,

All that was in the bedside cupboard
And a small green jar she'd had for flowers.

My father's were in an envelope:
A khaki lanyard, crushed handkerchief,
Twelve cigarettes, a copying-pencil,
All he had on him when he was killed
Or all my mother wanted to keep.

I put them together seven years ago.
Now that we've moved, my wife and I,
To a house of our own, I've taken them out.
Until we can find another spare drawer
They're packed in a cardboard box in the hall.

So this dead, middle-aged, middle-class man
Killed by a misfired shell, and his wife
Dead of cirrhosis, have left one son
Aged nine, aged nineteen, aged twenty six,
Who has buried them both in a cardboard box.

THE COMPASSES

Baroque-handled and sharp
With blunt lead in their lips
And their fluted legs together
My father's compasses
Lie buried in this flat box.

I take it out of its drawer,
Snap old elastic bands
And rub the frayed leatherette:
It smells faintly of smoke:
The broken hinges yawn.

As I level the case to look
A yellowed protractor claps
Against black-papered board,
Sliding loose in the lid
Behind a torn silk flap.

I look in the base at the dusty
Velvet cavities:
Dead-still, stiff in the joints
And side by side they lie
Like armoured knights on a tomb.

One by one I lift
Them out in the winter air
And wipe some dust away:
Screw back their gaping lips
And bend the rigid knees.

In an inch of hollowed bone
Two cylinders of lead
Slither against each other
With a faint scurrying sound.
I lay them carefully back

And close the case. In Crookes
My father's bones are scattered
In a measured space of ground:
Given his flair for drawing
These compasses should be there

Not locked away in a box
By an uninstructed son
But like an Egyptian king's
Ready shield and swords
Beside his crumbling hand.

BEDTIME STORY

Long long ago when the world was a wild place
Planted with bushes and peopled by apes, our
Mission Brigade was at work in the jungle.
  Hard by the Congo

Once, when a foraging detail was active
Scouting for green-fly, it came on a grey man, the

Last living man, in the branch of a baobab
  Stalking a monkey.

Earlier men had disposed of, for pleasure,
Creatures whose names we scarcely remember—
Zebra, rhinoceros, elephants, wart-hog,
  Lion, rats, deer. But

After the wars had extinguished the cities
Only the wild ones were left, half-naked
Near the Equator: and here was the last one,
  Starved for a monkey.

By then the Mission Brigade had encountered
Hundreds of such men: and their procedure,
History tells us, was only to feed them:
  Find them and feed them;

Those were the orders. And this was the last one.
Nobody knew that he was, but he was. Mud
Caked on his flat grey flanks. He was crouched, half-
  Armed with a shaved spear

Glinting beneath broad leaves. When their jaws cut
Swathes through the bark and he saw fine teeth shine,
Round eyes roll round and forked arms waver
  Huge as the rough trunks

Over his head, he was frightened. Our workers
Marched through the Congo before he was born, but
This was the first time perhaps that he'd seen one.
  Staring in hot still

Silence, he crouched there: then jumped. With a long
    swing
Down from his branch, he had angled his spear too
Quickly, before they could hold him, and hurled it
  Hard at the soldier

Leading the detail. How could he know Queen's
Orders were only to help him? The soldier

Winched when the tipped spear pricked him. Unsheath-
　　ing his
Sting was a reflex.

Later the Queen was informed. There were no more
Men. An impetuous soldier had killed off,
Purely by chance, the penultimate primate.
　　When she was certain,

Squadrons of workers were fanned through the Congo
Detailed to bring back the man's picked bones to be
Sealed in the archives in amber. I'm quite sure
　　Nobody found them

After the most industrious search, though.
Where had the bones gone? Over the earth, dear,
Ground by the teeth of the termites, blown by the
　　Wind, like the dodo's.

James Michie

DOOLEY IS A TRAITOR

"So then you won't fight?"
"Yes, your Honour," I said, "that's right."
"Now is it that you simply aren't willing,
Or have you a fundamental moral objection to killing?"
Says the judge, blowing his nose
And making his words stand to attention in long rows.
I stand to attention too, but with half a grin
(In my time I've done a good many in).
"No objection at all, sir," I said.
"There's a deal of the world I'd rather see dead—
Such as Johnny Stubbs or Fred Settle or my last land-
　　lord, Mr. Syme.
Give me a gun and your blessing, your Honour, and I'll
　　be killing them all the time.

But my conscience says a clear no
To killing a crowd of gentlemen I don't know.
Why, I'd as soon think of killing a worshipful judge,
High-court, like yourself (against whom, God knows, I've
    got no grudge—
So far), as murder a heap of foreign folk.
If you've got no grudge, you've got no joke
To laugh at after."
                 Now the words never come flowing
Proper for me till I get the old pipe going.
And just as I was poking
Down baccy, the judge looks up sharp with "No smoking,
Mr. Dooley. We're not fighting this war for fun.
And we want a clearer reason why you refuse to carry a
    gun.
This war is not a personal feud, it's a fight
Against wrong ideas on behalf of the Right.
Mr. Dooley, won't you help to destroy evil ideas?"
"Ah, your Honour, here's
The tragedy," I said. "I'm not a man of the mind.
I couldn't find it in my heart to be unkind
To an idea. I wouldn't know one if I saw one. I haven't one
    of my own.
So I'd best be leaving other people's alone."
"Indeed," he sneers at me, "this defence is
Curious for someone with convictions in two senses.
A criminal invokes conscience to his aid
To support an individual withdrawal from a communal
    crusade
Sanctioned by God, led by the Church, against a godless,
    churchless nation!"
I asked his Honour for a translation.
"You talk of conscience," he said. "What do you know of
    the Christian creed?"
"Nothing, sir, except what I can read,
That's the most you can hope for from us jail-birds.
I just open the Book here and there and look at the words.
And I find when the Lord himself misliked an evil notion
He turned it into a pig and drove it squealing over a cliff
    into the ocean,
And the loony ran away
And lived to think another day.

There was a clean job done and no blood shed!
Everybody happy and forty wicked thoughts drowned
    dead.
A neat and Christian murder. None of your mad slaughter
Throwing away the brains with the blood and the baby
    with the bathwater.
Now I look at the war as a sportsman. It's a matter
    of choosing
The decentest way of losing.
Heads or tails, losers or winners,
We all lose, we're all damned sinners.
And I'd rather be with the poor cold people at the wall
    that's shot
Than the bloody guilty devils in the firing-line, in Hell and
    keeping hot."
"But what right, Dooley, what right," he cried,
"Have you to say the Lord is on your side?"
"That's a dirty crooked question," back I roared.
"I said not the Lord was on my side, but I was on the side
    of the Lord."
Then he was up at me and shouting,
But by and by he calms: "Now we're not doubting
Your sincerity, Dooley, only your arguments,
Which don't make sense."
('Hullo,' I thought, 'that's the wrong way round.
I may be skylarking a bit, but my brainpan's sound.')
Then biting his nail and sugaring his words sweet:
"Keep your head, Mr. Dooley. Religion is clearly not up
    your street.
But let me ask you as a plain patriotic fellow
Whether you'd stand there so smug and yellow
If the foe were attacking your own dear sister."
"I'd knock their brains out, mister,
On the floor," I said. "There," he says kindly, "I knew you
    were no pacifist.
It's your straight duty as a man to enlist.
The enemy is at the door." You could have downed
Me with a feather. "Where?" I gasp, looking round.
"Not this door," he says angered. "Don't play the clown.
But they're two thousand miles away planning to do us
    down.

Why, the news is full of the deeds of those murderers and
    rapers."
"Your Eminence," I said, "my father told me never to be-
    lieve the papers
But to go by my eyes,
And at two thousand miles the poor things can't tell truth
    from lies."
His fearful spectacles glittered like the moon: "For the last
    time what right
Has a man like you to refuse to fight?"
"More right," I said, "than you.
You've never murdered a man, so you don't know what it
    is I won't do.
I've done it in good hot blood, so haven't I the right to
    make bold
To declare that I shan't do it in cold?"
Then the judge rises in a great rage
And writes DOOLEY IS A TRAITOR in black upon a
    page
And tells me I must die.
"What, me?" says I.
"If you still won't fight."
"Well, yes, your Honour," I said, "that's right."

THREE DREAMS

1

Hair long, cheekbones high,
Unencumbered by manners, though clothed in the cos-
    tume of an age,
I meet you, have always known you, used cunning and
    knives to win you in primitive epochs and other lives,
Woman with a tinge of African or Spanish.
We give no sign of recognition, I single you out at parties,
    we face each other at crossroads, I swim round a
    headland and there you are on the beach, conscious
    of me,
Eyes wide open.
You swerve aside. I follow,
Tracking you through the old familiar wilderness,

Unhurried because there is no time, unanxious because I
    am sure to find you
Under the oak or catch you under the sea,
In sympathy unlike human sympathy, which is mixed with
    a grain of contempt,
With love not made a lie by the pert desire for discovery,
With love we do not need to name.

2

I see islands floating unknowingly on to the bows of for-
    eign ships and sunk
(Gone the name of the archipelago),
The wading ashore, the scuffle in the shallows or the cliff-
    side barrage;
The chief consults unruffled, trusting in the local science
And the latest modifications in the arrow.
His sons are soon dead. The women go to the mountain.
High above the sea-shore vegetation flies the morbid,
    multi-coloured flag.
I see the Roman in Bavaria
Baffled by the fir-devils, the miles of fir, the sneering
    ravens;
The Spaniard breathing with difficulty in Peru,
Or afraid, for fear of laughter, to skate on the Dutch canals.
The Hawaiian turns his face away from me, dying of the
    imported germ.
Crete swarms with a new shape of head,
Makers of the prettiest daggers the Minoans are aston-
    ished, killed to a man.

Wandering I visit the last Carib lying in a corner, the lost
    Etruscans,
And empty of Red Indians the cheerless plains.

3

The Siberian tiger sits on a cliff of snow
Casting a blue shadow bigger than himself
And destroys with his mouth the appealing, flying deer.
I too tear the haunches and eat the strings and the guts,
The glance of the victim still upon me.
Only I know the true wickedness of the tiger.

His whiskers and eye compel me. I must scurry to please
    him.

The sunny lawn is littered with deadly snakes,
Walk as warily as you may, you are bound to wake them.
Aimed elsewhere my sole treads on the slumbering ribbon,
My shoe squelches the puff adder, the mamba strikes
    through my leggings,
All around alarm of tongues, coilings, ill colours, outrage,
    directed malice,
Till I fall on the sunny lawn, a small Laocoön.

In a gap in the forest I come upon the lion and the wolf
Fighting to the death, the lion losing,
His face gory, righteous, amazed.
He is the king. He has no right to lose.
But the wolf, who is guilty of winning, with a long clever
    look
Tears down the lion.
Hiding in a tree,
I love the wolf for this unnatural revolt.

But I am seen. Suddenly a crowd assembles,
Inflamed country faces, farmers with their sons and dogs,
Their pursuit ponderous, full of apparatus.
Running, never quite flying,
Weak I watch my webbed prints in the wet sand recede
    behind me.
I kiss the befriending trees, I confide in the river, the cur-
    rents are on my side,
Storming through legs, assisting speed.
Perfect my hiding-place in the reeds till each time by
    chance discovered.
From deep in the mud-bank they haul me out straining to
    use my wings,
For spying to be done to death with sticks.

CLOSING TIME

Jerusalem Street and Paradise Square
Drive their drinkers home to bed.
Dreaming of fancy houses where
The sheets are white and the lanterns red,
Drunkards grouped round the baby grand
With moonlike face and waving hand
Leave. The seedy last who lingers
Through the tankard sees his fingers.

Turned out in boastful threes and twos,
The champions at darts and soccer
Have hearts that sink into the shoes
That lead them back towards the knocker,
Kick stones, throw sticks dejectedly,
And whistle disconnectedly.
And, as they think about their wives,
The rain returns into their lives.

Christopher Middleton

THE THOUSAND THINGS

Dry vine leaves burn in an angle of the wall.
Dry vine leaves and a sheet of paper, overhung
by the green vine.
From an open grate in an angle of the wall
dry vine leaves and dead flies send smoke up
into the green vine where grape clusters go
ignored by lizards. Dry vine leaves
and a few dead flies on fire
and a Spanish toffee spat
into an angle of the wall

make a smell that calls to mind
the thousand things. Dead flies go,
paper curls and flares,
Spanish toffee sizzles and the smell
has soon gone over the wall.

A naked child jumps over the threshold,
waving a green spray of leaves of vine.

MALE TORSO

Before I woke, the customed thews
Alighted on strangeness.
Crammed over booms of vine,
The once buxom canvas quilled.

From his hot nest, before I woke,
The snowgoose flew, in skyward rings;
And funnelled air that filled my mouth
Rang with his wingbeat.

The customed eyes, before I woke, were glass:
A bleating queen whose legs were sheaths
Of hammered moon fed swill to pigs;
With needle oars they swept her bark

Through floes of starfruit, dolphins cutting
Under her eyelid's bow blue arcs in air;
And the beat of their oars like drums
Fanned my hushabye head.

Before I woke, no savour was;
But three birds sang that song they piped as girls,
Of sweetness, golden-rinded, and the fountaintree,
For mortal grapes cooled in my hands.

Then down the quartz-walled galleries of ears I coiled,
Before I woke; cymbals clashing sliced their hill,
And there with bulls my skew-wigged mother trod
Her crocus dance around its axle;

Counterwheeling Horn and Bear
Shared in her coronal the thud of fingertips on flutes,
Until my customed silence dipped and rose,
And gall was mine and darkness was.

I live now in a hutch of mud,
Without a floor, nailed by the sun,
Now for the interminable writhing sea
A fair food housed in roofless marble.

But if I wake to sniff the air of clustered stars,
I'm clothed in dew, for babes to drink,
The snowgoose moors her nest on light,
And the small horned worms walk high with hope.

ALBA AFTER SIX YEARS

There was a winter
    dark fell by five
four noses ran
    and shouting children
she got so quickly in a rage.

Now when I wake
    through mist and petrol
birdsong cannonades
    blaze open-sighted
at a climbing sun.

Hopeful but prone
    I turn to face a wall
between me and that wall
    surprised to meet
wild arms which did not hold this way before.

NEWS FROM NORWOOD

Professor Palamedes darts down Westow Street.
Nothing explains how he avoids
Colliding with mutton, plastics, pianos.
Professor Palamedes, darting down Westow Street,
Tunnels through petrol fumes and tundra;
Rhomboid oysterbeds under his rubbers,
Sparrows and sandwiches scatter before him.

Where is he going, Professor Palamedes?
It's well past three. What has he forgotten?
What can he have forgotten, Professor Palamedes,
Who stood with Agur by Solomon's elbow,
Who flogged the sea, full of nymphs and sheep,
Whom meat moods or helpful harmonies do not perplex?

Let us say he is going toward the stranger.
Again: he is going toward the stranger.
No matter who. The stranger. Who showed his face.
Who showed his face over Solomon's shoulder;
Who saw at Salamis, as planks buckled and the nymphs
Cheered, how sheep just went on cropping grass,
Side by side, to a tinkling of bells.

THINKING OF HÖLDERLIN

(HILLS NEAR HEIDELBERG)

Never mind avarice; the hills
squander at least a sprawl
of steep oak. Speak
of the moroccan green
pines that fetlock them; of rumps,
rutted by axes; of bristling stung flanks,
flushed by puffs of cloud—

for first and last
who saw them crammed the air
with hawk and temple;
and what fetched them avarice, in the interim,
cannot change their green
bulk and butts of sandstone,
let alone rot the wits, killing,

as hawk and temple, his, for the crime
of being put, by them, wise to the least thing.
No, not in his name
do I join these crooked words, lest I miss
for him, more than temple, his hawk,
now lofted by their hot gusts, now
plucking the crowded vermin from their folds.

From *HERMAN MOON'S HOURBOOK*

ABASIS

Walking docile as you do down the empty street
The shadow-crowded granite, glow of sodium seas
It may shake the pavement under your feet
May drum with fists on air beside you
Mirage at your back may corrupt the clarity before you
May knock on your door when guests have turned and
    gone
May trouble your dream in the house (angel or monster
Figures recoil then into the cavity of the dream)
Dissolving bastions you had made sure were solid
Dispensing the life that is casual (not good but average)
May issue a spectre out of the throat of morning
A mask of sweat at noon
Forbidding the ecstasy that rides the noon's brow
Perplexing the cool that lays the dust at evening
Hollowing the tranced hill where you squat at sundown

Happy with friends to watch the turning of the stars.

THE ANT SUN

The ant sun rams
Its ivory egg.
Grinding gears
Mix: it trundles on.
Slow river loomed,
A barge bellows;
Exhaust oils
Banked cloud of stone.

Sleep and waking
Swop lefts:
Old men tenderly
Thrump their brides
Of decades gone:
For white robes
They wait and stew,
The crowding misty girls.

And a day comes
And a day comes
With brisk birds.
A swab slops
Over dud marble.
Harder day comes
(Purity. Purity!)
With sweetly reeking coins.

THE FORENOON

All the long forenoon, the loitering of insects;
Their invisible wings, whirring in choir and alley,
By lemon pyramids, in domes of organpounded air,
Over golden loaves that cool on glass in Greek Street.

One has flown to the vine slopes of a gated city,
One is crushed in a tube; one is a foreign king,
Stern in his carriage, popular, waving;

One with a whip stumbled after office girls,
And woke smiling. In iron shade
To one on a bench his nostril's curlew pipings bring
Concomitant visions of vacant moors.
One has dwelled among the springs and heard
A throbbing in the ark above their mountain.
One sidesteps a banker with a beak
And a dead baby dangling on a string from it.
One wisecracks. One darts giggling under a hat,
To munch a matchstick. One reads words
ARBOGAST FACTION PACT BUT HEAT RISES.

One: severed from the great root the strong shrivel
One: the voluminous black fire answers their cry of terror
One: the plumed waves have burst long enough on this
    shore
One: scattering the blind swarms that drink at the carcass.

ODE ON CONTEMPLATING CLAPHAM JUNCTION

All day rain fell. Morning:
one dusky liquid nymphless cave.

By noon the cave was crammed with ocean.
Two trains, full tilt, great whistling mackerel,
raced in an X under whaleshaped shadow.

Umbrellas, propped in halls, by tea,
behaved across the floor, like puppies.

All fall, by day, had rained. As late
as nine now moist sun
ushers a fearful agitation in

through curtain after lifting curtain.
Some thrush or other aches to sing.

Joy. One thrush. One overhasty . . . No.
The sun mistaken, rising upside down?
Washed clean, no, space begins, unfolding

a million brilliant swishing fans
of bluish nothing.

Draughts of tomorrow
drawn slow
into empty lungs.

WATERLOO BRIDGE

The rolled umbrella on my wrist,
How much air, crushed in the folds,
Aches for expulsion? What is starved
Between my hat's crown and my own
Of angering freshness deep, deep down?

Chimney and sailor, ship and star
Strangely belong. The cobbled lanes
Rib the long river: wet flint mounds
Tug at its roots; and cranes that inch
Athwart thick rooves, suppose this freedom.

Horns blast the ear, like anchors flung
By fluke through sludge to block
Derision riding seaward with the sun.
A meal of rats, doled out by love:
Crushed by the silence, bolt it down.

POINTED BOOTS

At three in the morning
A quietness descends on central railway stations.
A mail van, or an ambulance, may be there;
A man in pointed boots, a Miss Carew.
Quietness keeps them apart,
The quietness that descends on central railway stations.

It is not meant for me.
It is not meant for you.

Dom Moraes

SONG

The gross sun squats above
A valley full of shadows:
The wizard plays his flute
And lizards in green meadows
And archers in pursuit
Of antelope and dove
Grow dumb and cannot move.

Now dancers, stones for eyes
And meadowgrass for hair,
To whom the four winds kneel,
Wheel in unspoken prayer.
Only this prayer seems real.
Lightly the flute sighs:
No living voice replies.

But breezes talk to trees
While seasons come and go
And in frail winter light
Pale feathers of the snow
Will flutter and alight
Bearing a branch of peace,
And dance and flute will cease.

GIRL

They told me first she was a tree
So tall, no man could ever climb
Into her branches, there to see
The folded rose untouched by Time.

In the dark wood where my thoughts move
She stood: I dared not go too close,
But dreamt for days of courtly love,
And took more trouble with my clothes.

Then weather for the death of Christ
—No wind at all, and rain like spears—
Came on the hillside, with a mist
As blinding as a mist of tears.

The geese sailed over with a cry.
The forest raised its arms above
Her bent head, where she stood: and I
Went close and stammered out my love.

We lay together in the mist
On clods the colour of wet bread.
My hand enclosed her hand: we kissed:
She trembled then and turned her head.

She whispered to me, I must go.
And absence came upon the land,
Cold, foreign, like the drifted snow.
The rose had shrivelled in my hand.

I stood and wished I had more wit,
There in the dripping wood, alone.
I took a stone and, fingering it,
Wished that I too could turn to stone.

LULLABY

With lights for eyes, our city turns
Its secret face towards the hill,
Where yet the sacred fire burns
And the sad priest lopes out to kill
At midnight, when the plains are still.

Limp flowers fester in those plains.
Our city stands there, and the deep

River moves gently in your veins
Until you are adrift on sleep,
Your cares put elsewhere: they will keep.

If bad dreams visit you, be still.
Turn on your side; they were not sent.
Those owl-eyed watchers on the hill,
Terrible in their lofty tent,
Keep no watch on the innocent.

I see far off the priest-king chase
The wounded doe until it dies.
He lifts a pale and guilty face.
The crows have eaten out his eyes.
Who suffers may perhaps be wise.

I doubt it, but shall climb to see
And find some black and monstrous thing
Dictating from a blasted tree
In thunder to the prostrate king.
You will not hear it. Sleep, my darling.

QUEEN

The queen went from me while I slept.
It was the hour before light breaks.
It was the last of my mistakes,
The promise that I never kept.

Mailed reptile, I had hissed and struck
This way and that at fresh alarms,
Kissed men to death, and pressed my arms
Tighter around her for good luck,

Who now, surrendered to her dream,
White fingers laid on boulder-scars,
Climbs the unwinding rock-hewn stair,

The sheep's path to the hidden stream.
The fallen rain glitters like stars
In the dark river of her hair.

THE FINAL WORD

Since I was ten I have not been unkind
To anyone save those who were most close:
Of my close friends one of the best is blind
One deaf, and one a priest who can't write prose.
None has a quiet mind.

Deep into night my friends with tired faces
Break language up for one word to remain,
The tall forgiving word nothing effaces,
Though without maps it travel, and explain
A pure truth in all places.

Yet death, if it should fall on us, would be
Only the smallest settling into beds:
Our last words lost because Eternity
Made its loud noise above our lifted heads
Before we ceased to see.

But, all made blind and deaf, the final word
Bequeathed by us, at the far side of
Experience, waits: there neither man nor bird
Settles, except with knowledge, or much love.
There Adam's voice is heard.

And my true love, a skylark in each eye,
Walks the small grass, and the small frightened things
Scurry to her for comfort, and can't die
While she still lives, and all the broken Kings
Kneel to her and know why.

Because she turns, her love at last expressed,
Into my arms; and then I cannot die.
I have furnished my heart to be her nest
For even if at dusk she choose to fly
Afterwards she must rest.

Peter Redgrove

ON CATCHING A DOG-DAISY
IN THE MOWER

After the death of a close friend in an accidental fall

"Well, that was silly; too near the edge:
White flesh goes flying and the bee escapes.
It was an old flower anyway and not a prize,
Inside, the shade of good tobacco finely-grained.
What a shock the bee got though, snatching away
His stool like that as he sat down.
I'll clear it up; so white a flesh
Against the green; I'll let it char,
But tuck the mangled neck back again
Right out of sight, behind the crowded bush
Of roses red as—how they shine: it seems to hum."
So I buzzed about my jobs, mumbling my mind,
Stringing sentences and trying words
And soon forgot whose flesh was white, and shreds
Charred back to soil, and what roses were as red as,
And summer dry as, now, and how swift
The tawny humming bee snapped away.
"I'd better pick the white bits up,
And put them on the heap, for tidiness."

SHEARING GRASS

The long grass searches the wind.
Her rust grit shears snap. She leaves
A broad path behind
Like a barber's matted floor. A squab mouse flees
In a quiver of hair. She's

Fatal. The fumbling beetle on its flower
Cracks its back as the crisp stalk falls.
Yoke-muscles under her tumbling hair
Squeeze shut. Some foot-splaying grass moves on with her
    heels
Stuck in its sap. The long tree-polyps snatch
Their birds.
Flowers, spread on their safe beds, watch.
In its bulk a black laurel stills
The air, leaves piled like an audience regard the stage,
Or as the breeze breathes its lines, applauds.
The sun draws rich oils from her hair,
Through her shirt pours in its rage
From the electric softness of her flesh distils
More there that through the warm cloth wind.
Later I take her up the stair;
We stride in the house above the garden where
Two blisters at the third finger-roots left
And paid for a ravaged festering weft.

BEDTIME STORY FOR MY SON

Where did the voice come from? I hunted through the
    rooms
For that small boy, that high, that head-voice,
The clatter as his heels caught on the door,
A shadow just caught moving through the door
Something like a school-satchel. My wife
Didn't seem afraid, even when it called for food
She smiled and turned her book and said:
"I couldn't go and love the empty air."

We went to bed. Our dreams seemed full
Of boys in one or another guise, the paper-boy
Skidding along in grubby jeans, a music-lesson
She went out in the early afternoon to fetch a child
    from.
I pulled up from a pillow damp with heat
And saw her kissing hers, her legs were folded

Far away from mine. A pillow! It seemed
She couldn't love the empty air.

Perhaps, we thought, a child had come to grief
In some room in the old house we kept,
And listened if the noises came from some especial room,
And then we'd take the boards up and discover
A pile of dusty bones like charcoal twigs and give
The tiny-sounding ghost a proper resting-place
So that it need not wander in the empty air.

No blood-stained attic harboured the floating sounds,
We found they came in rooms that we'd warmed with our
    life.
We traced the voice and found where it mostly came
From just underneath both our skins, and not only
In the night-time either, but at the height of noon
And when we sat at meals alone. Plainly, this is how we
    found
That love pines loudly to go out to where
It need not spend itself on fancy and the empty air.

STORY FROM RUSSIAN AUTHOR

"How did you know her?"
  "*By the soft flux of worry
  Round her mouth.*"

"What did you give her?"
  "*The simple necessity
  Of bread in the mouth.*"

"How was she sick?"
  "*Dark blood
  Rose in her mouth.*"

"Where did you find her?"
  "*Unmelting wedged
  Snow in her mouth.*"

CORPOSANT

A ghost of a mouldy larder is one thing: whiskery bread,
Green threads, jet dots,
Milk scabbed, the bottles choked with wool,
Shrouded cheese, ebony eggs, soft tomatoes
Cascading through their splits,
Whitewashed all around, a chalky smell,
And these parts steam their breath. The other thing
Is that to it comes the woman walking backwards
With her empty lamp playing through the empty house,
Her light sliding through her steaming breath in prayer.

Why exorcise the harmless mouldy ghost
With embodied clergymen and scalding texts?
Because she rises shrieking from the bone-dry bath
With bubbling wrists, a lamp and steaming breath,
Stretching shadows in her rooms till daybreak
The rancid larder glimmering from her corpse
Tall and wreathed like moulds or mists,
Spoiling the market value of the house.

THE GHOSTLY FATHER

He'd had enough of lying in the furze.
He combed gnats out of his beard,
Shrugged tendrils off his habit.

He'd try the road. But Goodness!
He was hungry. He wrung
The hem of his robe and sipped dew.

His bare feet had worn through. Thorns shivered on them,
They sank in the pasture and rattled flints
As he padded to the blot of a distant town.

He knew his face was seamed with pollen and earth,
But, peering over a smooth puddle,
Saw only the moon, blown to the full.

The trees enrolled him overhead.
A religious should not jump at shadows.
He rattled his rosary. A traveller glimpsing, ran.

This was discouraging. He sought the ditch
And burrowed through turf and fetched against bed-rock:
He would not walk, but lay blinking on packed roots;
Perhaps one day men would be more spiritual.

I STROLL

My grey-barked trees wave me in
In my stout double-breasted with the buttons winking,
Shirt blue as the thistle-heads, grey-barked stick
To swing great circles on the morning
And eyes glistening green as the pool.
The dog leaves thundering as I glance at him;
I beam back at the sun, my hair is grey as gossamer;
The bird-shadows hunt like rats through the grass.
A cobweb plashes my face
And plucks a frown from my nature, but that will pass.

My trees, grey-barked, waft me in. . . .
But the holly, stiff as carving, lashes my hand—
Lèse-majesté—I flick the blood-drop at its roots and listen
    to it wither
Like tissue-paper from my path.

My trees draw back and bristle as I enter the open space,
Dog growls because the couples do not rise,
But I motion silence, and walk among them considering
    offspring,
And the sun hides his face:

They shall have a boy, and those a statesman,
That one will miscarry, and that die in infancy,

A whore for the blond ones, and a centenarian under the
    hedge,
And no issue for the one that lies on his side and sneers at
    his partner;
I finish, and the sun ducks out of hiding. . . .

As I stroll among my human creation
In my park along my walks, disguised,
Waggling my fat caterpillar-eyebrows,
Evening mist-tides hissing past my brogues.

Alastair Reid

IN MEMORY OF MY UNCLE TIMOTHY

His name, they told me afterwards, was Able,
and he came, in yellow boots and a hat, and stood by the
    table
beside my Uncle Timmy, who went mad
later, and was a trouble to my Dad.
Uncle Tim said shakily "God, it's not you!"
but whoever he was, it was. So Tim took off his shoe,
shook it, and held it upside down. Out fell
a photograph of Grace, a sprig of fennel,
a bent crown piece, and a small gold key as well.
Tim spilt them in this man's lap, and he
—you'll not believe it—took out his eye
(glass, it was), and turned it over. On the back
was a crooked keyhole and a lock.
So he took Tim's key (he did, he did!)
and put it in. Up sprung a kind of lid.
He shoved it under Tim's nose. "Holy God!"
cried Tim. I looked, in the nick, before it closed.

Inside, upside down, was a tiny man
in a hat like Able's, with yellow boots on,
the spitting image of this living Able,

and there were Tim and me, upside down at the table,
and in the man's hand . . . but he quickly locked his eye,
tucking carefully away the key,
and put the thing crookedly back in his face,
gave Uncle the coin and the photograph of Grace,
stuck the sprig of fennel in his hat,
and off he went. "Uncle Tim" I cried, "what was that?"
I remember his face, but now I forget what he said.
Anyway, now Tim's dead.

GHOSTS' STORIES

That bull-necked blotch-faced farmer from Drumlore
would never dream (or so we heard him boast
to neighbours at the lamb sales in Kirkcudbright)
of paying the least attention to a ghost.

Were we to blame for teaching him a lesson?
We whored his daughter, spaded all his ewes,
brought a blight on his barley, drew the sea
rampaging over his sod. . . .

If we had any doubt that he deserved it,
that went when we heard him stamp his ruined acres
and blame it all on God.

When we went on and frightened Miss McQueen
for keeping children in on Halloween,
and wailed all night in the schoolhouse, she, poor woman,
sent for the Fire Brigade.
And so we made
fire lick from her hair, till they put her out.

The children knew what it was all about.

THE TALE THE HERMIT TOLD

It was one afternoon when I was young
in a village near here, which no one now remembers—
why, I will tell you—an afternoon of fiesta,
with the bells of the hermitage echoing in the mountains,
and a buzz of voices, and dogs barking. Some said
it could all be heard as far as Calatayud.
I was a boy then, though at that perilous point
when tiny things could terrify and amaze me.
The dust in the village square had been watered down,
and we waited, laughing and jostling
the satin rumps of the gipsy dancers.
Across from us, the girls, all lace and frills,
fluttered like tissue paper. Then at a signal,
as the charcoal-burner's dog rolled over and over,
shedding its ribbons, the village band
blundered into tune, and the day began.
   The dancing dizzied me. There was one gipsy
unlike the others, tall, who spun on her feet,
laughing to herself, lost in her own amazement.
I watched her as though in a dream. All round,
my uncles and other men were calling *olé*
while the women tittered and pouted.
There were more feet than shoes, more wine than glasses,
and more kisses than lips. The sun was burning.
Next came a magician, an ugly sly-eyed man
not from our district. "Fiesta, fiesta" he called,
then, chanting a kind of spell, he swore
he would conjure a live dove out of the air.
I saw the dove's wing peeping from his pocket,
so I wandered away, hating the sound of him,
among the tables, heavy with food and wine.
And there was the gipsy girl, standing alone,
head turned away to listen, as though she heard
bells in the hills. She saw me, and her eyes,
which were azure, not black, mocked me.
I could not stop looking. Lightly she danced across
and, keeping her eyes on mine, poured out

a glass of golden wine, and put it before me.
　I glanced from her eyes to the wine. In it, the sun
was a small gold coin, the people looked like nuts.
The band were brass buttons, the towering mountains
the size of pebbles, the houses, matchboxes
about the thumbnail square. A miniature magician
was letting loose a dove, which floated upwards,
and there, in that golden, glass-held afternoon,
were those mocking eyes. Time in that moment hung
upside down. In a gulp, I drank the wine.
　　What happened next? You must listen.
Goggling boys, girls, dogs, band, gipsies, village,
dove, magician, all rolled down my throat.
Even the music glugged once and was gone.
I was standing nowhere, horrified, alone,
waiting for her eyes to appear and laugh
the afternoon back, but nothing moved or happened.
Nothing, nothing, nothing.
　　All that night, I lay in a clump of pines
and seemed to hear the hunters with their dogs
(unribboned now) closing to flush me out.
I hid my face in the needles. All the next day,
I tried to wish the village back, to vomit
the wine, to free the white dove and the music.
I could not. And as time passed,
I lived on bitter nuts and bark and grasses,
and grew used to the woods. I am still here
on this barren mountainside. The years are nothing.
　　Yet I am sure of this—
that somewhere in my body there is fiesta,
with ribboned dogs, balloons, and children dancing
in a lost village, that only I remember.
Often I have visions, and I hear
voices I know call out. Was it the false magician
who tempted me to magic? Or was it
the gipsy girl who dropped her eyes in a glass
and asked me to work wonders?
Even now, in age, I wait to see her,
still a girl, come spiralling through the woods,

bringing her mystery to me, and with her eyes
teaching me to undream myself, and be
a boy again, believing in a dove
made out of air, that circles overhead
on a lost afternoon of fiesta.

OUTLOOK UNCERTAIN

No season
brings conclusion.

Each year,
through heartache, nightmare,

true loves alter,
marriages falter,

and lovers illumine
the antique design,

apart, together,
foolish as weather,

right as rain,
sure as ruin.

Must you, then, and I
adjust the whole sky

over every morning;
or else, submitting

to cloud and storm,
enact the same

lugubrious ending,
new lives pending?

Jon Silkin

FURNISHED LIVES

I have been walking today
Where the sour children of London's poor sleep
    Pressed close to the unfrosted glare,
Torment lying closed in tenement,
    Of the clay fire; I
Have watched their whispering souls fly straight to God:

"O Lord, please give to us
A dinner-service, austere, yet gay: like snow
    When swans are on it; Bird,
Unfold your wings until like a white smile
    You fill this mid-white room."
I have balanced myself on the meagre Strand where

Each man and woman turn,
On the deliberate hour of the cock
    As if two new risen souls,
Through the cragged landscape in each other's eyes.
    But where lover upon lover
Should meet—where sheet, and pillow, and eiderdown

Should frolic and breathe
As dolphins on the stylized crown of the sea
    Their pale cerements lie.
They tread with chocolate souls and paper hands,
    They walk into that room
Your gay and daffodil smile has never seen:

Not to love's pleasant feast
They go, in the mutations of the night,
    But to their humiliations

Paled as a swan's dead feather scorched in the sun.
    I have been walking today
Among the newly paper-crowned, among those

    Whose casual, paper body
Is crushed between fate's fingers and the platter;
    But Sir, their perpetual fire
Was not stubbed out, folded on brass or stone
    Extinguished in the dark,
But burns with the drear dampness of cut flowers.

    I cannot hear their piped
Cry. These souls have no players. They have resigned
    The vivid performance of their world.
        And your world, Lord,
            Has now become
Like a dumb winter show, held in one room,

    Which must now reek of age
Before you have retouched its lips with such straight fire
    As through your stony earth
Burns with ferocious tears in the world's eyes:
Church-stone, door-knocker and polished railway lines
    Move in their separate dumb way
        So why not these lives:
I ask you often, but you never say?

THE RETURN

    I have carried for five years
In me, your country cupped with oval leaves.
    It is a land quickened with streams
Which have no confluence, yet they now firmly flow
    One liquid star in my blood;
It is as a jewel there. It is fearful and

    Strange to attend you
For I once fled through your pattern, I who now cup
    Your shape in my palm, and I

Burst from the green veins of your delicate country
  Move into the grey
Borders of the town who crouches in her shadows.

  I revisit you now and find
There is nothing changed in you but myself, I am
  Like a bird
That lightly perches on the angular
  Chimneys of London; I see
The sour hands of that woman folded into her lap.

  And I divine I now shall
Not be admitted easily to your source.
  That image of your streams met in me—
As the confluence of the stars meets in the one eye—
  This I got when I saw
The white shoulder of your profound hill. You were

  Then simple to me, but my thought
That now so distorts you, helped by the sensual flesh
  That exudes its particular scent,
The scent that the flesh gives out, and the flower exudes,
  As they are loved—the gesture
Of the heart and the movement of the flower are the
  same—

  That starlike thought of you
Still treads through my head as a dream treads, quietly
  And with precision,
Unendingly real because impossible;
  That thought and that image of you
You now deny. I am refused by you.

  There are a thousand stones in
The shallows of the Avon but must I tender them,
  Become again the intimates of
Your intimates before I begin where you
  Began? The day's
Shadow has lengthened and the red sun stirring

  Its more recent beams, in the evening
Grinds up its heat still; and in between the sheltering
  Walls of the town

Where the poor's tears are dropped without the leaf
    For their comfort or even
The stalk for their pity, it pierces. May I attend

    These stones, as tears should be
Tendered. Say if you will admit me although
    My image of you is false.
Then your jewels, flat and poor, will have my tenderness;
    I will become their friend
Who fold over and over the fragile white rounds
    Of your demanding country.

RESPECTABILITIES

Many liberals don't just
Make love, they first ask each other;
And either is free to decline
What the other wishes;
That is, unmitigated
Possession of the beloved's flesh.
Nothing hasty, nothing unconsidered
Catches the liberal by
The hairs of lust. Nothing.
And this consideration
For those feelings
Of the approached one naked
In love or in hunger
Is extended to all.
He will, for instance, ask
A starving man if he
Would eat, pressing
For the particulars
Of hunger. And enquire
Why he is deficient
In bread. All men are treated
With such perception as stones
Get in subjection to
Their shaper, as their use fits
To his. Men are chosen to meet
That judged compassion which

A liberal has. A wounded man
Receives the ointments of love
From matrons, with respect.
Sex, the inhuman hunger,
Demands courteous
Submission, polite domination.
In fact, the turning world,
A stone delicately
Veined with acceptable
Colours, deficient just because
Another stone has gouged
A bit from its flesh
Demands the liberal heart;
Though another stone
Brutal in the untamed
Components—a misshapen
Tongue of useless rock—
Merits, and gets
A frank dismissal.
And this, too, is fair;
Though more than half the earth
Is denied purchase on
That delicate conscience
Cash gives: a fair if privileged
Mind veined with gold.

Burns Singer

STILL AND ALL

I give my word on it. There is no way
Other than this. There is no other way
Of speaking. I am my name. I find my place
Empty without a word, and my word is
Given again. It is nothing less than all
Given away again, and all still truly
Returned on a belief. Believe me now.
There is no other. There is no other way.

These words run vertical in their slim green tunnels
Without any turning away. They turn into
The first flower and speak from a silent bell.
But underneath it is as always still
Truly awakening, slowly and slowly turning
About a shadow scribbled down by sunlight
And turning about my name. I am in my
Survival's hands. I am my shadow's theme.

My shadow's ground feeds me with roots, and rhymes
My statement over. Its radius feeds my flames
Into a cool tunnel. And I who find your ways
About me (In every part I find your ways
Of speech.) pierce ground and shadow still. The light
Is struck. Its definition makes me my quiet
Survival's answer. All still and all so truly
Wakening underneath me and turning slowly.

It's all so truly still. I'll take you into
The first statement. I'll take you along cool tunnels
That channelled light and petalled an iridescent
Symmetry over my bruised shadow. And yes
I'll take you, and your word will follow me,
Till definitions gather distilled honey
And make their mark the fingerprints of light.
I am, believe me then, the name I write.

I lie here still. Yes, truly still. And all
My deliberate identities have fallen
Away with the word given. I find my place
In every place, in every part of speech,
And lie there still. I let my statements go.
A cool green tunnel has stepped in the light of my shadow
There is no way round it. It leads to the flower
Bell—that swings slowly and slowly over.

WORDS MADE OF WATER

Men meet and part;
But meeting men today

I find them frightened,
Frightened and insolent,
Distrustful as myself.
We turn arrogantly toward one another,
Caged in dogmatical dazzle.
Our eyes shine like thin torchlight.
Conflicting truths, we dazzle one another.
Never lately have I known men meet
With only darkness, quite anonymous,
Perched up between them on a song no bird
Would answer for in sunlight.
I have watched carefully but never once
Have I seen the little heaps,
The co-ordinated fragments of muscle, brain, and bone,
Creep steadfastly as ants across the planet,
Quite lost in their own excess of contraries,
Make signals, ask for answers,
Humbly and heavily from those they know
Are equally ignorant.

Looking about the streets I find the answers,
Thin blobs of light, enamelled pricelists, brawling,
An impatient competition
Between all those who all know all the answers.

I find also certain bits of paper,
Matchsticks, sodden or cracked or still with safety heads,
Cigarette douts and their empty packets,
And also water,
Water that is stagnant
Or water flowing slowly down the gutter.

I sometimes think that dead men live in water,
That their ghosts inhabit the stagnant puddles,
Their barges float with the gutter water,
That they are waiting patiently as water
Until the world is redeemed by doubt,
By each man's love for all those different answers
Dead men have dropped on sundry bits of paper,
From glances blue as smoke, now quite extinguished.

My womenfolk find these thoughts troubling.
Action becomes impossible: choice is impossible
To those who think such things.
On thoughts like these no man ever grew fat.

From SONNETS FOR A DYING MAN

XV

The old man dozed. The hospital quietened.
Nurses went whispering past his unmade bed:
While Mr. Childs, who has no stomach, yawned
And those with papers put them by, unread.
It went all right till tea-time. Then the trays
Trickling like iron water through the ward
Wakened the old man and in prompt relays
The nurses gathered to be reassured.
The old man wakened but to what old tales
Of overwork or underpay or hate
We'll never know. By now it is too late.
But Mr. Childs, who has no stomach, swore
The old man rose and tried to shout before
His eyes went slimy with the look of snails.

XXX

To see the petrel cropping in the farmyard
Among brown hens, trying in vain to cluck,
Trying to rouse the rooster, trying too hard,
And cursing its enormous lack of luck,
That, or to watch it stalling over snow
Starved, as at last, its energies pegged out,
Its fluttering perishes, and it does not know
What water this is though it cannot doubt,
That is not all enough. Remember then
The black bird, white bird, waltzing, gale and all
Fetch, lunge, soar, paddle, with an Atlantic squall
Or semi-Arctic blizzard, until an
Immense sea breaks you and the gunwals grip
And one storm petrel rises like a whip.

XXXIII

Those flaming Christians with their hygienic rose
Tattooed upon the lavatory tiles,
Who bends the penis to a sexless pose
And think of childbirth as a sort of piles;
Those gentlemen with asterisks in their hearts,
Those ladies without lamps, those virgin ones
Who don't quite have the conviction of their sins,
They are the negatives where damnation starts.
It is not all in death: there is no end
To the sweating, swivelling consciousness of that loss.
It is in life: to die is to defend
Life by that loss of laboured nothingness.
Those who deny it, though they cannot live,
Possess, but finally, a life to give.

XXXIX

Christ comes to mind and comes across the mind
And ankle-deep like stitches through a wound
Wades words through anger, and He steps behind
The meaning of the movement of the sound
That we had heard as silence. His boulder rolls
Gruffly across our thoughts. Our actions think
Suddenly for us, and the beatitudes slink
Like butlers towards us with His blood in bowls.
All graces air today in the long park
Grass grows more mellow, and our words decay
Into the mystery that we cannot say
As naturally as daylight turns to dark.
We are so close, the world has grown so wide,
That we don't know which one of us has died.

XLVIII

I promise you by the harsh funeral
Of thoughts beleaguered in a spun desire,
And by the unlatched hour, and by the fall
Of more than bodies into more than fire:
And by the blackbird with its throat alive,
And by the drowned man with his tongue distended,
By all beginnings never to be ended,
And by an end beyond what we contrive:

I promise you on an authority
Greater, more sure, more hazardous than my own,
Yes, by the sun which suffers in the sky
I promise you—that words of living bone
Will rise out of your grave and kneel beside
A world found dying of the death you died.

Iain Crichton Smith

END OF THE SEASON
ON A STORMY DAY—OBAN

In the dead park a bench sprawls drunkenly.
Buoys bob in the bay.
The ghostly waters rise in laddered spray.

Blank-faced hotels stand stiffly by the shore
in the dead silence after crockery falls.
Their sighing landscapes sink into the walls,
the visitors being gone, the season ended.

Boats lag on the waves untenanted.
There's thinner patter of walking on the winded
grey extended front. The soldier draws
into his Great War stone from loose applause.

A motor boat, stern-flagged, drives steadily through
the seething waters. Braced to a splayed poise
a yellow sailor digs his cockerel claws.

And so! And so! His harvest in his hold
he weathers another season, drives through cold
towards his roped stone quay, his dead fish fold.

THE WINDOW

We walked that night between the piled houses.
It was late and cold. Frost gleamed on the road
like the sheen of over-learning. Beaked and bowed,
the lamp posts lectured light, dispensed discourses.

All windows were dark. As on the edge of a cliff
we warily walked, stepping on steeps of silence
except for the click-click-click of our heels, the parlance
of stones that down a well make a crooked graph.

A bus like a late planet turned a corner.
There was nothing else, we and darkness merely.
These ancient houses had never stood in an early
atmosphere or radiance of summer.

At day's end they sank heavily into slumber
as a man sleeps open-mouthed at his fire when
too much light and heat exhaust his brain.
He floats on darkness like a tired swimmer.

None but we two, walking almost as over
a world's end. Yellow light sang and sang
into our coats, our faces, skin and tongue.
We thought each other shook with a yellow fever.

Then she said: "Look, there's a light up there"
and, slowly climbing the cliff-face, my eyes came
to a square light that shone with a blunt flame.
It was solid and dull and red in the yellow air.

And I wondered whose it was—a sleepless man
turning and turning between a window and bed
cursing his sleeplessness and the huge dread
shrill light that pecked at his bemused brain?

Or was it perhaps one studious and grave
who, grasping his pale book, would listen to

the sound it made, the authentic echo
of words returning what he thought and gave?

Or was it a mother, waking for her child,
who could not sleep because of the cold air,
and stumbled between dull bed and dull chair
in the red light imperious and wild?

At least the light was human: and we looked
into each other's eyes shyly as if
a house had suddenly sprung from a dead cliff
and it was all our searching spirits lacked.

OLD WOMAN

And she, being old, fed from a mashed plate
as an old mare might droop across a fence
to the dull pastures of its ignorance.
Her husband held her upright while he prayed

to God who is all-forgiving to send down
some angel somewhere who might land perhaps
in his foreign wings among the gradual crops.
She munched, half dead, blindly searching the spoon.

Outside, the grass was raging. There I sat
imprisoned in my pity and my shame
that men and women having suffered time
should sit in such a place, in such a state

and wished to be away, yes, to be far away
with athletes, heroes, Greeks or Roman men
who pushed their bitter spears into a vein
and would not spend an hour with such decay.

"Pray God," he said, "we ask you, God," he said.
The bowed back was quiet. I saw the teeth
tighten their grip around a delicate death.
And nothing moved within the knotted head

but only a few poor veins as one might see
vague wishless seaweed floating on a tide
of all the salty waters where had died
too many waves to mark two more or three.

A YOUNG HIGHLAND GIRL
STUDYING POETRY

Poetry drives its lines into her forehead
like an angled plough across a bare field.
I've seen her kind before, of the live and dead
who bore humped creels when the beating winds were
    wild.

Nor did they know much poetry but were skilful
at healing children, bringing lambs to birth.
The earth they lived from did not make them soulful.
The foreign rose abated at their mouth.

Yet they were dancers too and feared the season
when "pale Orion shook the seas with fire."
Peculiar waters had their inner reasons
for curing wastrels of a mental star.

And she—like them—should grow along these valleys
bearing bright children, being kind to love.
Simple affection needs no complex solace
nor quieter minds abstractions of the grave.

For most must walk though some by natural flying
learn from the bitter winds a kind of praise.
These fruits are different. She will know one dying
but he by many deaths will bless her days.

SCHOOLGIRL ON SPEECH-DAY
IN THE OPEN AIR

Here in their health and youth they're sitting down
on thick tight grass while bald official men,

heavy with sunshine, wear a moment's crown
and put it by reluctantly again.

I look at one who lies upon her side,
wearing bright yellow for the clasping light.
No ring of shadow has engaged her pride
or wolfed her, fallen, in the circling night.

Her scorn springs out like swords. A smile plays round
her unstained lips, as if a joke would spill.
She turns her shining head into that sound
which stumbles downward from low hill to hill.

And then I turn again and see how one
dangles her will from every word he spins
and think how thirty years can fence a man
by what he loses and by what he wins

into a little ground where he can see
the golden landlords, pursed with luck, stride past.
And schoolgirls flashing by are far and free
as fish he played for but new men will taste.

And the timed applause which falls from rock to rock
and then to silence is the way he came.
She gathers, like necessity, her cloak.
The schoolgirl rises—and must do the same.

Anthony Thwaite

RITES FOR A DEMAGOGUE

She turns the pillow, smoothes the rumpled bed,
Her hand gentle, her palm cool and dry.
The great head lolling on the linen there
Rolls over. From the corner of his eye
He sees the preparations for one dead.

Not to die here among such meddling ways
Is all his wish. He feels the governing hands
Smother the energy on which he broods,
While all around the cramping air expands
Into the dreams where he would end his days.

The cliché comforts him. "To end my days . . ."
It is the edge of battle, where the line
Wavers against the forces he controlled.
A dream advances, and the dreamer slays
The anarch, Death, who jibbed at discipline.

But in a dream. Waking, he sees them come,
The surgeons, the precise, the disciplined.
The stubborn lip and the imperious fist
Sags loose, unclenches. The bull throat is dumb.
And yet the orating brain is not resigned

But still must at its own constriction rail,
Blundering through his lungs, be struggling lest
The dark come down on silence. In the dark
He makes his violent testament . . . The pale
Hirelings are summoned . . . He will protest, protest.

To die fighting, and fighting most for breath—
Was this to earn plaudits, to convince the crowd
Under the balcony? Or will it seem
Merely the self-duped mind's harangue at Death,
The stock-response still raging in the shroud?

CHILD CRYING

My daughter cries, and I
Lift her from where she lies,
Carry her here and there,
Talk nonsense endlessly.
And still she cries and cries
In rage, mindlessly.

A trivial anguish, found
In every baby-book.
But, at a fortnight old,
A pink and frantic mound
Of appetites, each look
Scans unfamiliar ground.

A name without a face
Becomes a creature, takes
A creature's energies.
Raging in my embrace,
She takes the world and shakes
Each firm appointed place.

No language blocks her way,
Oblique, loaded with tact.
Hunger and pain are real,
And in her blindness they
Are all she sees: the fact
Is what you cannot say.

Our difference is that
We gauge what each cry says,
Supply what need demands.
Or try to. All falls flat
If cure is wrong or guess
Leaves her still obdurate.

So through uncertainties
I carry her here and there,
And feel her human heart,
Her human miseries,
And in her language share
Her blind and trivial cries.

AT BIRTH

Come from a distant country,
Bundle of flesh, of blood,
Demanding painful entry,

Expecting little good:
There is no going back
Among those thickets where
Both night and day are black
And blood's the same as air.

Strangely you come to meet us,
Stained, mottled, as if dead:
You bridge the dark hiatus
Through which your body slid
Across a span of muscle,
A breadth my hand can span.
The gorged and brimming vessel
Flows over, and is man.

Dear daughter, as I watched you
Come crumpled from the womb,
And sweating hands had fetched you
Into this world, the room
Opened before your coming
Like water struck from rocks
And echoed with your crying
Your living paradox.

LOOKING ON

Hearing our voices raised—
Perhaps in anger,
Or in some trivial argument
That is not anger—
She screams until we stop
And smile, and look at her,
Poised on the sheer drop
Which opens under her.

If these, her parents, show
How the gods can fail,
Squabbling on Olympus,
How can she fail
To see that anarchy

Is what one must expect,
That to be happy
One must be circumspect?

But the reverse is true
Also, when we kiss,
Seeing herself excluded
Even from that kiss.
The gods' too gross affairs
Made myths for innocent men,
So the innocent eye stares
At love in its den.

Like a strange motley beast
Out of an old myth,
Anger and love together
Make up her own myth
Of these two who cherish,
Protect, feed, deny,
In whose arms she will flourish
Or else will die.

Charles Tomlinson

OBSERVATION OF FACTS

Facts have no eyes. One must
Surprise them, as one surprises a tree
By regarding its (shall I say?)
Facets of copiousness.

The tree stands.

The house encloses.

The room flowers.

These are fact stripped of imagination:
Their relation is mutual.

A dryad is a sort of chintz curtain
Between myself and a tree.
The tree stands: or does not stand:
As I draw, or remove the curtain.

The house encloses: or fails to
Signify, as being bodied over against one,
As something one has to do with.

The room flowers once one has introduced
Mental fibre beneath its elegance,
A rough pot or two, outweighing
The persistence of frippery
In lampshades or wallpaper.

Style speaks what was seen,
Or it conceals the observation
Behind the observer: a voice
Wearing a ruff.

Those facets of copiousness which I proposed
Exist, do so when we have silenced ourselves.

PARING THE APPLE

There are portraits and still-lives.

And there is paring the apple.

And then? Paring it slowly,
From under cool-yellow
Cold-white emerging. And . . . ?

The spring of concentric peel
Unwinding off white,
The blade hidden, dividing.

There are portraits and still-lives
And the first, because "human"
Does not excell the second, and
Neither is less weighted
With a human gesture, than paring the apple
With a human stillness.

The cool blade
Severs between coolness, apple-rind
Compelling a recognition.

MORE FOREIGN CITIES

"Nobody wants any more poems about foreign cities. . . ."
(*From a recent disquisition on poetics*)

Not forgetting Ko-jen, that
Musical city (it has
Few buildings and annexes
Space by combatting silence),
There is Fiordiligi, its sun-changes
Against walls of transparent stone
Unsettling all preconception—a city
For architects (they are taught
By casting their nets
Into those moving shoals); and there is
Kairouan, whose lit space
So slides into and fits
The stone masses, one would doubt
Which was the more solid
Unless, folding back
Gold segments out of the white
Pith globe of a quartered orange,
One may learn perhaps
To read such perspectives. At Luna
There is a city of bridges, where
Even the inhabitants are mindful
Of a shared privilege: a bridge
Does not exist for its own sake.
It commands vacancy.

A MEDITATION ON JOHN CONSTABLE

*"Painting is a science, and should be pursued as an inquiry into
the laws of nature. Why, then, may not landscape painting be
considered as a branch of natural philosophy, of which pictures
are but the experiments?"*
        —JOHN CONSTABLE: The History of Landscape Painting

He replied to his own question, and with the unmannered
    Exactness of art; enriched his premises
By confirming his practice: the labour of observation
    In face of meteorological fact. Clouds
Followed by others, temper the sun in passing
    Over and off it. Massed darks
Blotting it back, scattered and mellowed shafts
    Break damply out of them, until the source
Unmasks, floods its retreating bank
    With raw fire. One perceives (though scarcely)
The remnant clouds trailing across it
    In rags, and thinned to a gauze.
But the next will dam it. They loom past
    And narrow its blaze. It shrinks to a crescent
Crushed out, a still lengthening ooze
    As the mass thickens, though cannot exclude
Its silvered-yellow. The eclipse is sudden,
    Seen first on the darkening grass, then complete
In a covered sky.
                    Facts. And what are they?
He admired accidents, because governed by laws,
    Representing them (since the illusion was not his end)
As governed by feeling. The end is our approval
    Freely accorded, the illusion persuading us
That it exists as a human image. Caught
    By a wavering sun, or under a wind
Which moistening among the outlines of banked foliage
    Prepares to dissolve them, it must grow constant;
Though there, ruffling and parted, the disturbed
    Trees let through the distance, like white fog
Into their broken ranks. It must persuade
    And with a constancy, not to be swept back

To reveal what it half-conceals. Art is itself
   Once we accept it. The day veers. He would have
      judged
Exactly in such a light, that strides down
   Over the quick stains of cloud-shadows
Expunged now, by its conflagration of colour.
   A descriptive painter? If delight
Describes, which wrings from the brush
   The errors of a mind, so tempered,
It can forgo all pathos; for what he saw
   Discovered what he was, and the hand—unswayed
By the dictation of a single sense—
   Bodied the accurate and total knowledge
In a calligraphy of present pleasure. Art
   Is complete when it is human. It is human
Once the looped pigments, the pin-heads of light
   Securing space under their deft restrictions
Convince, as the index of a possible passion,
   As the adequate gauge, both of the passion
And its object. The artist lies
   For the improvement of truth. Believe him.

THE RUIN

Dissolving, the coals shift. Rain swaddles us
   And the fire, driving its shadows through the room
Recalls us to our intention as the flames
   That, by turns, sink guttering or mount
To pour red light through every crater,
   Threaten the galleries of crumbling ash.

The ruins sag, then sift downwards,
   Their fall so soundless that, for the first time,
We distinguish the unbroken, muffled sibilance
   Rain has accompanied us with. Our talk
Recovers its theme—the ruin we should have visited
   Abandoned, now, in its own emptiness.

For the morning promised what, through the darkening
     air,
   Afternoon retracted, nor will the evening

Welcome us under its turmoil of wet leaves
   Where we have lost the keenness of such acridity
As a burnt ruin exhales long afterwards
   Into the coolness when rain has ceased.

It stands on the hill-slope. Between green and green
   There is the boundary wall that circles
And now hides it. Within, one can see nothing
   Save the third, chequered indefinite green
Of tree-tops—until, skirting those limits
   One discovers, open upon the emptied confine, the
      gate.

For a week, the swift traffic of demolition
   That mottled with oil their stagnant rain,
Advanced through the deepening ruts,
   Converged on the house, disjointed, reassembled
And carted, flung (what had sprawled unhinged)
   The door into the wreckage and burnt both.

The door which, though elegant, leaned from the true
   A little to one side, was shamed
By the nearby, slender but rigid elm—
   An unchanging comedy, varied
Only as the seasons thought fit and as the days
   Under their shifting lights reviewed it.

The house was not ancient, but old: deserted,
   The slewed door had focused its rotting style
And, as proportion tugged from decrepitude
   A faint self-respect, it was the door
With the firmness of an aged but practised arbiter
   Bestowed it back over the entire ruin.

Impartial with imperfections, it could accuse
   By this scant presence its clustering neighbours
Gross with the poverty of utility. Thus challenging, it
      stayed,
   A problem for the authorities, a retreat for urchins
Until the urchins burnt half and the authorities
   Publicly accomplished what their ally had attempted
      by stealth.

There remains now the levelled parapet of earth,
  The bleak diagram of a foundation, a hearth
Focussing nothing and, cast into it, the filigree ghost
  Of an iron fanlight. Could we assemble
Beside its other fragments, that last grace
  Under this meaner roof, they would accuse us still—

And accusing, speak from beyond their dereliction
  Out of their life; as when a vase
Cracked into shards, would seem
  Baldly to confess, "Men were here,"
The arabesque reproves it, tracing in faint lines:
  "Ceremonies and order were here also."

Nor could we answer: our houses
  Are no longer ourselves; they dare not
Enter our hopes as the guests of meditation
  To reanimate, warmed by this contact,
The laric world where the bowl glistens with presence
  Gracing the table on which it unfolds itself.

Thus fire, renewed at our hearth, consumes
  Yet it cannot create from the squalor of moderation
A more than fortuitous glory, multiplying its image
  Over the projections of lacquered wood. Charged with
    their past,
Those relics smoulder before they are compounded
  And turned by the spade under a final neatness.

The window lightens. The shell parts
  Beyond between cloud and skyline.
Thunder-light, flushing the walls, yellows them
  Into a more ardent substance than their own
And can do no more. The effect is nature's
  Who ignores it, and in whose impoverishment we domi-
    cile.

LE MUSÉE IMAGINAIRE

An Aztec sacrifice,
   beside the head of Pope—
     eclectic and unresolvable.
We admire the first
   for its expressiveness, the second
     because we understand it—
can re-create
   its circumstances, and share
     (if not the presuppositions)
the aura
   of the civilities surrounding it.
     The other, in point
at any rate, of violence
   touches us more nearly.
     And yet . . . it is cruel
but unaccountably so; for the temper of awe
   demanded by the occasion, escapes us:
     it is not
better than we are—
   it is merely different.
     Expressive, certainly. But of what?
Our loss is absolute, yet unfelt
   because inexact. The head
     of Alexander Pope,
stiller, attests the more tragic lack
   by remaining
     what it was meant to be;
intelligible,
   it forbids us to approach it.

THE HAND AT CALLOW HILL FARM

Silence. The man defined
The quality, ate at his separate table
Silent, not because silence was enjoined

But was his nature. It shut him round
Even at outdoor tasks, his speech
Following upon a pause, as though
A hesitance to comply had checked it—
Yet comply he did, and willingly:
Pause and silence: both
Were essential graces, a reticence
Of the blood, whose calm concealed
The tutelary of that upland field.

ODE TO ARNOLD SCHOENBERG

On a Performance of His Concerto for Violin

At its margin
   the river's double willow
     that the wind
variously
   disrupts, effaces
     and then restores
in shivering planes:
   it is
     calm morning.
The twelve notes
   (from the single root
     the double tree)
and their reflection:
   let there be
     unity—this,
however the winds rout
   or the wave disperses
     remains, as
in the liberation of the dissonance
   beauty would seem discredited
     and yet is not:
redefined
   it may be reachieved,
     thus to proceed
through discontinuities
   to the whole in which
     discontinuities are held

like the foam in chalcedony
  the stone, enriched
    by the tones' impurity.
The swayed mirror
  half-dissolves
    and the reflection
yields to reflected light.
  Day. The bell-clang
    goes down the air
and, like a glance
  grasping upon its single thread
    a disparate scene,
crosses and recreates
  the audible morning.
    All meet at cockcrow
when our common sounds
  confirm our common bonds.
    Meshed in meaning
by what is natural
  we are discontented
    for what is more,
until the thread
  of an instrument pursue
    a more than common meaning.
But to redeem
  both the idiom and the instrument
    was reserved
to this exiled Jew—to bring
  by fiat
    certainty from possibility.
For what is sound
  made reintelligible
    but the unfolding word
branched and budded,
  the wintered tree
    creating, cradling space
and then
  filling it with verdure?

John Wain

THE NEW SUN

The new sun rises in the year's elevation,
Over the low roofs' perspective.

It reveals the roughness of winter skin
And the dinginess of winter clothes.

It draws, with a hard forefinger,
a line under the old ways.

Finis! the old ways have become obsolete,
The old skin, the old clothes.

This same sun, like a severe comet,
rises over old disappointments.

It makes us cry out in agony,
this peeling away of old sorrows.

When the sun foretells the death of an old sorrow,
the heart prophetically feels itself an orphan;

a little snivelling orphan, and the sun
its hard-hearted parish officer.

Dear gods, help us to bear the new sun!
Let our firm hearts pray to be orphaned!

AU JARDIN DES PLANTES

The gorilla lay on his back,
One hand cupped under his head,
Like a man.

Like a labouring man tired with work,
A strong man with his strength burnt away
In the toil of earning a living.

Only of course he was not tired out with work,
Merely with boredom; his terrible strength
All burnt away by prodigal idleness.

A thousand days, and then a thousand days,
Idleness licked away his beautiful strength,
He having no need to earn a living.

It was all laid on, free of charge.
We maintained him, not for doing anything,
But for being what he was.

And so that Sunday morning he lay on his back,
Like a man, like a worn-out man,
One hand cupped under his terrible hard head.

Like a man, like a man,
One of those we maintain, not for doing anything,
But for being what they are.

A thousand days, and then a thousand days,
With everything laid on, free of charge,
They cup their heads in prodigal idleness.

ANNIVERSARY

These are my thoughts on realising
That I am the same age as my father was
On the day I was born.

As a little scarlet howling mammal,
Crumpled and unformed, I depended entirely on someone
Not very different from what I am to-day.

When I think this over,
I feel more crumpled and unformed than ever:
I ask myself what I have done to compare with *that*.

It also makes me aware, inescapably,
Of having entered upon the high table-land,
The broad flat life of a mature man.

Where everything is seen from its actual distance,
E.g. childhood not so remote as to seem a boring myth,
Nor senility as something that awaits other people.

But deeper than that,
It is like entering a dark cone,
The shadow thrown across my life by the life it derives
    from.

And deeper than that still,
It is the knowledge that life is the one communicable
    thing.
It called. I heard it from where I slept in seed and liquid.

The patterns of seed and brine coalesced in a solemn
    dance,
Whence my life arose in the form of a crest,
And has carried itself blindly forward until now.

In ignorance of its uniqueness until now,
Until I stumbled over these thoughts solid as bricks,
And like bricks fearsome in their everyday squareness.

APOLOGY FOR UNDERSTATEMENT

Forgive me that I pitch your praise too low.
Such reticence my reverence demands,
For silence falls with laying on of hands.

Forgive me that my words come thin and slow.
This could not be a time for eloquence,
For silence falls with healing of the sense.

We only utter what we lightly know.
And it is rather that my love knows me.
It is that your perfection sets me free.

Verse is dressed up that has nowhere to go.
You took away my glibness with my fear.
Forgive me that I stand in silence here.

It is not words could pay you what I owe.

POEM WITHOUT A MAIN VERB

Watching oneself
being clever, being clever:
keeping the keen equipoise between *always* and *never;*

delicately divining
(the gambler's sick art)
which of the strands must hold, and which may part;

playing off, playing off
with pointless cunning
the risk of remaining against the risk of running;

balancing, balancing
(alert and knowing)
the carelessly hidden with the carefully left showing;

endlessly, endlessly
finely elaborating
the filigree threads in the web and the bars in the grating;

at last minutely
and thoroughly lost
in the delta where profit fans into cost;

with superb navigation
afloat on that darkening, deepening sea,
helplessly, helplessly.

NEW POETS
OF AMERICA

Edited by Robert Pack

INTRODUCTION BY
ROBERT PACK

Dividing American poetry today into two camps, the Academics and the Beats, has obscured the distinction between good and bad, honest and pretentious writing, and it has corrupted the unprofessional audience concerned with modern poetry by turning their attention from the poem to the personality of the poet. The assumption that led *Life* to do an article on the Beats is that gossip is more interesting than poetry; and *Time* despises whatever does not sell itself to popular taste: "Talented poets in this generation seem aware that readers outnumber poets, and seem willing to write something that might interest them. The poets apparently want to rejoin the human race," and, in its usual manner, reduces criticism to innuendo: "Most poets' friends are poets; usually even their wives are poets." Would that be *Time*'s last word on Wordsworth, the Brownings, or Yeats? How long will the cowardly practice of writing unsigned articles of opinion pass as objective reporting? A poet is interesting to *Time* only *after* he is *successful*; he is interesting to the public, whose attitudes are shaped by such media, if he drinks himself to death, if he undresses at a poetry reading, or if he takes part in a presidential inauguration, but not for what his poems say or for their quality.

Robert Lowell has cleaved poetry into the "cooked" and the "uncooked." The connotations attached to "cooked" are: prepared, digestible, tamed, civilized—in effect, academic, dry, the emotion boiled out. The connotations attached to "uncooked" are: raw (as raw-brutal-sexy in the daily movie ads, implying that the truth at last will be told), barbaric (implying that the repressions of society have been broken), and original, liberated, and natural. Unfortunately, the metaphor of cooked and uncooked cannot escape its literal aspect (nor does Lowell, I believe, intend it to)—food, after all, is to be eaten. We end with both terms as pejorative.

The idea of raw, unaffected, or spontaneous poetry misleads the reader as to what is expected of him. It encourages laziness and passivity. He too can be spontaneous, just sit back and respond. A good poem, rather, is one that deepens upon familiarity; it continues to release your feelings and to engage your thoughts. Attention, which may begin as passive, becomes active—you are asked to remember, to associate, to consider, to comprehend, to speculate—you become involved. This is the challenge it offers, and this is the inescapable difficulty of poetry. It is not enough to let a poem echo through your being, to play mystical chords upon your soul. The poem must be understood and felt in its details; it asks for attention before transport.

The school of criticism that sees the work of art as the sum of the social or psychological forces acting upon the artist (failing to regard the artist as a creator, the inventor of his own life, and, in part, his own age) has inevitably led to the regarding of the artist and his work as social phenomena, as cultural fact. This is condescending—it is out of love with art. For example, a notable magazine, which "hopes to encourage original creative endeavor in the various fields of culture," has given up publishing poetry, but it continues to publish reviews and articles *about* poets and poetry. In other words, the poet and his work are merely of social interest.

Harold Rosenberg speaks of "the dungeons of the university monks engaged in grinding [poetry] to dust." Here is the typical glib and perfervid generalization. It is another variation on the "ivory tower" theme. The accuser would appropriate reality as exclusively his own. His is the I-have-suffered-more-than-thou kind of snobism. His vicious—against life—blunder is that he sees as valid (what is worth writing about) only the hysterical extreme. Are the poets represented here who teach at universities, who write about desire, joy, marriage, divorce, despair, war, death, and God to be considered "monks"? "Denmark's a prison," cries Hamlet, "O God, I could be bounded in a nutshell, and count myself a king of infinite space, were it not that I have bad dreams." There is enough reality, enough suffering to go around. One finds them wherever one works, loves, and dies. The poet is distinguished by his ability to sing out or dramatize his realities compactly and eloquently, and by nothing else.

The poems in this anthology are characterized first by their variety, in subject, outlook, and style. Only after asserting this am I willing to venture a few generalizations. Love, in these pages, is experienced more in the contexts of sexual desire, need, marriage and divorce, than in the contexts of romance or spiritual striving. The traditional theme of unfaithfulness has become more specifically adultery; parting has become divorce; union (transcendence) has become harmony, compatibility. Nowhere has Marx or any social ideology taken the place of God. For most of these poets, nothing has. Where God is loved or feared, the emphasis is on the poet's personal emotion as a Jew or a Christian. There is no esoteric wisdom, no erudite reference to Eastern religions, no easy, half-assimilated mysticism. There is social and political concern in the writing of many of these poets, but none is Utopian, their diagnosis does not imply a cure. This, surely, indicates a disillusion with reform, except for the man alone with his conscience. The crucial thing is the recognition of evil and the engagement with it in the battlefield of one's own life.

The terms and concepts of psychology are crucial in helping these poets define what it is to be a man, in portraying his nature. But man is seen as free: not to the extent that he has faced his own psychic history, nor because he is made free and creative in the image of God, but because he experiences himself that way, because he feels responsible, and because he wants and chooses to be.

The poems here are set as much in the country as in the city. The forests are still "red in tooth and claw" or a place of welcome isolation and ecstatic imagery. The city too is seen in opposing ways: a wasteland of nervous apathy, corrupt ambition, and lust, but also as the edifice that makes possible human exchange and striving. Rather than part animal, part angel, man is seen as part animal, part machine—but conscious. He cannot escape from his own words.

What are his rewards? Work, friendship, love, writing poems. There are few who find meaning in abstract concepts of purpose or believe in salvation or nirvana. What are their despairs? Bodily or neurotic sickness, love that has failed, a world out of control, physical death.

And as for style, the love (fascination mixed with distrust) these poets have for their craft is everywhere apparent. Experimentation with form, as always, is the endless quest for a personal language of feeling, accuracy, and honesty. Blundering, being lucky, revising, contriving, blurting ahead—these are all part of it. And the careful reader will be astounded by the diversity of voices, of tight and of free forms that these poets have found—not as a policy, but depending on the need of a particular poem. There is no retreat behind the merely formal or the mere breaking down of form, within a pose, or an attitude.

The necessity for style, for control, is that it focuses feeling: economy makes emotion directly felt, and control is a function of the mind. The poet, no matter how intuitive, cannot bypass it. Yeats, in "Adam's Curse," describing how he writes, says: "A line will take us hours maybe; / Yet if it does not seem a moment's thought/ Our stitching and unstitching has been naught." Here then is the crux, the crucial paradox of poetry: it must *seem* spontaneous, but to make it seem so, one must labor, one must contrive the effect. And this paradox has its mirror image: the more the reader dwells upon the poem—perceives the interrelationships of its images, both progressing through narrative and reading backwards as each new image changes what has gone before—the more he responds spontaneously to the poem. Which is to say, he becomes in touch with what is there. The sentimentalization of art, rescuing it from the academy into the sanctum of the coffee house, seeking to free it (whatever comes of itself is good) actually denies art by confusing it with life. And, in the end, those who would make of art a religion, a way of life, retreat from the flesh which they appear to affirm, by substituting the poem for the historical moment which alone cannot be revised.

Although the criticisms of tameness and uniformity made

against the non-Beat poets (for that is all they have in common) seem to me a result of ignorance or of the failure to read with care; nevertheless, it is true that the charge of almost unrelieved solemnity and seriousness is valid. But the same charge can be made against Dante, Milton, and Wordsworth. It is the quality of their solemnity which alone is to be judged, for each is serious in a distinctive way—unlike the Beats who, conventionally irreverent, push a poor substitute for satirical humor, while their sympathies come too easily (a disguised form of self-pity and self-indulgence), as if the goof-off, the slob, the criminal, were more human and more lovable than anyone else.

Lack of scope and of universality is perhaps the most formidable accusation made against contemporary poetry. But to what degree scope is a more valuable attribute than concentration is a personal matter, one might say personal to our age as well. And the demand for greatness seems to me a pretentiousness of the critical mind, for it results from a *comparative* judgment, while goodness is absolute, for it marks the effectiveness of the poem itself. The assumption behind the question of greatness is that one is to be stranded on a desert island with ten favorite books to be chosen in advance. As for *universality*, it remains for me a vague and useless concept, like saying that God is infinite. The poem lives only in its particulars. But if by universality one means nobility over pettiness, I would suggest that there is only one nobility, and it is available to king or beggar—the willingness to pay the price of consciousness. The true poet burns with this willingness.

There are, however, good poems with bad ideas and bad poems with good ideas: poetry is not capsule philosophy, though a poem that we take to be true, whose statements or beliefs we give assent to, will have an additional value to us. But what a poem argues or propounds *must* be understood if we are to get at what the poem offers as sensation, as feeling. Thought and feeling are not separable. For every sensation there is a mental (conscious or unconscious) response, and for every thought there is an accompanying sensation or passion. To be conscious is to be divided, to be in conflict with yourself. And to deny this is to deny the very condition without which art is impossible—the awareness of disorder (art more often than not brings bad news) and the need to choose and to organize. Thus the most characteristic human act, making a decision, is brought to a heightened pitch in the composing of a poem. The unwillingness to choose, the wish to make the production of art "spontaneous," as if it just "happens" to you, is the sentimentalization of both art and life, for it avoids the difficulty of commitment, of being in one place at one time with time itself running out; it belies the fact of our mortality and the division (I want to know, but not to face my own death) which this consciousness enforces upon us.

The personality that is constitutionally grounded in opposition—sentimentalism in reverse—has a facile subject in hand, and lightly finds fluency in complaint. The shriek against the world adds no wisdom to what is obvious. I say this because there is always a movement in the Arts that tries to be new for the sake of newness, or makes a protest for the sake of protest. Individuality, uniqueness of style, are not so easily achieved. Nor is it honest to despise your audience and ask that you be loved for it.

The problem of an audience—of a community of informed and open discussion and dissent, concerned and yet free from commercial or vested interest—is inseparable from the question of the vitality of any art. In our time, the university, rather than the literary cliques, the poetry societies, the incestuous pages of little magazines, is capable of nurturing and supporting such an audience. For it is alone the place where past and present live together. And one finds among one's students a genuine responsiveness, not yet spoiled, to art. They are there to give this response, to have it deepened through learning, and through sharing it, to have it encouraged that they may never lose their love for all forms of human knowledge and expression. Anyone who has had the privilege of teaching the young knows this is true. Of course there is pettiness, dryness, and reaction in the universities—as everywhere else—but the feeling which today draws so many poets to it is that here an audience may be cultivated which will be both passionate and detached, responsive and yet willing to judge.

It is the value of the individual poem that I wish to reaffirm here in the hope that there will be a growing audience to receive it. And I believe that many of these poets will leave behind them the kind of statement that will guide the future, if there will be one, in the only way that art guides—by opening and extending each man's capacity for sensation and awareness, in pleasure or in pain, to those with the will and the power to listen.

A number of poets whose work I have greatly enjoyed have not been included because of limited space. And I am sorry too that the representations here could not have been larger. But this book is meant to serve a practical purpose—to whet readers' appetites—not to make a definitive and exclusive selection.

Gene Baro

THE HORSEMEN

Those lathered horses galloping past
with breathless riders come not this way back:
we look, scanning the east, searching the west;
only an old mule walks the muddy track.

Under grey skies promising rain again,
we hear the pounding hooves, or so it seems;
but there comes again only drumming rain
and we are sunk in wayside country dreams.

Sometimes, lying in love, or close to sleep,
the heart heaves suddenly and thunders on.
Those wild horsemen had not that furious leap;
a cry is at the lips, and then is gone.

NORTHWIND

No, no, this bitterness is no new thing:
light dazzles on the butterfly's brief wing;
These golden flakes yield autumn's coloring.

Interminable summers rage and close
at last, deserting nightingale and rose,
and all the while the northwind grows and grows.

You who have loved beauty will invent
some new distraction for your discontent,
the dun earth and the leaden firmament.

What if this cold wind scour the cold sky clean,
if the trees of the forest break or lean?
What will another raging season mean?

Old time will bring the stars and statues down;
the sea will dry up and the land will drown,
and yet the brutal heart beat on and on.

You who have loved beauty may confess
how, too, you love terror and ugliness,
and the year's cruel turning on the merciless.

LAMENT FOR BETTER OR WORSE

The hour told by the owl and the moon
through the chinks of the ruined clock tower
in the creaky wood may find the witch of the world
confused, the wizard world-weary. There is a time
when even the evil are far from cheery
in the evil business of brooms and spells, when
even the trusty familiar seems a stranger, and when the
     monster
most formidable howls his loneliness in boozy self-pity.

The black and the white of things are not, in fact,
for such a night. Gray hairs come sometimes
early to the surly fiend, who wants a friend only;
lumbago may afflict the mad virago; and a Fury
may know the pangs of penury. Such nights are shadowy,
haunted, when from the tear-stained pillow Medusa's
     head
arises blubbering because she is no lovely thing:
sometimes, the Gorgon rushes to the mirror that will kill
     her.

Think: the selfish giant may have no choice
but to be aggressive, self-reliant; the princesses,
perhaps, are shrieking and not shrinking, and he
is restless, anxious, planning, wishing—wondering,
dare he shut down the dungeon and go fishing?

An ogre with an ulcer has no answer
better than you or I. Night vapors come,
and Time that knits the sleeve of care may leave us bare.

Those tyrants who with shouts of "Bravo!"
greet the headsman; torturers who spend their Sundays
brushing up on bastinado; and the simplest victim—
all have their introspective troubles. Misunderstood, the
    mind
and not the cauldron bubbles; who from the iron maiden
with the squeaky hinges gets the worser twinges?
Are things, then, what they seem? Why does the raven
    scream?
The bats have fled the tower. Now hoots the sleepless
    hour.

JUDGES, JUDGES

The themes of love and death I have rehearsed.
Another child, a face among the rest,
and now another man, and not the first
to know himself rejected and unblessed
by what is godlike in his manhood's breast,
I have my longing and God's love reversed
and, like a coward, put life to the test.
I am the prodigal small wisdom cursed.

Judges, judges, be judges if you dare.
I stand upon the threshold, swing wide
the door, and wait the wanderer everywhere.
What else is there of mercy, what of pride?
He broke his heart with loving and he died.
Let flesh swing open! Let the ghost abide!

THE LADDER

Tumbling among its stones,
a ghost of the forest green,

under the leaning ferns,
the stream purls on unseen.
A trembling of the leaves,
only a thread of sound—
like quiverings of light
among the trees is wound,
like flutterings of wings,
quick dapplings of the sun—
a brilliance singing there
and there, and quickly gone.
Echoes of moonlight sent
into the limpid dark,
like a thousand fireflies,
repeat a velvet spark;
the stream's voice suddenly
is vistas far, yet near
it hesitates and bends
to whisper at the ear;
or else, out of the mist
of morning is released
a mirthful sound of waters
by the waking birds increased,
increased by early sun
that, golden-bright and brief,
has touched the wind awake
upon each darting leaf,
as if the forest stretched itself into a cry
of grown and tangled voices
under the unseen sky!
Yet how distinctly clear
the waters dropping low
repeat upon the stones
a progress as they go;
and if they hurry on,
their mingling with the rain
seems but a turning wheel
that spins a coarser skein;
and yet the waters' thread
sometimes is silken-spare,
a glowing silken ladder
raised on the vibrant air;
between the unseen and unknown,

far on in the forest, there
rises a silken ladder
into the depthless air.

A NORTHERN SPRING

Across the greening lawn,
blankets and pillows lie
with daffodil and crocus
in the new sun's eye.

Storm windows have come down:
the house now drinks its fill
of the brimming Maytime wind
at the swept window sill;

but, like old winds, indeed,
like branches at the pane,
stiff brush and broom are making
a wintery refrain,

a music that will die
upon the well-scrubbed air
when, hands on hips in her doorway,
my mother stands there

and dreams her August roses
have flowered pink and red
and sees the harvest making
and the fresh season's bread,

sees smoke again from the chimneys,
sees seasons that are past,
new leaves and snowflakes falling
in the kindred northwind's blast.

This is a winter country,
its spring just a cleaning day,
though my mother will stand in her doorway
and pass half an hour away.

Philip Booth

WAS A MAN

Was a man, was a two-
faced man, pretended
he wasn't who he was,
who, in a men's room,
faced his hung-over
face in a mirror hung
over the towel rack.
The mirror was cracked.
Shaving close in that
looking glass, he nicked
his throat, bled blue
blood, grabbed a new
towel to patch the wrong
scratch, knocked off
the mirror and, facing
himself, almost intact,
in final terror hung
the wrong face back.

THE TOWER

Strangers ask,
always, how tall
it is. Taller,
the natives say,
than any other.
Watching it sway,
slightly, in a brisk
wind, you believe
them and feel,

well, smaller
than you once
did, or would have,
even had they woken
somebody's father,
who remembers
every specification,
they say, having fought
against this location,
in the last elections
before it was built.
It is enough
to see it, canted
over you, as
you approach
the strange base:
a cement stilt
set in a rough
patch of marsh;
on that, a ball
with numbers
etched on it,
perhaps a date,
on which the steel
frame, in one
brave unbroken
line, seems to stretch
for heaven itself,
in three diminishing
sections. The balance
is fantastic,
or seems so, until
you recall the elastic
web of guy wires
that, slanted
beyond you, support
the tower in nine
equal directions.
The local women,
hanging their wash
on a wet line,
Monday, report

that it's hidden
in clouds, out
of mind, until,
in a sudden
wind and vanishing
fog, they look up:
not to worship,
but, more, from habit;
the way, once left
home when their men
went to rivet
the thing, they said
morning prayers.
Even on Sunday,
now, of course,
they accept how
the shadow swings
down, leaning
in and away
in elliptic rings
like a sundial.
Or so a high
state official
told them it did,
when they, craning
that broken sky,
sat assembled
there for the long
dedication:
it resembled,
he said, nothing
so much; and laughing
then, said if you
knew where you were
(they laughed too),
and perhaps how far
from the solstice,
you could almost tell
what time it was,
by when the shadow
fell on your house.
Not that the tower

itself would fall,
ever, on such
a quiet meadow
of homes, nor would
the isogonic reaction
affect, even touch,
their elm trees;
the theta conductors
were shielded, at
his personal direction,
he said, so not
to entail any risk
for them, or their families.
A man, then, stood
tall, as if to ask
a first question, but
near him a guard
preserved order.
There was, the speaker
admitted, an odor
caused by the breaker
circuits, but this
was the new power,
in essence, and, as
designed, wouldn't last.
A solar device,
he called it, strong
as the Nation
itself, which, because
of such structures,
would stand until
Kingdom Come.
They were proud there,
then; and still are,
when their children,
or children's children,
home from municipal
lectures, recite,
without prompting,
the smallest detail:
the interval
of each warning light,

and how, just
at dawn, the strange
orange glow
on top will go
out, with something
suspended, like
lazing snow
in the morning air;
not much, a flake
here, a flake there,
which dissolves
to a kind of dust
and settles, daily,
around the globular
base. And, daily,
the child who puts up
the flag is assigned,
also, to sweep.
Once every year
they make wreaths
(of jagged cut felt,
shaped like elm leaves)
and lay them here,
between the new sidewalk
and Main Street.
Otherwise, nothing
is changed: home
is the same, talk
still revolves
around the same
people. Government
studies, given
every control,
have proven
this. The report
is unanimous,
to every intent:
there's been neither
famine nor war.
Their original
fear of the fall
is gone, the range

of the shadow
seems less, the weather
more clear. The meadows
are full of new flowers;
stakes are aligned
on most lawns, shaped
like sundials.
Women count hours
still; they repeat
household trials,
and gossip. But
except for
the fool who tried
climbing the tower,
few have died;
most have escaped
the usual town
diseases; misbegotten
children are
fewer, the suicide
rate is down.
Indeed, nothing
is ominous
here, unless
you take stock
of their dreams:
waking, sometimes,
they say, it hangs
over them: not
exactly the tower
itself, but what
they've forgotten,
something above
the tower, like
a dance tune
they can't quite
remember, or name.
They are used to
the circuit breakers
now; they admit
it, even to
Government

census-takers,
who wake them—
women weeping
over their sleeping
men, at dawn—
since only then,
before day
begins, will they
try to show,
without words,
but pointing towards
the tower, that what
they can't name
is, like waking
itself, or making
love, not different,
no, but in spite
of the Government,
yes, not quite
the same.

Jane Cooper

THE FAITHFUL

Once you said joking slyly, "If I'm killed
I'll come to haunt your solemn bed,
I'll stand and glower at the head
And see if my place is empty still, or filled."

What was it woke me in the early darkness
Before the first bird's twittering?
A shape dissolving and flittering
Unsteady as a flame in a drafty house.

It seemed a concentration of the dark burning
By the bedpost at my right hand,

While to my left that no-man's land
Of sheet stretched palely as a false morning. . . .

All day I have been sick and restless. This evening
Curtained, with all the lights on,
I start up—only to sit down.
Why should I grieve after ten years of grieving?

What if last night I was the one who lay dead,
While the dead burned beside me
Trembling with passionate pity
At my blameless life and shaking its flamelike head?

THE GRAVEYARD

Where five old graves lay circled on a hill
And pines kept all but shattered sunlight out
We came to learn about
How each had sinned, loved, suffered, lost until
He met the other and grew somehow still.

Under those soughing, rumor-speaking trees
Full of dead secrets, on the August ground,
We leaned against a mound
Not touching; there, as we could, gave keys
To open midnight vaults that no one sees.

All that had shaped us thirty years or more
We tried to offer—not as brave youngsters do
Who need an echo, who
See in their fathers' sins a canceled score—
But as two grieving inmates tapping at the door.

Gifts of the self which were but bids for power,
Gifts of the innocent self—stripped, bound and torn—
A rare child wrongly born
And our best strivings turned, with age, half-sour:
Such darkness we unlocked within an hour.

Those five old graves lay speechless while the sun
Gradually stroked them with its flickering arm,
The smell of pines grew warm.
We walked away to watch a fresh stream run
As free as if all guilts were closed and done.

OBLIGATIONS

Here where we are, wrapped in the afternoon
As in a chrysalis of silken light,
Our bodies kindly holding one another
Against the press of vision from outside,
Here where we clasp in a stubble field
Is all the safety either of us hopes for,
Stubbornly constructing walls of night
Out of the ordered energies of the sun.

With the same gratitude I feel the hot
Dazzle on my eyelids and your hand
Carefully opening my shaded breasts.
The air is very high and still. The buzz
And tickle of an insect glow and fuse
Into the flicker of a pulse. We rest
Closed in the golden shallows of a sound.
Once, opening my eyes, I betray your trust.

Startled, I break apart a shining blade
Of stubble as you bend to look at me.
What can your eyes lay claim to? What extreme
Unction after love is forced upon us?
The sun is setting now after its fullness,
While on the horizon like a fiery dream
Wakes the long war, and shared reality,
And death and all we came here to evade.

FOR A VERY OLD MAN,
ON THE DEATH OF HIS WIFE

So near to death yourself
You cannot justly mourn
For one who was beautiful
Before these children were born.
You only remember her
Poised by the edge of the sea
As you stalked heron-legged,
Chairing the baby high
(Red-capped, hilarious)
Through the ecstatic surf,
And all the boardwalk flags
Clapped to her seaward laugh.

Or perhaps she would pretend
To lose you over the edge
Of that great curve of blue
Distinct as a cliffy ledge,
And cry and wave and cry
Until with a little breath
She spied the red-capped head
Of the pledge both flung at death;
Then she would swing her hat
With her graceful arm held high
As if she would top the flags
And the flags could sweep the sky.

Now it is she who is gone
And you wait on the sand:
The place itself has changed,
The boardwalks are torn down.
For places curve with time
Over the horizon's rim;
Only a seabird flies
Lower and seems to skim
All that has been or is. . . .
No one is left to share

Those windless flags you see,
Alone in the dying glare.

Henri Coulette

THE ATTIC

We have ascended to this paradise,
Make-believe angels hurrying to our choirs.
Imagination is our Sunday vice;
We are alone, alone with our desires.

We are enchanted by the sound of rain;
Darkness, half-light, and light combine and blur.
This is the national treasury of Cockaigne,
Of which we are the keepers, as it were.

Time is our Midas. We are of his line;
His touch descends to us on either side—
That golden touch. One gesture will refine
This dust into such realms as dust would hide.

These beads are pearls disguised as imitations.
This broken chair, my dear? It is a throne
From which you may survey the lesser nations,
Those lands that cannot claim you as their own.

This box contains the music of the spheres;
Its Swiss machinery records the stars.
Ever the listener given to fancy hears
The strings of Venus and the drum of Mars.

Time and Imagination—what are they?
They are, my dear, the pseudonyms of Change,
The smooth, indifferent author of our play,
Master of both the common and the strange.

My sister, it is autumn in Cockaigne,
And we are weary, for we've come so far
— Too far to be enchanted by the rain.
We are alone, alone with what we are.

From THE WAR OF THE
SECRET AGENTS

*A lighthouse keeper, a schoolgirl, an alcoholic, and a red-headed
ghost—they were agents of the British in France during World
War II. They were betrayed by London (Buckmaster), by their
chief (Prosper), by each other, and by themselves. They do not
understand this, but they try to, and they speak . . .*

VI. CINEMA, AT THE LIGHTHOUSE

I admire the driven, those who rise from choice
as from a sickbed.
I was of that company,
as you are, as he is whom you seek.
What little I know you must know, or have guessed.
Prosper, I assume, is dead;

we last met beside the train that brought us
into Germany.
We came upon each other
in the steam of the brakes, and his eyes
were those of a blindman or a cuckold. We passed
each other without speaking.

The other one I met once on an airfield
my first night in France.
If I remember rightly,
we did not speak; perhaps we nodded;
perhaps his hand touched my elbow. I recall
only the scent of the cut hay

and the overwhelming sensual delight
I knew momently
under the dangerous moon.
Your prey was of the breathing darkness

wherein, without father, Cinema was born—
he was midwife at that birth.

A ghost of a cockney with a gift of tongues,
what did I become?
Whatever Cinema did,
and he did it well. And when I slept,
I could hear the nations underneath my ear,
and my dreams were of pure light.

This has the ring of nonsense about it, no?
How can I tell you?
How can I explain to one
never there? I was a courier
and rode the Métro, disguised differently
every day. I was no one,

I was what I seemed, I did not have to think.
This house is the grave
of Cinema, and this light
his epitaph. How can I explain
the dead? The dead are an extravagant cheese,
nor have the sad gift of tongues.

VIII. DENISE: A LETTER NEVER SENT

Desiree,
        I find it most bitter that you,
my sister, my twin,
should set your heart against me.
Gilbert is my love, my protection;
I am no streetwalker in a scarlet sheath
tripping through the Place Pigalle.

How stupid, how petite-bourgeoise to unleash
such rabid, convent-
bred imaginings upon
me—your own sister, your twin!
I had thought to share the sweetness of my love.
How carefully I chose words!

I wanted so to tell you of this strange gift,
for I must conceive
of love as something given—
I wanted to tell you of Gilbert,
of how he crams my very being with such joy,
and of his marvelous eyes.

Now you have come between me and my mirror.
How can I behold
my image—yes, our image—
without rancor? I must school myself
to be an only child, beyond reflection,
marvelous to his marvelous eyes.

IX. PHONO, AT THE BOAR'S HEAD

Thanks, I will.
                You understand he wasn't mad?
even in the end?
Oh, I was there, I saw him,
I saw his mind become more lucid
hour by hour, thought by thought, lucid as the flesh
of the old, the very old,

a Chinese wisdom. I give you the Chinese.
I give you nothing
you can't find out for yourself,
except the last look of Archambault:
the delicate, livid face of a red-head,
with one brown eye, and one blue.

We knew at Mauthausen that we were to die.
My fear kept me sane;
I talked to it in my head.
Show these bastards how to die, I said.
My days were like dreams in which I dreamt my death.
I lived like a coward.

And all the while Archambault lay there smiling
Like a god damn saint.
There is nothing left to lose,

he said. *Nothing but my frigging life,*
I said, but he didn't hear me, or he heard
and knew there was nothing left.

Did you know, he laughed, *they captured us in bed,*
in Denise's bed?
I woke up with their torches
in my face. I dreamed they would be there,
and they were, and I wasn't afraid. I sighed,
I think, with satisfaction.

I rose. I stood stock still. I read the letter-
ing on the light bulb.
I saw Denise's nipples,
taut, purple, oddly oval. I heard
the embarrassed creaking of the German coats.
I smelled the oil on their guns.

I saw the world, and I gave back what I saw.
I was a mirror,
nothing more. I was faithful;
I gave an eye for an eye. Can they
execute a mirror? There will be gunfire
and an end to reflection.

—*Show these Gothic bastards how to die,* I said.
—*You show them,* he said,
and don't forget to say "cheese."
—*Fuck your brown eye, and your blue,* I said,
and in the morning, the guards took him outside
and shot him, and I waited,

knowing I would be next, saying, *Show them how* . . .
I waited nine months,
and the Americans came.
It was 80 days before I walked.
I was Lazarus come to Piccadilly,
unseeing among strangers,

among the accusing Buckmasters of London,
among the whispers
of *treason, treason.* —*Bad show,*

a bad show best forgotten old man,
Buckmaster said. He was embarrassed for me;
I had neglected to die.

It's madness, I know, but they wanted us dead.
Are the files neater
if you die? What Prosper did
when he dickered with that German crank
was to save a few lives—oh, not the best lives,
but a few; that was his crime.

And when you ask me why I drink, I must say
I don't know. Is it
in memory of Prosper,
of silly Prosper? Do I follow
Archambault by fifths, a brown eye, and a blue?
The Buckmasters of this world—

do I drink to stomach them? Or the coward
who waited nine months
and the Americans came?
Well, I give you the Americans.
Now one more for the road, and do count your change;
the publican is a cheat.

XII. EPILOGUE: AUTHOR TO READER

Reader, we are getting ready to pull out.
Archambault has packed
the transmitter in an old
suitcase. Denise is combing her hair.
We are meeting Phono and Cinema downtown
in a second-rate bistro.

Prosper has been worrying about Phono;
he has a bad cough.
—And Cinema, I worry
about Cinema, who must insist
on a trenchcoat, of all things. But life goes on,
even here, in its own way.

Reader, you have been as patient as an agent
waiting at midnight
outside a deserted house
in a cold rain. You will ask yourself,
What does it all mean? What purpose does it serve,
my being here in this rain?

Reader (you will be known henceforth by that name),
there is no meaning
or purpose; only the codes.
So think of us, of Prosper, silly
Prosper, of Archambault of the marvelous eyes,
of Denise combing her hair.

James Dickey

WALKING ON WATER

Feeling it with me
On it, barely float, the narrow plank on the water,
I stepped from the clam-shell beach,
Breaking in nearly down through the sun
Where it lay on the sea,
And poled off, gliding upright
Onto the shining topsoil of the bay.

Later, it came to be said
That I was seen walking on water,
Not moving my legs
Except for the wrong step of sliding:
A child who leaned on a staff,
A curious pilgrim hiking
Between two open blue worlds,

My motion a miracle,
Leaving behind me no footprint,
But only the shimmering place

Of an infinite step upon water,
In which sat still and were shining
Many marsh-birds and pelicans.
Alongside my feet, the shark

Lay buried and followed,
His eyes on my childish heels.
Thus, taking all morning to stalk
From one littered beach to another,
I came out on land, and dismounted,
Making marks in the sand with my toes
Which truly had walked there, on water,

With the pelicans beating their shadows
Through the mirror carpet
Down, and the shark pursuing
The boy on the burning deck
Of a bare single ship-wrecked board.
Shoving the plank out to sea, I walked
Inland, on numb sparkling feet,

With the sun on the sea unbroken,
Nor the long quiet step of the miracle
Doing anything behind me but blazing,
With the birds in it nodding their heads,
That must ponder that footstep forever,
Rocking, or until I return
In my ghost, which shall have become, then,

A boy with a staff,
To loose them, beak and feather, from the spell
Laid down by a balancing child,
Unstable, tight-lipped, and amazed,
And, under their place of enthrallment,
A huge, hammer-headed spirit
Shall pass, as if led by the nose into Heaven.

THE CALL

Through the trees, with the moon underfoot,
More soft than I can, I call.
I hear the king of the owls sing
Where he moves with my son in the gloom.
My tongue floats off in the darkness.
I feel the deep dead turn
My blind child round toward my calling,
Through the trees, with the moon underfoot,

In a sound I cannot remember.
It whispers like straw in my ear,
And shakes like a stone under water.
My bones stand on tiptoe inside it.
Which part of the sound did I utter?
Is it song, or is half of it whistling?
What spirit has swallowed my tongue?
Or is it a sound I remember?

And yet it is coming back,
Having gone, adrift on its spirit,
Down, over and under the river,
And stood in a ring in a meadow
Round a child with a bird gravely dancing.
I hear the king of the owls sing.
I did not awaken that sound,
And yet it is coming back,

In touching every tree upon the hill.
The breath falls out of my voice,
And yet the singing keeps on.
The owls are dancing, fastened by their toes
Upon the pines. Come, son, and find me here,
In love with the sound of my voice.
Come calling the same soft song,
And touching every tree upon the hill.

TREES AND CATTLE

Many trees can stand unshaded
In this place where the sun is alone,
But some may break out.
They may be taken to Heaven,
So gold is my only sight.

Through me, two red cows walk;
From a crowning glory
Of slowness they are not taken.
Let one hoof knock on a stone,
And off it a spark jump quickly,

And fire may sweep these fields,
And all outburn the blind sun.
Like a new light I enter my life,
And hover, not yet consumed,
With the trees in holy alliance,

About to be offered up,
About to get wings where we stand.
The whole field stammers with gold;
No leaf but is actively still;
There is no quiet or noise;

Continually out of a fire
A bull walks forth,
And makes of my mind a red beast
At each step feeling how
The sun more deeply is burning

Because trees and cattle exist.
I go away, in the end.
In the shade, my bull's horns die
From my head; in some earthly way
I have been given my heart:

Behind my back, a tree leaps up
On wings that could save me from death.
Its branches dance over my head.
Its flight strikes a root in me.
A cow beneath it lies down.

ON THE HILL BELOW THE LIGHTHOUSE

Now I can be sure of my sleep;
I have lost the blue sea in my eyelids.
From a place in the mind too deep
For thought, a light like a wind is beginning.
  Now I can be sure of my sleep.

When the moon is held strongly within it,
The eye of the mind opens gladly.
Day changes to dark, and is bright,
And miracles trust to the body,
  When the moon is held strongly within it.

A woman comes true when I think her.
Her eyes on the window are closing.
She has dressed the stark wood of a chair.
Her form and my body are facing.
  A woman comes true when I think her.

Shade swings, and she lies against me.
The lighthouse has opened its brain.
A browed light travels the sea.
Her clothes on the chair spread their wings.
  Shade swings, and she lies against me.

Let us lie in returning light,
As a bright arm sweeps through the moon.
The sun is dead, thinking of night
Swung round like a thing on a chain.
  Let us lie in returning light.

Let us lie where your angel is walking
In shadow, from wall onto wall,

Cast forth from your off-cast clothing
To pace the dim room where we fell.
Let us lie where your angel is walking,

Coming back, coming back, going over.
An arm turns the light world around
The dark. Again we are waiting to hover
In a blaze in the mind like a wind
Coming back, coming back, going over.

Now I can be sure of my sleep;
The moon is held strongly within it.
A woman comes true when I think her.
Shade swings, and she lies against me.
Let us lie in returning light;
Let us lie where your angel is walking,
Coming back, coming back, going over.

THE PERFORMANCE

The last time I saw Donald Armstrong
He was staggering oddly off into the sun,
Going down, of the Philippine Islands.
I let my shovel fall, and put that hand
Above my eyes, and moved some way to one side
That his body might pass through the sun,

And I saw how well he was not
Standing there on his hands,
On his spindle-shanked forearms balanced,
Unbalanced, with this big feet looming and waving
In the great, untrustworthy air
He flew in each night, when it darkened.

Dust fanned in scraped puffs from the earth
Between his arms, and blood turned his face inside out,
To demonstrate its suppleness
Of veins, as he perfected his role.
Next day, he toppled his head off
On an island beach to the south,

And the enemy's two-handed sword
Did not fall from anyone's hands
At that miraculous sight,
As the head rolled over upon
Its wide-eyed face, and fell
Into the inadequate grave

He had dug for himself, under pressure.
Yet I put my flat hand to my eyebrows
Months later, to see him again
In the sun, when I learned how he died,
And imagined him, there,
Come, judged, before his small captors,

Doing all his lean tricks to amaze them—
The back somersault, the kip-up—
And at last, the stand on his hands,
Perfect, with his feet together,
His head down, evenly breathing,
As the sun poured up from the sea

And the headsman broke down
In a blaze of tears, in that light
Of the thin, long human frame
Upside down in its own strange joy,
And, if some other one had not told him,
Would have cut off the feet

Instead of the head,
And if Armstrong had not presently risen
In kingly, round-shouldered attendance,
And then knelt down in himself
Beside his hacked, glittering grave, having done
All things in this life that he could.

Donald Finkel

GIVE WAY

Give way to the man coming at you:
He is probably organized, or he
Is a Mason, so much the worse
For you. The child ahead of you
Walks carefully, does not step
On a crack. She knows. Keep
Close to the buildings, stick
To the well-lit avenues, give way

"Man that is born of woman is of
Few days, and full of trouble.
He cometh forth like a flower,
And is cut down: he fleeth also
As a shadow, and continueth not."
Your path will be covered with cracks;
Beware of a tall man who will bring
Ill fortune; beware of a short man:
He will be armed.

             Or, better yet,
Organize, call meetings, make speeches,
Pay dues. With the dues, acquire
A public address system, and make
Louder speeches. Cast ballots, win.

It you will notice, now, the tall
Man, he tests the microphones,
The short man insures with his gun
The collection of dues; everyone
Is stepping between the cracks.
However, nobody is fully satisfied:
Keep close to the buildings, give way;
The man coming at you may be armed.

TARGET PRACTICE

On the first day good enough father and son
Went out with the new gun
And rode for miles in Iowa.

No. That spring, city-bred and new to sun,
We went out in the car in Iowa
And parked at last between
Two farms and walked, through mud, to the place.

Neither is right, the fiction
Or the fact. It is as if
What happened were good enough, as if the place,
If I described it, might produce
Shoots between the wagon-ruts,
As the spring works, yearly, miracles in Iowa.
No poem grows anything.
The hands of words are tender,
False to work, as you and I were false, in Iowa,
To mud and gun, were neither
Farmer's son nor father,
Whose ancient secrets back away from words
Like huge and hungry birds
That have no use for song.

A poem is the least kind of honesty. Words
Have their sense and semblance.
When I saw, over the place,
The huge bird angling, I said, It's a hawk,
It's a hawk, and you could
Shoot then, at something,
Even if it was a crow we saw, and not a hawk
At all.

But a poem is the least
kind of honesty. It's to subsist
In woods for weeks on weeds to tell your friends
How you and nature are like

That. One must, to speak
Directly, have, at first, something to say to friends,
To sons. That spring in Iowa
We shot skyward at the hawk,
The crow, in a copse between two farms. We hit
Nothing, I think, though three
Times the big bird suddenly,
For a silent moment, fell, as if we'd really hit
Him, then changed direction
And wheeled off, screaming.

We did not hit him, I think, and I don't know
If it was a hawk or a crow
We didn't hit that day,
Between two populated farms, and I don't know
Where the bullets finally
Went, or if they killed
Some farmer, maybe, or his son, someone who knew
Hunting, mud, knew guns, who
Spoke little, having little
To say, could tell a hawk from a crow, and knew
His father, maybe, the way you
Don't know me, or I know you.

SOLO FOR BENT SPOON

*He figured as long as he couldn't be a successful anything else,
at least he could be a first-class junky.*

He saw beneath the bughouse wall
The consummate platonic sun
Craftily veneer the hill
A golder green where it had been
But only for a little while
Greengold and then before that green.

Inside his groin another sun
Burned a perfect charless hole
and squinting at a golden thumb
Painted on his stomach wall

An accurate academic scene
With trees of bile and hills of gall.

He saw in Mexico the twins
Who hid themselves for years until
With bits of glass they blew and spun
On molehill Calvary to scale
A careful crucifixion
Down to the painful last detail

With redeyed vultures and black nails
And real dice for the centurions.
He saw himself on the gold hill
Sporting a hypodermic crown,
Fixed by the needle in his bowels
Just as the literal sun went down.

KING MIDAS HAS ASSES' EARS

Under his careful crown he keeps
His psyche safe, and every day
In a kingdom of eyes he makes his way.
Only at midnight when his subjects sleep
In easy ignorance he stands before
His mirror, running his soft ears
Through his hands. Below the stairs
Servants like recriminations stir
In their beds, and the night birds
Scream Ears, ears! in mounting minor thirds.

Nobody hears, but yet he royally must
Be shaved in the mornings, nightly undressed;
Sunlight through his window-blind commands
The drawing near of strange impolitic hands.
His valet knocks: now like a whore he suffers
The hands, the eyes, of an untimely lover.

The barber stands behind his chair
And works the secrets from his hair;
As in a dim confessional,

The secular professional
Passive uncomprehending ear
Hears more than it was meant to hear.

I am a king who tells you this. Just so,
I keep them under my hat, all day
My kingdom course, between the hands and eyes;
At night before my mirror watch them grow
Softer and taller. Yet cannot keep
My peace: it is not servants merely
Who run and tell. I tell them daily
When they cut my hair, drag up my steep
Stair ice, my laundry. I confide
To urchins in the street who clean my shoes,
Stretch on a couch each morning and accuse
Myself of murder, mayhem, fratricide.
I am a king who tells you this: they know
Us better than we know ourselves, and rightly so.

THE IMBECILE

He is not the wise man, who comes
round to it only the long way.
He has not yet crept out of his mind,
which he inhabits like a snake
a well. No. Like water the shape
of the well. Any stone shakes
him, is him: then fear like a memory
of fading ripples to remind
him.

However, there is a moment they come
to him real as stones, there is a way
he can see, out of the corner of his mind,
and for a moment they stay. No snake
is as subtle, then, or as slight a shape,
shaking only as the wind shakes
him, softly, for passers beneath his tree
are few, and the least breath can confound
them.

His is a balance the wise man comes
to only by fumes and potions, or the way
or whirling in circles, until the mind
is water and the world is a shuddering snake
upon it, one last terrestrial shape,
then nothing: then the mind shakes
and settles, and no ark, though the sea
fall back from Ararat, can land
him.

S. S. Gardons

THE MOTHER

She stands in the dead center like a star;
They form around her like her satellites
Who take her energies, her heat, light
And massive attraction on their paths, however far.

Born of her own flesh; still, she feels them drawn
Into the outer cold by dark forces;
They are in love with suffering and perversion,
With the community of pain. Thinking them gone,

Beyond her reach, she is consoled by evil
In children, neighbors, in the world she cannot change,
That lightless universe where they range
Out of the comforts of her disapproval.

If evil did not exist, she would create it
To die in righteousness, her martyrdom
To that sweet dominion they have bolted from.
At last, she can believe that she is hated

And is content. Things can decay, break,
Spoil themselves; who cares? She'll gather the debris

With loving tenderness to give them; she
Will weave a labyrinth of waste, wreckage,

Of hocus-pocus; leave free no fault
Or cornerhole outside those lines of force
Where she and only she can thread a course.
All else in her grasp grows clogged and halts.

Till one by one, the areas of her brain
Switch off and she has filled all empty spaces;
Then she hallucinates in their right places
Their after-images, reversed and faint,

And the drawn strands of love, spun in her mind,
Turn dark and cluttered, precariously hung
With the black shapes of her mates, her sapless young,
Where she moves by habit, hungering and blind.

TO A CHILD

We've taken the dog for his walk
To the practice football field;
We sit on a dead branch, concealed
  In the tall grass and the trees
Near the old spring; we talk the usual talk
  About the birds and the bees.

How strange we should come here.
In the thick, matted grass, ten feet away
Some twenty years ago I lay
  With my first girl; half-dead
Or half-demented by my fear,
  I left her there and fled.

I always seem to choose
Odd spots; we used to go stone dapping
On the riverbanks where lovers lay
Abandoned in each others' arms all day
  By their beached green canoes;
  You asked why were they napping.

We've sat on cemetery
Stones to sing; found a toad
    Flat on the graveyard road
That no one had seen fit to bury;
    There we deciphered dark
Names carved in stone, names carved in white birch bark.

    We've waded up the creek
Over sharp stones, and through deep
Slime, to its source; caught a turtle
    And carried him home to keep.
    At best, he lived a week;
We said *that* ought to make the garden fertile.

We've named the animals in the park;
    Watched a caged squirrel caper,
    Patted the baby tapir,
Fed milk to the llamas, fawns and goats that roam
Loose, in a sort of Noah's Ark
    Or home away from home.

We heard a bantie chick there that had wandered
    Into the wrong pen;
It kept on peeping, scurrying
    To a huge indignant hen
    That fled. You said we'd bring
Our feather duster for it to crawl under.

    And I mailed you long letters
Though you were still too young to read;
Sent you the maple wings that fly,
Linden gliders and torqued ailanthus seeds,
    The crisp pine flyers that flutter
    Like soft moths down the sky;

    Told you how Fall winds bear
The tree seeds out, like airmailed letters,
To distant ground so, when they come up later,
    They may find, possibly,
The rain they need, some sun and air,
    Far from the parent tree.

They threw my letters out.
They said I had probably forgotten.
We have seen the sheen and glow of rotten
Wood, the glimmering being that consumes
    The flesh of a dead trout.
    We've been in livingrooms;

    We have seen the dodder,
That parasitic pale love-vine that thrives
Coiling the zinnias in the ardor
    Of its close embrace.
    We have seen men abase
Themselves to their embittered wives;

And I have let you see my mother,
    That old sow in her stye
    Who would devour her farrow;
We have seen my sister in her narrow
Grave. Without love we die;
    With love we kill each other.

    You are afraid, now, of dying;
    Sick of change and loss;
You think of your own self lying
Still in the ground while someone takes your room.
Today, you felt the small life toss
    In your step-mother's womb.

I sit here with you in the summer's lull
By the lost handkerchiefs of lovers
    To tell you when your brother
    Will be born; how, and why.
I tell you love is possible.
    We have to try.

Donald Hall

THE SNOW

Snow is in the oak.
Behind the thick, whitening
air which the wind drives,
the weight of the sun
presses the snow
on the pane of my window.

I remember snows and my walking
through their first fall in cities,
asleep or drunk
with the slow, desperate falling.
The snow blurs in my eyes,
with other snows.

Snow is what must
come down, even if it struggles
to stay in the air with the strength
of the wind. Like an old man,
whatever I touch I turn
to the story of death.

Snow is what fills
the oak, and what covers
the grass and the bare garden.
Snow is what reverses
sidewalk, house and lawn
into the substance of whiteness.

So the watcher sleeps himself
back to the baby's eyes.
The tree, the breast, and the floor
are limbs of him, and from

his eyes he extends a skin
which grows over the world.

The baby is what must
have fallen, like snow. He resisted,
the way the old man
struggles inside the airy tent
to keep on breathing.
Birth is the fear of death

and the source of an old hope.
Snow is what melts. I distrust
the cycles of water.
The sun has withdrawn itself
and the snow keeps falling,
and something will always be falling.

THE LONG RIVER

The musk-ox smells
in his long head
my boat coming. When
I feel him there,
intent, heavy,

the oars make wings
in the white night,
and deep woods are close
on either side
where trees darken.

I rowed past towns
in their black sleep
to come here. I passed
the northern grass
and cold mountains.

The musk-ox moves
when the boat stops,
in hard thickets. Now

the wood is dark
with old pleasures.

IN THE OLD HOUSE

In the kitchen of the old house, late,
I was making some coffee
  and I day-dreamed sleepily of old friends.
Then the dream turned. I waited.
  I walked alone all day in the town
where I was born. It was cold,
  a Saturday in January
when nothing happens. The streets
  changed as the sky grew dark around me.
The lamps in the small houses
  had tassels on them, and the black cars
at the curb were old and square.
  A ragman passed with his horse, their breaths
blooming like white peonies,
  when I turned into a darker street
and I recognized the house
  from snapshots. I felt as separate
as if the city and the house
  were closed inside a globe which I shook
to make it snow. No sooner
  did I think of snow, but snow started
to fill the heavy darkness
  around me. It reflected the glare
of the streetlight as it fell
  melting on the warmth of the sidewalk
and frozen on frozen grass.
  Then I heard out of the dark the sound
of steps on the bare cement
  in a familiar rhythm. Under
the streetlight, bent to the snow,
  hatless, younger than I, so young that
I was not born, my father
  walked home to his bride and his supper.
A shout gathered inside me
  like a cold wind, to break the rhythm,

to keep him from entering
   that heavy door—but I stood under
a tree, closed in by the snow,
   and did not shout, to tell what happened
in twenty years, in winter,
   when his early death grew inside him
like snow piling on the grass.
   He opened the door and met the young
woman who waited for him.

THE CHILD

He lives among a dog,
a tricycle, and a friend.
Nobody owns him.

He walks by himself, beside
the black pool, in the cave
where icicles of rock

rain hard water,
and the walls are rough
with the light of stone.

He hears some low talking
without words.
The hand of a wind touches him.

He walks until he is tired
or somebody calls him.
Then he leaves right away.

Later when he plays with his friend
he stops suddenly
to hear the black water.

NEW HAMPSHIRE

A bear sleeps in the cellar hole, where pine needles
heap over the granite doorstep. And the well brims
with acorns and the broken leaves of the oak tree
that has grown where the anvil rusted in the forge.

When my eyes close, I can see another summer:
a bark of rust grows on the trees of the gas pumps,
and the EAT signs gather like leaves in the shallow
cellars of diners, and a wildcat waits for deer

on the roof of a car. Blacktop buckled by frost
starts goldenrod from the highway. Fat honey bees
meander among raspberries, where a quarrel
of vines crawls into the spilled body of a plane.

THE THREE MOVEMENTS

It is not in the books
that he is looking, nor for
a new book, nor
documents of any kind, nor
does he expect it to be like the wind,
that, when you touch it, tears
without a sound of tearing, nor
like the rain
water
that becomes
grass in the sun. He
expects that when he finds it
it will be
like a man, visible, alive
to what has happened and what
will happen, with
firmness in its face, seeing
exactly what is, without

measure of change, and not
like documents,
or rain in the grass.

But what, he says,
if it is not
for the finding, not
what you most expect, nor even
what you dread, nothing
but the books, the endless
documents, the banked
volumes that repeat
mile after mile
their names,
their information?
Perhaps there is nothing
except the rain
water
becoming the grass, the
sustenance. What
a man should do is
accumulate
information
until he has gathered, like a
farmer, as much
as his resources can contain.

Yet perhaps, he thinks,
I speak
with knowledge, but perhaps
forgetting the movement
that intrigues
all thinking. It is
the movement which works through,
which discovers itself
in alleys, in
sleep, not
expected and not
in the books of words and phrases
nor the various paints and edges
of scenery.

It is, he says,
familiar when come upon,
glimpsed
as in a mirror
unpredicted,
and it appears
to understand. It is
like himself, only visible.

Anthony Hecht

THE END OF THE WEEKEND

A dying firelight slides along the quirt
Of the cast-iron cowboy where he leans
Against my father's books. The lariat
Whirls into darkness. My girl, in skin-tight jeans,
Fingers a page of Captain Marryat,
Inviting insolent shadows to her shirt.

We rise together to the second floor.
Outside, across the lake, an endless wind
Whips at the headstones of the dead and wails
In the trees for all who have and have not sinned.
She rubs against me and I feel her nails.
Although we are alone, I lock the door.

The eventual shapes of all our formless prayers,
This dark, this cabin of loose imaginings,
Wind, lake, lip, everything awaits
The slow unloosening of her underthings.
And then the noise. Something is dropped. It grates
Against the attic beams.
                              I climb the stairs,

Armed with a belt.
                          A long magnesium strip

Of moonlight from the dormer cuts a path
Among the shattered skeletons of mice.
A great black presence beats its wings in wrath.
Above the boneyard burn its golden eyes.
Some small grey fur is pulsing in its grip.

"MORE LIGHT! MORE LIGHT!"

Composed in the Tower before his execution
These moving verses, and being brought at that time
Painfully to the stake, submitted, declaring thus:
"I implore my God to witness that I have made no crime."

Nor was he forsaken of courage, but the death was
      horrible,
The sack of gunpowder failing to ignite.
His legs were blistered sticks on which the black sap
Bubbled and burst as he howled for the Kindly Light.

And that was but one, and by no means one of the worst;
Permitted at least his pitiful dignity;
And such as were by made prayers in the name of Christ,
That shall judge all men, for his soul's tranquility.

We move now to outside a German wood.
Three men are there commanded to dig a hole
In which the two Jews are ordered to lie down
And be buried alive by the third, who is a Pole.

Not light from the shrine at Weimar beyond the hill
Nor light from heaven appeared. But he did refuse.
A Lüger settled back deeply in its glove.
He was ordered to change places with the Jews.

Much casual death had drained away their souls.
The thick dirt mounted toward the quivering chin.
When only the head was exposed the order came
To dig him out again and to get back in.

No light, no light in the blue Polish eye.
When he finished a riding boot packed down the earth.
The Lüger hovered lightly in its glove.
He was shot in the belly and in three hours bled to death.

No prayers or incense rose up in those hours
Which grew to be years, and every day came mute
Ghosts from the ovens, sifting through crisp air,
And settled upon his eyes in a black soot.

THE DOVER BITCH

A CRITICISM OF LIFE

So there stood Matthew Arnold and this girl
With the cliffs of England crumbling away behind them,
And he said to her, "Try to be true to me,
And I'll do the same for you, for things are bad
All over, etc., etc."
Well now, I knew this girl. It's true she had read
Sophocles in a fairly good translation
And caught that bitter allusion to the sea,
But all the time he was talking she had in mind
The notion of what his whiskers would feel like
On the back of her neck. She told me later on
That after a while she got to looking out
At the lights across the channel, and really felt sad,
Thinking of all the wine and enormous beds
And blandishments in French and the perfumes.
And then she got really angry. To have been brought
All the way down from London, and then be addressed
As a sort of mournful cosmic last resort
Is really tough on a girl, and she was pretty.
Anyway, she watched him pace the room
And finger his watch-chain and seem to sweat a bit,
And then she said one or two unprintable things.
But you mustn't judge her by that. What I mean to say is,
She's really all right. I still see her once in a while
And she always treats me right. We have a drink
And I give her a good time, and perhaps it's a year
Before I see her again, but there she is,

Running to fat, but dependable as they come.
And sometimes I bring her a bottle of *Nuit d'Amour*.

THIRD AVENUE IN SUNLIGHT

Third Avenue in sunlight. Nature's error.
Already the bars are filled and John is there.
Beneath a plentiful lady over the mirror
He tilts his glass in the mild mahogany air.

I think of him when he first got out of college,
Serious, thin, unlikely to succeed;
For several months he hung around the Village,
Boldly T-shirted, unfettered but unfreed.

Now he confides to a stranger, "I was first scout,
And kept my glimmers peeled till after dark.
Our outfit had as its sign a bloody knout.
We met behind the museum in Central Park.

Of course, we were kids." But still those savages,
War-painted, a flap of leather at the loins,
File silently against him. Hostages
Are never taken. One summer, in Des Moines,

They entered his hotel room, tomahawks
Flashing like barracuda. He tried to pray.
Three years of treatment. Occasionally he talks
About how he almost didn't get away.

Daily the prowling sunlight whets its knife
Along the sidewalk. We almost never meet.
In the Rembrandt dark he lifts his amber life.
My bar is somewhat further down the street.

BEHOLD THE LILIES OF THE FIELD

And now. An attempt.
Don't tense yourself; take it easy.

Look at the flowers there in the glass bowl.
Yes, they are lovely and fresh. I remember
Giving my mother flowers once, rather like those
(Are they narcissus or jonquils?)
And I hoped she would show some pleasure in them
But got that mechanical enthusiastic show
She used on the telephone once in praising some friend
For thoughtfulness or good taste or whatever it was,
And when she hung up, turned to us all and said,
"God, what a bore she is!"
I think she was trying to show us how honest she was,
At least with us. But the effect
Was just the opposite, and now I don't think
She knows what honesty is. "Your mother's a whore,"
Someone said, not meaning she slept around,
Though perhaps this was part of it, but
Meaning she had lost all sense of honor,
And I think this is true.

But that's not what I wanted to say.
What was it I wanted to say?
When he said that about Mother, I had to laugh,
I really did, it was so amazingly true.
Where was I?
Lie back. Relax.
Oh yes. I remember now what it was.
It was what I saw them do to the emperor.
They captured him, you know. Eagles and all.
They stripped him, and made an iron collar for his neck,
And they made a cage out of our captured spears,
And they put him inside, naked and collared,
And exposed to the view of the whole enemy camp.
And I was tied to a post and made to watch
When he was taken out and flogged by one of their
    generals
And then forced to offer his ripped back
As a mounting block for the barbarian king
To get on his horse;
And one time to get down on all fours to be the royal
    throne
When the king received our ambassadors
To discuss the question of ransom.

Of course, he didn't want ransom.
And I was tied to a post and made to watch.
That's enough for now. Lie back. Try to relax.
No, that's not all.
They kept it up for two months.
We were taken to their outmost provinces.
It was always the same, and we were always made to
    watch,
The others and I. How he stood it, I don't know.
And then suddenly
There were no more floggings or humiliations,
The king's personal doctor saw to his back,
He was given decent clothing, and the collar was taken off,
And they treated us all with a special courtesy.
By the time we reached their capital city
His back was completely healed.
They had taken the cage apart—
But of course they didn't give us back our spears.
Then later that month, it was a warm afternoon in May,
The rest of us were marched out to the central square.
The crowds were there already, and the posts were set up,
To which we were tied in the old watching position.
And he was brought out in the old way, and stripped,
And then tied flat on a big rectangular table
So that only his head could move.
Then the king made a short speech to the crowds,
To which they responded with gasps of wild excitement,
And which was then translated for the rest of us.
It was the sentence. He was to be flayed alive,
As slowly as possible, to drag out the pain.
And we were made to watch. The king's personal doctor,
The one who had tended his back,
Came forward with a tray of surgical knives.
They began at the feet.
And we were not allowed to close our eyes
Or to look away. When they were done, hours later,
The skin was turned over to one of their saddle-makers
To be tanned and stuffed and sewn. And for what?
A hideous life-sized doll, filled out with straw,

In the skin of the Roman Emperor, Valerian,
With blanks of mother-of-pearl under the eyelids,

And painted shells that had been prepared beforehand
For the fingernails and toenails,
Roughly cross-stitched on the inseam of the legs
And up the back to the center of the head,
Swung in the wind on a rope from the palace flag-pole;
And young girls were brought there by their mothers
To be told about the male anatomy.
His death had taken hours.
They were very patient.
And with him passed away the honor of Rome.

In the end, I was ransomed. Mother paid for me.
You must rest now. You must. Lean back.
Look at the flowers.
Yes. I am looking. I wish I could be like them.

John Hollander

THE GREAT BEAR

Even on clear nights, lead the most supple children
Out onto hilltops, and by no means will
They make it out. Neither the gruff round image
From a remembered page nor the uncertain
Finger tracing that image out can manage
To mark the lines of what ought to be there,
Passing through certain bounding stars, until
The whole massive expanse of bear appear
Swinging, across the ecliptic; and, although
The littlest ones say nothing, others respond,
Making us thankful in varying degrees
For what we would have shown them: "There it is!"
"I see it now!" Even "Very like a bear!"
Would make us grateful. Because there is no bear

We blame our memory of the picture: trudging
Up the dark, starlit path, stooping to clutch

An anxious hand, perhaps the outline faded
Then; perhaps could we have retained the thing
In mind ourselves, with it we might have staged
Something convincing. We easily forget
The huge, clear, homely dipper that is such
An event to reckon with, an object set
Across the space the bear should occupy;
But even so, the trouble lies in pointing
At any stars. For one's own finger aims
Always elsewhere: the man beside one seems
Never to get the point. "No! The bright star
Just above my fingertip." The star,

If any, that he sees beyond one's finger
Will never be the intended one. To bring
Another's eye to bear in such a fashion
On any single star seems to require
Something very like a constellation
That both habitually see at night;
Not in the stars themselves, but in among
Their scatter, perhaps, some old familiar sight
Is always there to take a bearing from.
And if the smallest child of all should cry
Out on the wet, black grass because he sees
Nothing but stars, though claiming that there is
Some bear not there that frightens him, we need
Only reflect that we ourselves have need

Of what is fearful (being really nothing)
With which to find our way about the path
That leads back down the hill again, and with
Which to enable the older children standing
By us to follow what we mean by "This
Star," "That one," or "The other one beyond it."
But what of the tiny, scared ones?— Such a bear,
Who needs it? We can still make do with both
The dipper that we always knew was there
And the bright, simple shapes that suddenly
Emerge on certain nights. To understand
The signs that stars compose, we need depend
Only on stars that are entirely there
And the apparent space between them. There

Never need be lines between them, puzzling
Our sense of what is what. What a star does
Is never to surprise us as it covers
The center of its patch of darkness, sparkling
Always, a point in one of many figures.
One solitary star would be quite useless,
A frigid conjecture, true but trifling;
And any single sign is meaningless
If unnecessary. Crab, bull, and ram,
Or frosty, irregular polygons of our own
Devising, or finally the Great Dark Bear
That we can never quite believe is there—
Having the others, any one of them
Can be dispensed with. The bear, of all of them,

Is somehow most like any one, taken
At random, in that we always tend to say
That just because it might be there; because
Some Ancients really traced it out, a broken
And complicated line, webbing bright stars
And fainter ones together; because a bear
Habitually appeared—then even by day
It is for us a thing that should be there.
We should not want to train ourselves to see it.
The world is everything that happens to
Be true. The stars at night seem to suggest
The shapes of what might be. If it were best,
Even, to have it there (such a great bear!
All hung with stars!), there still would be no bear.

A LION NAMED PASSION

". . . the girl had walked past several cages occupied by
other lions before she was seized by a lion named Passion. It
was from his cage that keepers recovered the body."
                    —The New York Times, May 16, 1958

Hungering on the gray plain of its birth
For the completion of the sunny cages
To hold all its unruly, stretching forth
Its longest streets and narrowest passages,

The growing city paws the yielding earth,
And rears its controlling stones. Its snarl damages
The dull, unruffled fabric of silences
In which the world is wrapped. The day advances
And shadows lengthen as their substances
Grow more erect and rigid, as low hearth
And high, stark tower rise beneath the glances
Of anxious, ordered Supervision. North
Bastion and eastern wall are joined, and fences
Are finished between the areas of Mirth
And the long swards of Mourning. Growth manages
At once vigor of spurts, and the rigor of stages.

If not the Just City, then the Safe one: sea
And mountain torrent warded off, and all
The wildest monsters caged, that running free,
The most exposed and open children shall
Fear no consuming grasp. Thus the polity
Preserves its fast peace by the burial
Of those hot barbarous sparks whose fiery, bright
Eruption might disturb blackness of night
And temperateness of civil love. The light
Of day is light enough, calm, gray, easy
And agreeable. And beasts? The lion might
Be said to dwell here, but so tamed is he,
Set working in the streets, say, with no fright
Incurred by those huge paws which turn with glee
A hydrant valve, while playing children sprawl
And splash in the bright spray, dribbling a shiny ball;

So innocent he is, his huge head, high
And chinny, pointed over his shoulder, more
A lion rampant, blazoned on the sky,
Than monster romping through the streets, with gore
Reddening his jaws; so kind of eye
And clear of gaze is that sweet beast, that door
Need never shut, nor window bar on Him.
But look! Look there! One morning damp and dim
In thick, grey fog, or even while the slim
And gaily tigering shadows creep on by
The porch furniture on hot noons, see him
Advancing through the streets, with monstrous cry,

Half plea, half threat, dying in huff of flame;
This must be some new beast! As parents spy,
Safe, from behind parked cars, he damps his roar—
It is the little children he is making for!

When elders, not looking at each other, creep
Out of their hiding places, little men,
Little women, stare back, resentment deep
Inside their throats at what had always been
A Great Place for the Kids: infants asleep
And growing, boys and girls, all, all eaten,
Burned by the prickly heat of baby throbbing,
Already urging scratching hands; the sobbing
After certain hot hurts in childhood; stabbing
Pulses and flashing floods of summer that leap
Out, in the dusk of childhood, at youth, dabbing
At the old wounds from which fresh feelings seep.
"O help me! I am being done!" the bobbing
Hip and awakened leg, one day, from heap
Of melting body call. Done? No, undone!
Robbing the grave of first fruits, the beast feeds again.

Burning is being consumed by flaming beasts,
Rebellious and unappeasable. The wind
Of very early morning, finally, casts
A cool sweet quenching draught on hunger's end,
Those ashes and whitened bones. Each day, to lists
Of dead and sorely wounded are assigned
The tasks of memory. Mute crowds push by
The useless cages and restraining, high,
(But not retaining) walls. Against the sky
Only these ruins show at dawn, like masts,
Useless in ships becalmed, but hung with dry
Corpses; or like unheeded fruit that blasts
High in trees, wasted. Menacing, wild of eye,
The city, having missed its spring, now feasts,
Nastily, on itself. Jackals attend
The offal. And new cities raven and distend.

Robert Huff

RAINBOW

After the shot the driven feathers rock
In the air and are by sunlight trapped.
Their moment of descent is eloquent.
It is the rainbow echo of a bird
Whose thunder, stopped, puts in my daughter's eyes
A question mark. She does not see the rainbow,
And the folding bird-fall was for her too quick.
It is about the stillness of the bird
Her eyes are asking. She is three years old;
Has cut her fingers; found blood tastes of salt;
But she has never witnessed quiet blood,
Nor ever seen before the peace of death.
I say: "The feathers— Look!" but she is torn
And wretched and draws back. And I am glad
That I have wounded her, have winged her heart,
And that she goes beyond my fathering.

THE SMOKER

Sitting down near him in the shade,
I watch him strike a match on his white cane.
He burns his finger but displays no pain.
This smiling blind man with a hearing aid

Smokes by the hour. Now he's blowing rings.
He measures in the smoke and takes much care
To shape his mouth for pumping circled air.
He fathers hundreds of round hoverings.

I offer: It's too warm; it ought to rain.
His only comment is a smiling cough.
Maybe he's got his hearing aid turned off
To keep such interference from his brain,

Or can't hear through the haze, or won't let sound
Disturb his gentle passion. Who can tell
What he envisions with his sense of smell
Heaving my presence at him by the pound?

I never blame him when he comes in dreams,
A slow smile smoking, circled to the thighs,
And screws both of his thumbs into my eyes
And will not stop to listen to my screams.

GETTING DRUNK WITH DAUGHTER

Caught without wife and mother, child,
We squat close, scratching gibberish in the sand,
Inspect your castle, peek into the pail
Where shells await your signal to attack
The stick gate, strike down squads of stones,
And storm the tower of the Feather Queen,
When, perchspine arrow in his head,
Lord Cork falls dead, his bride carted away.
And my pailful of ice is melting down
Around what will be two dead soldiers soon.

Odors remind me your cheeks reeked with kisses:
Whiskey, tobacco, dentures—sourdough—
When Father found you on the trail he misses.
Too bad the old man had to see you grow
Into my blonde wag with your woman's wishes,
Playing pretend wife, Daughter . . . even though
He threw himself to rags and knows his bliss is
Walking the sweaty mares he can't let go.

Precocious runt. Noting our shapely neighbor
Is amber from toenails to Brillo hair,

Has rolled, and drops her top and props her cleavage,
You grin above your army. Dear, her spine's
Not likely to compete with you or Bourbon
Since you're your mother's small ape from behind.
Oh, I know you know I know love likes beaches—
For blood outruns the heart, no doubt,
But mine runs to your lordship's mortal splinter.
I've one cork left. So let the spearmen start.

Tomorrow's going to come. We'll be together.
The sun will bake us, and we'll let our bones
Fly with the wastrel gulls, who love this weather,
Enlisting stronger sticks, more stalwart stones.
Your mother's got a feather where she itches.
Your daddy's got a fish bone in his brain.
The world lies down and waits in all its ditches.
But you and I aren't going to let it rain.

TRADITIONAL RED

Returning after dark, I thought,
The house will have grown small: noises
In the barn I knew, wood and field,
All tree tops visible. My eyes,
I thought, lied then or will lie now;
My ears, even my ears, will tell
Me: small. Then half awake I waited,
Half afraid of the sound light makes
With frost on windowpanes. But night
Birds carried fifteen years away
Like an abandoned nest, put them
To rest somewhere I couldn't see
Without undoing anything,
And when I woke the dawn I saw
Was on the farm as positive as God.

A rooster dipped in sunlight raised
His crown, called to the steaming barn,
Gigantic, red, until my blood

Roared for stupidity, and I
Ran down the path humble with hens
To kneel and stare dumb wonder
At his size. My pride! my pride! O
Jesus, bright dove call! I knelt there
In his thunder, white and small, watched
Him and rose to walk under trees
Whose tops I couldn't see for light,
Dense, golden, moving hosts of leaves
Answering that red cry. And when
I turned I saw the farm house roof
Raking an iron rooster through the sky.

Donald Justice

THE SNOWFALL

The classic landscapes of dreams are not
More pathless, though footprints leading nowhere
Would seem to prove that a people once
Survived for a little even here.

Fragments of a pathetic culture
Remain, the lost mittens of children,
And a single, bright detasseled snow-cap,
Evidence of some frantic migration.

The landmarks are gone. Nevertheless
There is something familiar about this country.
Slowly now we begin to recall

The terrible whispers of our elders
Falling softly about our ears
In childhood, never believed till now.

ON A PAINTING BY PATIENT B
OF THE INDEPENDENCE STATE
HOSPITAL FOR THE INSANE

1

These seven houses have learned to face one another,
But not at the expected angles. Those silly brown lumps,
That are probably meant for hills and not other houses,
After ages of being themselves, though naturally slow,
Are learning to be exclusive without offending.
The arches and entrances (down to the right out of sight)
Have mastered the lesson of remaining closed.
And even the skies keep a certain understandable distance,
For these are the houses of the very rich.

2

One sees their children playing with leopards, tamed
At great cost, or perhaps it is only other children,
For none of these objects is anything more than a spot,
And perhaps there are not any children but only leopards
Playing with leopards, and perhaps there are only the
    spots.
And the little maids from the windows hanging like
    tongues,
Calling the children in, admiring the leopards,
Are the dashes a child might represent motion by
    means of,
Or dazzlement possibly, the brilliance of solid-gold
    houses.

3

The clouds resemble those empty balloons in cartoons
Which approximate silence. These clouds, if clouds they
    are
(And not the smoke from the seven aspiring chimneys),
The more one studies them the more it appears
They too have expressions. One might almost say
They have their habits, their wrong opinions, that their

Impassivity masks an essentially lovable foolishness,
And they will be given names by those who live under
    them
Not public like mountains' but private like companions'.

TALES FROM A FAMILY ALBUM

How shall I speak of doom, and ours in special,
But as of something altogether common?
No house of Atreus ours, too humble surely,
The family tree a simple chinaberry
Such as springs up in Georgia in a season.
(Under it sags the farmer's broken wagon.)
Nor may I laud it much for shade or beauty,
Yet praise that tree for being prompt to flourish,
Spite of the worm and weather out of heaven.

I publish of my folk how they have prospered
With something in the eyes, perhaps inherent,
Or great-winged nose, bespeaking an acquaintance
Not casual and not recent with a monster,
Citing, as an example of some courage,
That aunt, long gone, who kept one in a bird-cage
Thirty-odd years in shape of a green parrot,
Nor overcame her fears, yet missed no feeding,
Thrust in the crumbs with thimbles on her fingers.

I had an uncle, long of arm and hairy,
Who seldom spoke in any lady's hearing
Lest that his tongue should light on aught unseemly,
Yet he could treat most kindly with us children
Touching that beast, wholly imaginary,
Which, hunting once, his hounds had got the wind of.
And even of this present generation
There is a cousin of no great removal
On whom the mark is printed of a forepaw.

How shall I speak of doom and not the shadow
Caught in the famished cheeks of those few beauties
My people boast of, being flushed and phthisic?

Of my own childhood I remember dimly
One who died young, though as a hag most toothless,
Her fine hair wintry, from a hard encounter
By moonlight in a dark wood with a stranger,
Who had as well been unicorn or centaur
For all she might recall of him thereafter.

There was a kinsman took up pen and paper
To write our history, whereat he perished,
Calling for water and the holy wafer,
Who had, ere that, resisted much persuasion.
I pray your mercy on a leaf so shaken,
And mercy likewise on these other fallen,
Torn from the berry-tree in heaven's fashion,
That there was somewhat in their way of going
Put doom upon my tongue and bade me utter.

ANOTHER SONG

Merry the green, the green hill shall be merry.
Hungry, the owlet shall seek out the mouse,
And Jack his Joan, but they shall never marry.

And snows shall fly, the big flakes fat and furry.
Lonely, the traveler shall seek out the house,
And Jack his Joan, but they shall never marry.

Weary the soldiers go, and come back weary,
Up a green hill and down the withered hill,
And Jack from Joan, and they shall never marry.

ANONYMOUS DRAWING

A delicate young Negro stands
With the reins of a horse clutched loosely in his hands;
So delicate, indeed, that we wonder if he can hold the
    spirited creature beside him
Until the master shall arrive to ride him.

Already the animal's nostrils widen with rage or fear.
But if we imagine him snorting, about to rear,
This boy, who should know about such things better
      than we,
Only stands smiling, passive and ornamental, in a fantas-
      tic livery
Of ruffles and puffed breeches,
Watching the artist, apparently, as he sketches.
Meanwhile the petty lord who must have paid
For the artist's trip up from Perugia, for the horse, for the
      boy, for everything here, in fact, has been delayed,
Kept too long by his steward, perhaps, discussing
Some business concerning the estate, or fussing
Over the details of his impeccable toilet
With a manservant whose opinion is that any alteration
      at all would spoil it.
However fast he should come hurrying now
Over this vast greensward, mopping his brow
Clear of the sweat of the fine Renaissance morning, it
      would be too late:
The artist will have had his revenge for being made to
      wait,
A revenge not only necessary but right and clever—
Simply to leave him out of the scene forever.

BUT THAT IS ANOTHER STORY

I do not think the ending can be right.
How can they marry and live happily
Forever, these who were so passionate
At chapter's end? Once they are settled in
The quiet country house, what will they do,
So many miles from anywhere?
Those blonde Victorian ghosts crowding the stair,
Surely they disapprove? Ah me,
I fear love will catch cold and die
From pacing naked through those drafty halls
Night after night. Poor Frank! Poor Imogene!
Before them now their lives
Stretch empty as great Empire beds

After the lovers rise and the damp sheets
Are stripped by envious chambermaids.

And if the first night passes brightly enough,
What with the bonfires lit with old love-letters,
That is no inexhaustible fuel, perhaps?
God knows how it must end, not I.
Will Frank walk out some day
Alone through the ruined orchard with his stick,
Strewing the path with lissome heads
Of buttercups? Will Imogene
Conceal in the crotches of old trees
Love-notes for grizzled gardeners and such?
Meanwhile they quarrel, and make it up,
Only to quarrel again. A sudden storm
Has pulled the fences down. The stupid sheep
Stand out all night now coughing in the garden
And peering through the windows where they sleep.

X. J. Kennedy

NUDE DESCENDING A STAIRCASE

Toe upon toe, a snowing flesh,
A gold of lemon, root and rind,
She sifts in sunlight down the stairs
With nothing on. Nor on her mind.

We spy beneath the banister
A constant thresh of thigh on thigh—
Her lips imprint the swinging air
That parts to let her parts go by.

One-woman waterfall, she wears
Her slow descent like a long cape
And pausing, on the final stair
Collects her motions into shape.

FIRST CONFESSION

Blood thudded in my ears. I scuffed,
  Steps stubborn, to the telltale booth
Beyond whose curtained portal coughed
  The robed repositor of truth.

The slat shot back. The universe
  Bowed down his cratered dome to hear
Enumerated my each curse,
  The sip snitched from my old man's beer,

My sloth pride envy lechery,
  The dime held back from Peter's Pence
With which I'd bribed my girl to pee
  That I might spy her instruments.

Hovering scale-pans when I'd done
  Settled their balance slow as silt
While in the restless dark I burned
  Bright as a brimstone in my guilt

Until as one feeds birds he doled
  Seven Our Fathers and a Hail
Which I to double-scrub my soul
  Intoned twice at the altar rail

Where Sunday in seraphic light
  I knelt, as full of grace as most,
And stuck my tongue out at the priest:
  A fresh roost for the Holy Ghost.

SOLITARY CONFINEMENT

She might have stolen from his arms
Except that there was nothing left

To steal. There was the crucifix
Of silver good enough to hock
But how far could she go on it
And what had he left her to pack
And steal away with and lay down
By someone new in a new town?

And so she put the notion back
And turned her look up where the clock,
Green ghost, swept round its tethered hand
That had made off with many nights
But no more could break from its shelf
Than she could quit this bed where breath
By breath these years he'd nailed her fast
Between two thieves, him and herself.

B NEGATIVE

M/60/5 FT 4/W PROT

You know it's April by the falling-off
In coughdrop boxes—fewer people cough—
    By daisies' first white eyeballs in the grass
And every dawn more underthings cast off.

Though plumtrees stretch recovered boughs to us
And doubledecked in green, the downtown bus,
    Love in one season—so your stab-pole tells—
Beds down, and buds, and is deciduous.

Now set down burlap bag. In pigeon talk
The wobbling pigeon flutes on the sidewalk,
    Struts on the breeze and clicks leisurely wings
As if the corn he ate grew on a stalk.

So plump he topples where he tries to stand,
He pecks my shoelaces, come to demand
    Another sack, another fifteen cents,
And yet—who else will eat out of my hand?

It used to be that when I laid my head
And body with it down by you in bed
    You did not turn from me nor fall to sleep
But turn to fall between my arms instead

And now I lay bifocals down. My feet
Forget the twist that brought me to your street.
    I can't make out your face for steamed-up glass
Nor quite call back your outline on the sheet.

I know how, bent to a movie magazine,
The hobo's head lights up, and from its screen
    Imagined bosoms in slow motion bloom
And no director interrupts the scene.

I used to purchase in the Automat
A cup of soup and fan it with my hat
    Until a stern voice from the changebooth crashed
Like nickels: *Gentlemen do not do that.*

Spring has no household, no abiding heat,
Pokes forth no bud from branches of concrete,
    Nothing to touch you, nothing you can touch—
The snow, at least, keeps track of people's feet.

The springer spaniel and the buoyant hare
Seem half at home reclining in mid-air—
    But, Lord, the times I've leaped the way they do
And looked round for a foothold—in despair.

The subway a little cheaper than a room,
I browse the *News*—or so the guards assume—
    And there half-waking, tucked in funny-sheets,
I hurtle in my mileaminute womb.

Down streets that wake up earlier than wheels
The routed spirit flees on dusty heels
    And in the soft fire of a muscatel
Sits up, puts forth its fingertips, and feels—

Down streets so deep the sun can't vault their walls,
Where one-night wives make periodic calls,

Where cat steals stone where rat makes off with child
And lyre and lute lie down under three balls,

Down blocks in sequence, fact by separate fact,
The human integers add and subtract
    Till in a cubic room in some hotel
You wake one day to find yourself abstract

And turn a knob and hear a voice: *Insist
On Jiffy Blades, they're tender to the wrist—*
    Then static, then a squawk as if your hand
Had shut some human windpipe with a twist.

I know how, lurking under trees by dark,
Poor loony stranglers out to make their mark
    Reach forth shy hands to touch some woman's hair—
I pick up after them in Central Park.

FACES FROM A BESTIARY

Suggested by the twelfth-century Livre des Créatures
of Philip de Thaun

1

The Lion sleeps with open eyes
That none may take him by surprise.
The Son of God he signifies

For when a Lion stillborn lies
His mother circles him and cries.
Then on the third day he will rise.

2

Hyena is a beast to hate.
No man hath seen him copulate.
He is unto himself a mate.

You who this creature emulate
Who with your mirrors fornicate
Do not repent. It is too late.

Galway Kinnell

THE WOLVES

Last night knives flashed. LeChien cried
And chewed blood in his bed.
Vanni's whittling blade
Had found flesh easier than wood.

Vanni and I left camp on foot. In a glade
We came on a brown blossom
Great and shining on a thorned stem.
"That's the sensitive briar," I said.

"It shrinks at the touch," I added.
Soon we found buffalo. Picking
A bull grazing by itself, I began
The approach: while the shaggy head

Was turned I sprinted across the sod,
And when he swung around his gaze
I bellyflopped in the grass
And lay on my heartbeat and waited.

When he looked away again I made
Enough yardage before he wheeled
His head: I kneeled, levelled
My rifle, and we calmly waited.

It occurred to me as we waited
That in those last moments he was,
In fact, daydreaming about something else.
"He is too stupid to live," I said.

His legs shifted and the heart showed.
I fired. He looked, trotted off,
He simply looked and trotted off,
Stumbled, sat himself down, and became dead.

I looked for Vanni. Amid the cows he stood,
Only his arms moving as he fired,
Loaded, and fired, the dumb herd
Milling about him sniffing at their dead.

I called and he retreated.
We cut two choice tongues for ourselves
And left the surplus. All day wolves
Would splash blood from those great sides.

Again we saw the flower, brown-red
On a thorn-spiked stem. When Vanni
Extended his fingers, it was funny,
It shrank away as if it had just died.

They told us in camp that LeChien was dead.
None of us cared. Nobody much
Had liked him. His tobacco pouch,
I observed, was already missing from beside his bed.

From THE AVENUE BEARING THE
INITIAL OF CHRIST INTO THE NEW
WORLD

Was diese kleine Gasse doch für ein Reich an sich war . . .

1

pcheek pcheek pcheek pcheek pcheek
They cry. The motherbirds thieve the air
To appease them. A tug on the East River
Blasts the bass-note of its passage, lifted
From the infra-bass of the sea. A broom
Swishes over the sidewalk like feet through leaves.
Valerio's pushcart Ice Coal Kerosene

Moves clack
      clack
         clack
On a broken wheelrim. Ringing in its chains
The New Star Laundry horse comes down the street
Like a roofleak whucking in a pail.
At the redlight, where a horn blares,
The Golden Harvest Bakery brakes on its gears,
Squeaks, and seethes in place. A propane-
gassed bus makes its way with big, airy sighs.

Across the street a woman throws open
Her window,
She sets, terribly softly,
Two potted plants on the windowledge
         tic   tic
And bangs shut her window.

A man leaves a doorway tic toc tic toc tic toc tic hurrah
    toc splat on Avenuce C tic etc and turns the corner.

Banking the same corner
A pigeon coasts 5th Street in shadows,
Looks for altitude, surmounts the rims of buildings,
And turns white.

The babybirds pipe down. It is day.

6

In the pushcart market, on Sunday,
A crate of lemons discharges light like a battery.
Icicle-shaped carrots that through black soil
Wove away lie like flames in the sun.
Onions with their shirts ripped seek sunlight
On green skins. The sun beats
On beets dirty as boulders in cowfields,
On turnips pinched and gibbous
From budging rocks, on embery sweets,
Peanut-shaped Idahos, shore-pebble Long Islands and
    Maines,
On horseradishes still growing weeds on the flat ends,
Cabbages lying about like sea-green brains

The skulls have been shucked from,
On tomatoes, undented plum-tomatoes, alligator-skinned
Cucumbers, that float pickled
In the wooden tubs of green skim milk—

Sky-flowers, dirt-flowers, underdirt-flowers,
Those that climbed for the sun in their lives
And those that wormed away—equally uprooted,
Maimed, lopped, shucked, and misaimed.

In the market in Damascus a goat
Came to a stall where twelve goatheads
Were lined up for sale. It sniffed them
One by one. Finally thirteen goats started
Smiling in their faintly sardonic way.

A crone buys a pickle from a crone,
It is wrapped in the *Mirror*,
At home she will open the wrapping, stained,
And stare and stare and stare at it.
And the cucumbers, and the melons,
And the leeks, and the onions, and the garlic.

10

It was Gold's junkhouse, the one the clacking
Carts that little men pad after in harnesses
Picking up bedbugged mattresses, springs
The stubbornness has been loved out of,
Chairs felled by fat, lampshades lights have burned
    through,
Linoleum the geometry has been scuffed from,
Carriages a single woman's work has brought to wreck,
Would come to in the dusk and unload before,
That the whole neghborhood came out to see
Burning in the night, flames opening out like
Eyelashes from the windows, men firing the tears in,
Searchlights coming on like streams of water, smashing
On the brick, the water blooming up the wall
Like pale trees, reaching into the darkness beyond.

Nobody mourned, nobody stood around in pajamas
And a borrowed coat steaming his nose in coffee.

It was only Gold's junkhouse.
                        But this evening
The neighborhood comes out again, everything
That may abide the fire was made to go through the fire
And it was made clean: a few twisted springs,
Charred mattresses (crawling still, naturally),
Perambulator skeletons, bicycles tied in knots—
In a great black pile at the junkhouse door,
Smelling of burnt rubber and hair. Rustwater
Hangs in icicles over the windows and door,
Like frozen piss aimed at trespassers,
Combed by wind, set overnight. Carriages we were
        babies in,
Springs that used to resist love, that gave in
And were thrown out like whores—the black
Irreducible heap, mausoleum of what we were—
It is cold suddenly, we feel chilled,
Nobody knows for sure what is left of him.

11

The fishmarket closed, the fishes gone into flesh.
The smelts draped on each other, fat with roe,
The marble cod hacked into chunks on the counter,
Butterfishes mouths still open, still trying to eat,
Porgies with receding jaws hinged apart
In a grimace of dejection, as if like cows
They had died under the sledgehammer, perches
In grass-green armor, spotted squeteagues
In the melting ice meek-faced and croaking no more,
Except in the plip plop plip plip in the bucket,
Mud-eating mullets buried in crushed ice,
Tilefishes with scales like chickenfat,
Spanish mackerels, buttercups on the flanks,
Pot-bellied pikes, two-tone flounders
After the long contortion of pushing both eyes
To the brown side that they might look up,
Brown side down, like a mass laying-on of hands,
Or the oath-taking of an army.

The only things alive are the carp
That drift in the black tank in the rear,
Kept living for the usual reason, that they have not died.

And perhaps because the last meal was garbage and they
    might begin stinking
On dying, before the customer was halfway home.
They nudge each other, to be netted,
The sweet flesh to be lifted thrashing in the air,
To be slugged, and then to keep on living
While they are opened on the counter.

Fishes do not die exactly, it is more
That they go out of themselves, the visible part
Remains the same, there is little pallor,
Only the cataracted eyes which have not shut ever
Must look through the mist which crazed Homer.

These are the vegetables of the deep,
The Sheol-flower of darkness, swimmers
Of denser darknesses where the sun's rays bend for the
    last time
And in the sky there burns this shifty jellyfish
That degenerates and flashes and re-forms.

Motes in the eye land is the lid of,
They are plucked out of the green skim milk of the eye.

Fishes are nailed on the wood,
The big Jew stands like Christ, nailing them to the wood,
He scrapes the knife up the grain, the scales fly,
He unnails them, reverses them, nails them again,
Scrapes and the scales fly. He lops off the heads,
Shakes out the guts as if they did not belong in the first
    place,
And they are flesh for the first time in their lives.

Dear Frau————:

    Your husband, ————, died in the Camp Hospital on
————. May I express my sincere sympathy on your
bereavement. ———— was admitted to the Hospital on
———— with severe symptoms of exhaustion, complaining
of difficulties in breathing and pains in the chest. Despite
competent medication and devoted medical attention, it
proved impossible, unfortunately, to keep the patient alive.
The deceased voiced no final requests.

                Camp Commandant, ————

On 5th Street Bunko Certified Embalmer Catholic
Leans in his doorway drawing on a Natural Bloom Cigar.
He looks up the street. Even the Puerto Ricans are Jews
And the Chinese Laundry closes on Saturday.

14

Behind the Power Station on 14th, the held breath
Of light, as God is a held breath, withheld,
Spreads the East River, into which fishes leak:
The brown sink or dissolve,
The white float out in shoals and armadas,
Even the gulls pass them up, pale
Bloated socks of riverwater and rotted seed,
That swirl on the tide, punched back
To the Hell Gate narrows, and on the ebb
Steam seaward, seeding the sea.

On the Avenue, through air tinted crimson
By neon over the bars, the rain is falling.
You stood once on Houston, among panhandlers and winos
Who weave the eastern ranges, learning to be free,
To not care, to be knocked flat and to get up clear-headed
Spitting the curses out. "Now be nice,"
The proprietor threatens; "Be nice," he cajoles.
"Fuck you," the bum shouts as he is hoisted again,
"God fuck your mother." (In the empty doorway,
Hunched on the empty crate, the crone gives no sign.)

That night a wildcat cab whined crosstown on 7th.
You knew even the traffic lights were made by God,
The red splashes growing dimmer the farther away
You looked, and away up at 14th, a few green stars;
And without sequence, and nearly all at once,
The red lights blinked into green,
And just before there was one complete Avenue of green,
The little green stars in the distance blinked.

It is night, and raining. You look down
Towards Houston in the rain, the living streets,
Where instants of transcendence
Drift in oceans of loathing and fear, like lanternfishes,

Or phosphorus flashings in the sea, or the feverish light
Skin is said to give off when the swimmer drowns at night.

From the blind gut Pitt to the East River of Fishes
The Avenue cobbles a swath through the discolored air,
A roadway of refuse from the teeming shores and ghettos
And the Caribbean Paradise, into the new ghetto and new
        paradise,
This God-forsaken Avenue bearing the initial of Christ
Through the haste and carelessness of the ages,
The sea standing in heaps, which keeps on collapsing,
Where the drowned suffer a C-change,
And remain the common poor.

Since Providence, for the realization of some unknown
        purpose, has
seen fit to leave this dangerous people on the face of the
        earth, and did not destroy it . . .

Listen! the swish of the blood,
The sirens down the bloodpaths of the night,
Bone tapping on the bone, nerve-nets
Singing under the breath of sleep—
We scattered over the lonely seaways,
Over the lonely deserts did we run,
In dark lanes and alleys we did hide ourselves . . .

The heart beats without windows in its night,
The lungs put out the light of the world as they
Heave and collapse, the brain turns and rattles
In its own black axlegrease—

                    In the nighttime
Of the blood, they are laughing and saying,
Our little lane, what a kingdom it was!

                    oi weih, oi weih

Carolyn Kizer

THE INTRUDER

My mother—preferring the strange to the tame:
Dove-note, bone marrow, deer dung,
Frog's belly distended with finny young,
Leaf-mould wilderness, hare-bell, toadstool,
Odd, small snakes roving through the leaves,
Metallic beetles rambling over stones: all
Wild and natural!—flashed out her instinctive love,
    and quick, she
Picked up the fluttering, bleeding bat the cat laid at her
    feet,
And held the little horror to the mirror, where
He gazed on himself, and shrieked like an old screen door
    far off.

Depended from her pinched thumb, each wing
Came clattering down like a small black shutter.
Still tranquil, she began, "It's rather sweet . . ."
The soft mouse body, the hard feral glint
In the caught eyes. Then we saw,
And recoiled: lice, pallid, yellow,
Nested within the wing-pits, cosily sucked and snoozed.
The thing dropped from her hands, and with its thud,
Swiftly, the cat, with a clean careful mouth
Closed on the soiled webs, growling, took them out to the
    back stoop.

But still, dark blood, a sticky puddle on the floor
Remained, of all my mother's tender, wounding passion
For a whole wild, lost, betrayed and secret life
Among its dens and burrows, its clean stones,
Whose denizens can turn upon the world
With spitting tongue, an odor, talon, claw,

To sting or soil benevolence, alien
As our clumsy traps, our random scatter of shot.
She swept to the kitchen. Turning on the tap,
She washed and washed the pity from her hands.

THE UNGRATEFUL GARDEN

Midas watched the golden crust
That formed over his streaming sores,
Hugged his agues, loved his lust,
But damned to hell the out-of-doors

Where blazing motes of sun impaled
The serried roses, metal-bright.
"Those famous flowers," Midas wailed,
"Have scorched my retina with light."

This gift, he'd thought, would gild his joys,
Silt up the waters of his grief;
His lawns a wilderness of noise,
The heavy clang of leaf on leaf.

Within, the golden cup is good
To heft, to sip the yellow mead.
Outside, in summer's rage, the rude
Gold thorn has made his fingers bleed.

"I strolled my halls in golden shift,
As ruddy as a lion's meat.
Then I rushed out to share my gift,
And golden stubble cut my feet."

Dazzled with wounds, he limped away
To climb into his golden bed.
Roses, roses can betray.
"Nature is evil," Midas said.

THE GREAT BLUE HERON

As I wandered on the beach
I saw the heron standing
Sunk in the tattered wings
He wore as a hunchback's coat.
Shadow without a shadow,
Hung on invisible wires
From the top of a canvas day,
What scissors cut him out?
Superimposed on a poster
Of summer by the strand
Of a long-decayed resort,
Poised in the dusty light
Some fifteen summers ago;
I wondered, an empty child,
"Heron, whose ghost are you?"

I stood on the beach alone,
In the sudden chill of the burned.
My thought raced up the path.
Pursuing it, I ran
To my mother in the house
And led her to the scene.
The spectral bird was gone.
But her quick eye saw him drifting
Over the highest pines
On vast, unmoving wings.
Could they be those ashen things,
So grounded, unwieldy, ragged,
A pair of broken arms
That were not made for flight?
In the middle of my loss
I realized she knew:
My mother knew what he was.

O great blue heron, now
That the summer house has burned
So many rockets ago,

So many smokes and fires
And beach-lights and water-glow
Reflecting pin-wheel and flare:
The old logs hauled away,
The pines and driftwood cleared
From that bare strip of shore
Where dozens of children play;
Now there is only you
Heavy upon my eye.
Why have you followed me here,
Heavy and far away?
You have stood there patiently
For fifteen summers and snows,
Denser than my repose,
Bleaker than any dream,
Waiting upon the day
When, like grey smoke, a vapor
Floating into the sky,
A handful of paper ashes,
My mother would drift away.

Melvin Walker La Follette

LOVE FOR A HARE

Nameless, he crept from the hutch of creation
And rode my childhood skys in clouds
Fluffy and white, or thunderheaded dark
He was the softness I wanted to touch
And could not. In my sleepless bed
I cried for him quietly nightly,
And during my days I talked to him,
Although he did not answer me.

My beautiful cat, the tiger that slept
In my heart, caught rabbits and I loved her
For it. Her quick white teeth made blood

At the throats of young bunnies. Sometimes,
She caught the old ones, too, but they
Were always dead on arrival at my play hospital.
Their ears hung limp from broken necks
And their glazed eyes stared at her live green ones.

Never in all my dreams, nor in all the nights
I slept at the side of my beautiful gray cat
Did I ever forget my love for the hare
That was part of the sky; sometimes I stroked
Her fur and thought of him; sometimes
My mother or my teacher chided me,
Catching me talking to him, and still
He did not answer me. After all,
A hare, except when dying, is dumb.

Once, at Eastertide, my uncle gave
Me a big white rabbit with pink eyes;
He squatted in the cage all day
And poked at the lettuce but would not eat;
That night I crept from bed and strangled him
Because he was stupid and tame and fat
And did not squeal, even when being killed.
They never found out what I had done,
But for a long time I was afraid.

Like tonight, I was afraid again—
The midnight mass of a new Easter—
And the priest saw me flinch, taking communion;
I took the wine and choked blood,
In my sticky throat the bread bounded,
Bounded and stopped in the shape of a hare
Paralyzed by my car's eyes; back
And forth, forth and back, his head
Reeled on a moveless body, and then
He answered me: I heard him squeal
Before he died beneath my wheel.

SPRING LANDSCAPE

Beautiful, through clear skies newly blue
The sleek, young jets leave fleecy trails
Shaming the antique geese who fly
Languid and stupid, in crude Vs northward.

Let us laugh at the clumsy spring lamb;
Funny thing, too bad he has no eyes,
Only black sockets pocking his white face;
His mother fed on radiant clover.

How happy, to sit with my newly taken wife
And dream of monstrous children, now unborn,
And watch this thing, growing from bombarded roots,
A tulip like a red badge of courage.

I KNEW A BOY
WITH HAIR LIKE GOLD

I knew a boy with hair like gold,
Sing, thrasher, sing, in the apple tree,
I knew a lad with a glad gold heart,
But he is lost to me.

He lived in the smile of a happy wood
And with the sweet songs he would sing
He charmed from the bear his grizzley growl
And honeyed the bee from his sting.

I knew a lad who flowers loved,
And at the springing of each year
He kissed the bloodroot for his blood,
Narcissus for his tear.

I knew a boy with hair like gold,
Sing, thrasher, sing, in the apple tree,

I knew a lad with a glad gold heart,
But he is lost to me.

One moony night, I missed him so
I asked of the owl on the cypress limb
But never in time would the tree breeze tell
What had become of him.

I followed the egret across the swamp,
And a thousand leopard frogs sang out,
I flogged me through briars to the flagged lake shore
When I thought I heard him shout.

I knew a boy with hair like gold,
Sing, thrasher, sing, in the apple tree,
I loved a lad with a glad gold heart,
But he is lost to me.

I saw him stand at the glacier's rim,
OH! he was all gold and ivory,
And dive like a tower to the lake's cold core—
You cannot comfort me.

Although, I remember the prismed trout
Had never so much grace as he;
Why must I weep for this long lost boy
Who sure is lost to me?

I loved a boy with hair like gold,
Laugh, lake loon, laugh, you cannot see
The blood hot tears in my cockled heart
For he is lost to me.

For he is lost to me, is lost
Like marigolds beneath the snow
And the tears of hell cannot heat my heart
When the white winds blow.

Denise Levertov

OBSESSIONS

Maybe it is true we have to return
to the black air of ashcan city
because it is there the most life was burned,

as ghosts or criminals return?
But no, the city has no monopoly
of intense life. The dust burned

golden or violet in the wide land
to which we ran away, images
of passion sprang out of the land

as whirlwinds or red flowers, your hands
opened in anguish or clenched in violence
under that sun, and clasped my hands

in that place to which we will not return
where so much happened that no one else noticed,
where the city's ashes that we brought with us
flew into the intense sky still burning.

SEEMS LIKE WE MUST
BE SOMEWHERE ELSE

Sweet procession, rose-blue,
and all them bells.

Bandstand red, the eyes
at treetop level seeing it. "Are we
what we think we are or are we
What befalls us?"

The people from an open window
the eyes
seeing it!   Daytime!   Or twilight!

Sweet procession, rose-blue.
If we're here let's be here now.

And the train whistle? who
invented that? Lonesome man, wanted the trains
to speak for him.

A SOLITUDE

A blind man. I can stare at him
ashamed, shameless. Or does he know it?
No, he is in a great solitude.

O, strange joy,
to gaze my fill at a stranger's face.
No, my thirst is greater than before.

In his world he is speaking
almost aloud. His lips move.
Anxiety plays about them. And now joy

of some sort trembles into a smile.
A breeze I can't feel
crosses that face as if it crossed water.

The train moves uptown, pulls in and
pulls out of the local stops. Within its loud
jarring movement a quiet,

the quiet of people not speaking,
some of them eyeing the blind man,
only a moment though, not thirsty like me,

and within that quiet his
different quiet, not quiet at all, a tumult
of images, but what are his images,

he is blind? He doesn't care
that he looks strange, showing
his thoughts on his face like designs of light

flickering on water, for he doesn't know
what *look* is.
I see he has never seen.

And now he rises, he stands at the door ready,
knowing his station is next. Was he counting?
No, that was not his need.

When he gets out I get out.
"Can I help you towards the exit?"
"Oh, alright." An indifference.

But instantly, even as he speaks,
even as I hear indifference, his hand
goes out, waiting for me to take it,

and now we hold hands like children.
His hand is warm and not sweaty,
the grip firm, it feels good.

And when we have passed through the turnstile,
he going first, his hand at once
waits for mine again.

"Here are the steps. And here we turn
to the right. More stairs now." We go
up into sunlight. He feels that,

the soft air. "A nice day,
isn't it?" says the blind man. Solitude
walks with me, walks

beside me, he is not with me, he continues
his thoughts alone. But his hand and mine
know one another,

it's as if my hand were gone forth
on its own journey. I see him
across the street, the blind man,

and now he says he can find his way. He knows
where he is going, it is nowhere, it is filled
with presences. He says, *I am.*

THE VIGIL

When the mice awaken
and come out to their work of searching
for life, crumbs of life,
I sit quiet in my back room
trying to quiet my mind of its chattering,
rumors and events, and find
life, crumbs of life, to nourish it
until in stillness, replenished,
the animal god within the
clutted shrine   speaks.   Alas!
poor mice—I have left
nothing for them, no bread,
no fat, not an unwashed plate.
Go through the walls to other kitchens;
let it be silent here.
I'll sit in vigil
awaiting the Cat
who with human tongue
speaks inhuman oracles
or delicately, with its claws, opens
Chinese boxes, each containing
the World and its shadow.

THE CHARGE

Returning
        to all the unsaid
   all the lost living untranslated
   in any sense,
   and the dead
   unrecognized, celebrated
   only in dreams that die by morning

is a mourning or ghostwalking only.
    You must make, said music

  in its voices of metal and wood
  in its dancing diagrams, moving
  apart and together, along
     and over and under a line
  and speaking in one voice,

            make
  my image.   Let be
  what is gone.

TO THE SNAKE

Green Snake, when I hung you round my neck
and stroked your cold, pulsing throat
    as you hissed to me, glinting
arrowy gold scales, and I felt
    the weight of you on my shoulders,
and the whispering silver of your dryness
    sounded close at my ears—

Green Snake—I swore to my companions that certainly
    you were harmless! But truly
I had no certainty, and no hope, only desiring
    to hold you, for that joy,
               which left
a long wake of pleasure, as the leaves moved
and you faded into the pattern
of grass and shadows, and I returned
smiling and haunted, to a dark morning.

THE OFFENDER

  The eye luminous
  in its box of ebony
saw the point of departure, a room

pleasant, bare, sunlit,
and space beyond it, time
extending to mountains, ending,
beginning new space beyond.

The eye, luminous, grayblue,
        a moonstone,
    brimmed over with mercury tears
that rolled and were lost in sunny dust.
    The world in the lustre of a
    black pupil moved its clouds
        and their shadows. Time
had gathered itself and gone. The eye
    luminous, prince of solitude.

THE PRESENCE

To the house on the grassy hill
where rams rub their horns against the porch

and your bare feet on the floors of silence
speak in rhymed stanzas to the furniture,

solemn chests of drawers and heavy chairs
blinking in the sun you have let in!

Before I enter the rooms of your solitude
in my living form, trailing my shadow,

I shall have come unseen. Upstairs and down with you
and out across road and rocks to the river

to drink the cold spray. You will believe
a bird flew by the window, a wandering bee

buzzed in the hallway, a wind
rippled the bronze grasses. Or will you

know who it is?

THE RAINWALKERS

An old man whose black face
shines golden-brown as wet pebbles
under the streetlamp, is walking
two mongrel dogs of dis-
proportionate size, in the rain,
in the relaxed early-evening avenue.

The small sleek one wants to stop,
docile to the imploring soul of the trashbasket,
but the young tall curly one
wants to walk on; the glistening sidewalk
entices him to arcane happenings.

Increasing rain. The old bareheaded man
smiles and grumbles to himself.
The lights change: the avenue's
endless nave echoes notes of liturgical red. He drifts

between his dogs' desires.
The three of them are enveloped—
turning now to go crosstown—in their
sense of each other, of pleasure,
of weather, of corners,
of leisurely tensions between them
and private silence.

Philip Levine

NIGHT THOUGHTS OVER A SICK CHILD

Numb, stiff, broken by no sleep,
I keep night watch. Looking for
signs to quiet fear, I creep

closer to his bed and hear
his breath come and go, holding
my own as if my own were
all I paid. Nothing I bring,
say, or do has meaning here.

Outside, ice crusts on river
and pond; wild hare come to my
door, pacified by torture.
No less ignorant than they
of what grips and why, I am
moved to prayer, the quaint gestures
which ennoble beyond shame
only the mute listener.

No one hears. A dry wind shifts
dry snow, indifferently;
the roof, rotting beneath drifts,
sighs and holds. Terrified by
sleep, the child strives toward
consciousness and the known pain.
If it were mine by one word
I would not save any man,

Myself or the universe
at such cost: reality.
Heir to an ancestral curse
Though fallen from Judah's tree,
I take up into my arms my hopes,
my son, for what it's worth give
bodily warmth. When he escapes
his heritage, then what have

I left but false remembrance
and the name. Against that day
there is no armor or stance,
only the frail dignity
of surrender, which is all
that can separate me now
or then from the dumb beast's fall,
unseen in the frozen snow.

THE DRUNKARD

FROM ST. AMBROSE

He fears the tiger standing in his way.
The tiger takes its time, it smiles and growls.
Like moons, the two blank eyes tug at his bowels.
"God help me now," is all that he can say.

"God help me now, how close I've come to God.
To love and to be loved, I've drunk for love.
Send me the faith of Paul, or send a dove."
The tiger hears and stiffens like a rod.

At last the tiger leaps, and when it hits
A putrid surf breaks in the drunkard's soul.
The tiger, done, returns to its patrol.
The world takes up its trades; the man his wits,
And, bottom up, he mumbles from the deep,
"Life was a dream, Oh, may this death be sleep."

THE NEGATIVES

On March 1, 1958, four deserters from the French Army of North Africa, August Rein, Henri Bruette, Jack Dauville, and Thomas Delain, robbed a government pay station at Orléansville. Because of the subsequent confession of Dauville the other three were captured or shot. Dauville was given his freedom and returned to the land of his birth, the U.S.A.

AUGUST REIN: FROM A
LAST CAMP NEAR ST. REMY

I dig in the soft earth all
afternoon, spacing the holes
a foot or so from the wall.
Tonight we eat potatoes,
tomorrow rice and carrots.
The earth here is like the earth

nowhere, ancient with wood rot.
How can anything come forth,

I wonder; and the days are
all alike, if there is more
than one day. If there is more
of this I will not endure.
I have grown so used to being
watched I can no longer sleep
without my watcher. The thing
I fought against, the dark cape

crimsoned with terror that
I so hated comforts me now.
Thomas is dead; insanity,
prison, cowardice, or slow
inner capitulation
has found us all, and all men
turn from us, knowing our pain
is not theirs or caused by them.

HENRI BRUETTE: FROM A HOSPITAL IN ALGIERS

Dear Suzanne: this letter will
not reach you because I can't
write it; I have no pencil,
no paper, only the blunt
end of my anger. My dear,
if I had words how could I
report the imperfect failure
for which I began to die?

I might begin by saying
that it was for clarity,
though I did not find it in
terror: dubiously
I entered each act, unsure
of who I was and what I
did, touching my face for fear
I was another: inside

my head I played back pictures
of my childhood, of my wife
even, for it was in her
I found myself beaten, safe,
and furthest from the present.
It is her face I see now
though all I say is meant
for you, her face in the slow

agony of sexual
release. I cannot see you.
The dark wall ribbed with spittle
on which I play my childhood
brings me to this bed, mastered
by what I was, betrayed by
those I trusted. The one word
my mouth must open to is *why*.

JACK DAUVILLE: FROM A HOTEL IN TAMPA, FLORIDA

From Orléansville we drove
south until we reached the hills,
        then east until
the road stopped. I was nervous
and couldn't eat. Thomas took
over, told us when to think
        and when to shit.
We turned north and reached Blida
by first dawn and the City

by morning, having dumped our
weapons beside an empty
        road. We were free.
We parted, and to this hour
I haven't seen them, except
in photographs: the black hair
        and torn features
of Thomas Delain captured
a moment before his death

on the pages of the world,
smeared in the act. I tortured
     myself with their
betrayal: alone I hurled
them into freedom, inner
freedom which I can't find
     nor ever will
until they are dead. In my mind
Delain stands against the wall

precise in detail, steadied
for the betrayal. "La France
     C'Est Moi," he cried,
but the irony was lost. Since
I returned to the U.S.
nothing goes well. I stay up
     too late, don't sleep,
and am losing weight. Thomas,
I say, is dead, but what use

telling myself what I won't
believe. The hotel quiets
     early at night,
the aged brace themselves for
another sleep, and offshore
the sea quickens its pace. I
     am suddenly
old, caught in a strange country
for which no man would die.

THOMAS DELAIN: FROM A JOURNAL
FOUND ON HIS PERSON

At night wakened by the freight
trains boring through the suburbs
of Lyon, I watched first light
corrode the darkness, disturb
what little wildlife was left
in the alleys: birds moved from
branch to branch, and the dogs leapt
at the garbage. Winter numbed

even the hearts of the young
who had only their hearts. We
heard the war coming; the long
wait was over, and we moved
along the crowded roads south
not looking for what lost loves
fell by the roadsides. To flee
at all cost, that was my youth.

Here in the African night
wakened by what I do not
know and shivering in the heat,
I listen as the men fight
with sleep. Loosed from their weapons
they cry out, frightened and young,
who have never been children.
Once merely to be strong,
to live, was moral. Within
these uniforms we accept
the evil we were chosen
to deliver, and no act
human or benign can free
us from ourselves. Wait, sleep, blind
soldiers of a blind will, and
listen for that old command
dreaming of authority.

John Logan

LINES TO HIS SON ON REACHING ADOLESCENCE

I've always thought Polonius a dry
And senile fop, fool to those he didn't love
Though he had given life to them as father—
To his beautiful young boy and beautiful
Young daughter; and loathed Augustine's

Lecherous old man who noticed that his son
Naked at his bath, was growing up
And told his wife a dirty joke. But
I have given my own life to you my son
Remembering my fear, my joy and unbelief
(And my disgust) when I saw you monkey
Blue and blooded, shrouded with the light down
Of the new born, the cord of flesh
That held you to my wife cut free from her
And from my own remote body,
And I could fill you up with epithets
Like Ophelia's father, full of warnings,
For I have learned what we must avoid
And what must choose and how to be of use.
My father never taught me anything
I needed for myself. It's no excuse,
For what he might have said I think
I would refuse, and besides (is it despair
I reach?) I feel we learn too late to teach.
And like Augustine's dad I have watched you bathe
Have seen as my own hair begins to fall
The fair gold beard upon your genital
That soon will flow with seed
And swell with love and pain (I almost add
Again). I cannot say to you whether
In a voice steady or unsteady, ah Christ
Please wait your father isn't ready.
You cannot wait, as he could not.
But for both our sakes I ask you, wrestle
Manfully against the ancient curse of snakes,
The bitter mystery of love, and learn to bear
The burden of the tenderness
That is hid in us. Oh you cannot
Spare yourself the sadness of Hippolytus
Whom the thought of Phaedra
Turned from his beloved horse and bow,
My son, the arrow of my quiver,
The apple of my eye, but you can save your father
The awful agony of Laocoön
Who could not stop the ruin of his son.
And as I can I will help you with my love.
Last I warn you, as Polonius,

Yet not as him, from now on I will not plead
As I have always done, for sons
Against their fathers who have wronged them.
I plead instead for us
Against the sons we hoped we would not hurt.

CONCERT SCENE

So he sits down. His host will play for him
And his hostess will come again, with wine.
He has a chance to see the room, to find
The source, defend himself against something
Beautiful, which hit him when he came in
And left him weak. On the baroque fireplace,
Whose stone has the turn of a living arm,
Some lacquer red poppies now are opened
In a copper bowl. Over the mantel
A warm oil against the white paneled wall.
An open coach; a girl and bearded man,
Both young, canter through a summer landscape
Soft with color, their faces full and flushed.
The Brahms on the piano is about
This. To the left a black coffee table
Topped with strips of crossed cane beside a green
Cloth couch. On this top a wicker horn leaks
Out white grapes by a tin of purple-wrapped
Candied nuts, and a thin white porcelain
Cream pitcher with a few, loosely figured
Very bright blue anemones and greens;
At the right of the fireplace a great teak
Desk has a red Chinese plume or feather
In a silver pitcher, then a clear, wine-
glass shaped, tall bowl—full of golden apples.
Still the music is Brahms: golds, blues, and wines
Of the stained glass panels in the far door,
A light behind. The hostess brings a tray
Of sherry and a jar of caviar
In ice, the thousand eggs writhing with light
Beside the lucent lemon slice. She sits
Upon the green or gold cloth couch. She holds

The thin stemmed glass, and now he looks at her,
Shook with the colors or the music or
The wine. Her hair is blue black and drops straight
From the part—directly in the middle
Of her skull—its long, moonwet waterfall.
Her smile is warm for him, lips large without
Paint, gentle eyes hollowed in the high bones
Of her white face. Now he sees above her
A graceful, black iron candelabra
On the white wall, green of its candles spin-
ning in the whorls of shiny surfaced leaves
At the top of a thin plant in the corner,
And in the jagged-necked, blown-glass bottle,
As big as a child, standing on the floor
By the piano. His hostess rises
To sing. (She doesn't know he's trembling.) Her
Voice is too strong. Suddenly the color
Is intense. And he finds no defense.

THE PICNIC

It is the picnic with Ruth in the spring.
Ruth was third on my list of seven girls
But the first two were gone (Betty) or else
Had someone (Ellen has accepted Doug).
Indian Gully the last day of school;
Girls make the lunches for the boys too.
I wrote a note to Ruth in algebra class
Day before the test. She smiled, and nodded.
We left the cars and walked through the young corn
The shoots green as paint and the leaves like tongues
Trembling. Beyond the fence where we stood
Some wild strawberry flowered by an elm tree
And Jack-in-the-pulpit was olive ripe.
A blackbird fled as I crossed, and showed
A spot of gold or red under its quick wing.
I held the wire for Ruth and watched the whip
Of her long, striped skirt as she followed.
Three freckles blossomed on her thin, white back
Underneath the loop where the blouse buttoned.

We went for our lunch away from the rest,
Stretched in the new grass, our heads close
Over unknown things wrapped up in wax papers.
Ruth tried for the same, I forget what it was,
And our hands were together. She laughed,
And a breeze caught the edge of her little
Collar and the edge of her brown, loose hair
That touched my cheek. I turned my face in-
to the gentle fall. I saw how sweet it smelled.
She didn't move her head or take her hand.
I felt a soft caving in my stomach
As at the top of the highest slide
When I had been a child, but was not afraid,
And did not know why my eyes moved with wet
As I brushed her cheek with my lips and brushed
Her lips with my own lips. She said to me
Jack, Jack, different than I had ever heard,
Because she wasn't calling me, I think,
Or telling me. She used my name to
Talk in another way I wanted to know.
She laughed again and then she took her hand;
I gave her what we both had touched—can't
Remember what it was, and we ate the lunch.
Afterward we walked in the small, cool creek
Our shoes off, her skirt hitched, and she smiling,
My pants rolled, and then we climbed up the high
Side of Indian Gully and looked
Where we had been our hands together again.
It was then some bright thing came in my eyes,
Starting at the back of them and flowing
Suddenly through my head and down my arms
And stomach and my bare legs that seemed not
To stop in feet, not to feel the red earth
Of the gully, as though we hung in a
Touch of birds. There was a word in my throat
With the feeling and I knew the first time
What it meant and I said, it's beautiful.
Yes, she said, and I felt the sound and word
In my hand join the sound and word in hers
As in one name said, or in one cupped hand.
We put back on our shoes and socks and we
Sat in the grass awhile, crosslegged, under

A blowing tree, not saying anything.
And Ruth played with shells she found in the creek,
As I watched. Her small wrist which was so sweet
To me turned by her breast and the shells dropped
Green, white, blue, easily into her lap,
Passing light through themselves. She gave the pale
Shells to me, and got up and touched her hips
With her light hands, and we walked down slowly
To play the school games with the others.

James Merrill

LABORATORY POEM

Charles used to watch Naomi, taking heart
And a steel saw, open up turtles, live.
While she swore they felt nothing, he would gag
At blood, at the blind twitching, even after
The murky dawn of entrails cleared, revealing
Contours he knew, egg-yellows like lamps paling.

Well then. She carried off the beating heart
To the kymograph and rigged it there, a rag
In fitful wind, now made to strain, now stopped
By her solutions tonic or malign
Alternately in which it would be steeped.
What the heart bore, she noted on a chart,

For work did not stop only with the heart.
He thought of certain human hearts, their climb
Through violence into exquisite disciplines
Of which, as it now appeared, they all expired.
Soon she would fetch another and start over,
Easy in the presence of her lover.

MIRROR

I grow old under an intensity
Of questioning looks. *Nonsense,*
I try to say, *I cannot teach you children
How to live.—If not you, who will?*
Cries one of them aloud, grasping my gilded
Frame till the world sways. *If not you, who will?*
Between their visits the table, its arrangement
Of Bible, fern and Paisley, all past change,
Does very nicely. If ever I feel curious
As to what others endure,
Across the parlor *you* provide examples,
Wide open, sunny, of everything I am
Not. You embrace a whole world without once caring
To set it in order. That takes thought. Out there
Something is being picked. The red-and-white bandannas
Go to my heart. A fine young man
Rides by on horseback. Now the door shuts. Hester
Confides in me her first unhappiness.
This much, you see, would never have been fitted
Together, but for me. Why then is it
They more and more neglect me? Late one sleepless
Midsummer night I strained to keep
Five tapers from your breathing. *No,* the widowed
Cousin said, *let them go out.* I did.
The room brimmed with gray sound, all the instreaming
Muslin of your dream . . .
Years later now, two of the grown grandchildren
Sit with novels face-down on the sill,
Content to muse upon your tall transparence,
Your clouds, brown fields, persimmon far
And cypress near. One speaks. *How superficial
Appearances are!* Since then, as if a fish
Had broken the perfect silver of my reflectiveness,
I have lapses. I suspect
Looks from behind, where nothing is, cool gazes
Through the blind flaws of my mind. As days,
As decades lengthen, this vision

Spreads and blackens. I do not know whose it is,
But I think it watches for my last silver
To blister, flake, float leaf by life, each milling-
Downward dumb conceit, to a standstill
From which not even you strike any brilliant
Chord in me, and to a faceless will,
Echo of mine, I am amenable.

SOME NEGATIVES: X. AT THE CHATEAU

Where skies are thunderous, by a cypress walk
Copied in snow, I have you: or
Sitting beside the water-jet that here
Is jet. You could be an Ethiop with hair
Powdered white as chalk.

Instead of simple diffidence on her tour
Of monuments. Yet these first
Images of images I shall keep.
Once they have testified, immersed
In a mild Lethe, to what you really are,

These insights of the mind in sleep,
May they recall you as you never were!—
Your charming face not lit
But charred, as by dark beams instructing it
In all to which you were the latest heir,

In lake, lawn, urn, and maze
Plotted by your dead rivals with no care
That I should love you next, find milky ways
To leave the grotto where I grieved for them.
Slowly you might have learned to bear

Estates no deed can alter. Only whim
Holds sway like gossamer
Till never breath dispels the water-wraith.
Here where no image sinks to truth
And the black sun kindles planets in noon air

The lover leads a form eclipsed, opaque,
Past a smoked-glass parterre
Towards the first ghostliness he guessed in her.
He bends her to a dazzling lake . . .
If the lens winks, it winds them who knows where.

A TIMEPIECE

Of a pendulum's mildness, with her feet up
My sister lay expecting her third child.
Over the hammock's crescent spilled
Her flushed face, grazing clover and buttercup.

Her legs were troubling her, a vein had burst.
Even so, among partial fullnesses she lay
Of pecked damson, of daughters at play
Who in the shadow of the house rehearsed

Her gait, her gesture, unnatural to them,
But they would master it soon enough, grown tall
Trusting that out of themselves came all
That full grace, while she out of whom these came

Shall have thrust fullness from her, like a death.
Already, seeing the little girls listless
She righted herself in a new awkwardness.
It was not *her* life she was heavy with.

Let us each have some milk, my sister smiled
Meaning to muffle with the taste
Of unbuilt bone a striking in her breast,
For soon by what it tells the clock is stilled.

HOTEL DE L'UNIVERS ET PORTUGAL

The strange bed, whose recurrent dream we are,
Basin, and shutters guarding with their latch
The hour of arrivals, the reputed untouched Square.

Bleakly with ever fewer belongings we watch
And have never, it each time seems, so coldly before

Steeped the infant membrane of our clinging
In a strange city's clear grave acids;
Or thought how like a pledge the iron key-ring
Slid overboard, one weighty calm at Rhodes,
Down to the vats of its eventual rusting.

And letters moulting out of memory, lost
Seasons of the breast of a snowbird . . .
One morning on the pillow shall at last
Lie strands of age, and many a crease converge
Where the ambitious dreaming head has tossed

The world away and turned, and taken dwelling
Withing the pillow's dense white dark, has heard
The lover's speech from cool walls peeling
To the white bed, whose dream they were.
Bare room, forever feeling and annulling,

Bare room, bleak problem set for space,
Fold us ever and over in less identity
Than six walls hold, the oval mirror face
Showing us vacantly how to become only
Bare room, mere air, no hour and no place,

Lodging of chance, and bleak as all beginning.
We had begun perhaps to lack a starlit Square.
But now our very poverties are dissolving,
Are swallowed up, strong powders to ensure
Sleep, by a strange bed in the dark of dreaming.

A VIEW OF THE BURNING

Righteous or not, here comes an angry man
Done up in crimson, his face blackened
If only by the smoke of a self-purifying flame.
Now he is thrusting his hand into the flame
To sear away not, as he said, a moment's folly

So much as his hand, the useful part of it.
I must confess this fails, after a bit,
To produce the intended effect on us.
We had loved each other freely, humanly
With our own angers and our own forgiveness
—Who now, made light of by his seriousness,
Gases on which flame feeds, are wafted up
With lyre and dart, public, hilarious,
Two cupids cuddling in a cupola.
Useless to say he is acting for our sakes.
One does not care for those who care for one
More than one cares for oneself. Divine or not,
At the end he calls upon justice. But, my dear,
Little shall startle from the embers, merely
A grinning head incensed, a succulence
On which to feast, grinning ourselves, I fear.

W. S. Merwin

BLIND GIRL

Silent, with her eyes
Climbing above her like a pair of hands drowning,
Up the tower stairs she runs headlong, turning
In a spiral of voices that grow no fainter, though
At each turn, through the tiny window,
The blood-shrieking starling, flaking into the trees,
Sound farther below.

Still, as she runs
Turn above turn round the hollow flights, so
Ringing higher, the towering voices follow,
Out of each room renewed as she passes,
To echo, hopeless: their shrieked entreaties
Singing their love, and their gross resonance
Her beauty's praises,

With no name too tender,
High, or childish to din their desperate
Invocations; confessing; swearing to dedicate
Their split hearts on salvers if only she
Will pause. Each raw plea raucous less to delay,
At last, than to claim her: "Though you turn for no other,
    Dear soul, this is me, me!"

But, buffetted and stunned
By their spun cries as in clambering water,
Now if she tried she could not remember
Which door among those, nor what care, crime,
Possession, name, she had bolted from,
Nor how, the way opening to her blind hand,
    She had slipped past them,

Nor how many centuries
Ago. Only tells herself over and over
That their winding calls cannot forever
Build, but at their shrill peak stairs, tower, all
Into the loose air sprung suddenly, will fall,
Breathless, to nothing, and instantly her repose
    Be silent and final.

GRANDMOTHER AND GRANDSON

As I hear it, now when there is company
Always the spindly granddam, stuck standing
In her corner like a lady clock long
Silent, out of some hole in the talk
Is apt to clack cup, clatter teeth, and with
Saucer gesturing to no one special,
Shake out her paper voice concerning
That pimply boy her last grandson: "Now who,
Who does he remind you of?"

                    (Who stuffs there
With cake his puffed face complected half
Of yellow crumbs, his tongue loving over
His damp hands to lick the sticky

From bitten fingers; chinless; all boneless but
His neck and nose; and who now rolls his knowing
Eyes to their attention.)

                In vain, in vain,
One after the other, their lusterless
Suggestions of faint likenesses; she
Nods at none, her gaze absent and more
Absent, as though watching for someone through
A frosted window, until they are aware
She has forgotten her own question.

When he is alone, though, with only her
And her hazy eyes in the whole house
To mind him, his way is to take himself
Just out of her small sight and there stay
Till she starts calling; let her call till she
Sounds in pain; and as though in pain, at last,
His answers, each farther, leading her
Down passages, up stairs, with her worry
Hard to swallow as a scarf-end, her pace
A spun child's in a blindfold, to the piled
Dust-coop, trunk- and junk-room at the top
Of all the stairs, where he hides till she sways
Clutching her breath in the very room, then
Behind her slips out, locking the door. His
Laughter down stair after stair she hears
Being forgotten. In the unwashed light,
Lost, she turns among the sheeted mounds
Fingering hems and murmuring, "Where, where
Does it remind me of?" Till someone comes.

PLEA FOR A CAPTIVE

Woman with the caught fox
By the scruff, you can drop your hopes:
It will not tame though you prove kind,
Though you entice it with fat ducks
Patiently to your fingertips
And in dulcet love enclose it

Do not suppose it will turn friend,
Dog your heels, sleep at your feet,
Be happy in the house,
                                        No,

It will only trot to and fro,
To and fro, with vacant eye,
Neither will its pelt improve
Nor its disposition, twisting
The raw song of its debasement
Through the long nights, and in your love,
In your delicate meats tasting
Nothing but its own decay
(As at first hand I have learned)
                                        Oh

Kill it at once or let it go.

THE BONES

It takes a long time to hear what the sands
Seem to be saying, with the wind nudging them,
And then you cannot put it in words nor tell
Why these things should have a voice. All kinds
Of objects come in over the tide-wastes
In the course of a year, with a throaty
Rattle: weeds, driftwood, the bodies of birds
And of fish, shells. For years I had hardly
Considered shells as being bones, maybe
Because of the sound they could still make, though
I knew a man once who could raise a kind
Of wailing tune out of a flute he had,
Made from a fibula: it was much the same
Register as the shells'; the tune did not
Go on when his breath stopped, though you thought it
      would.
Then that morning, coming on the wreck,
I saw the kinship. No recent disaster
But an old ghost from under a green buoy,
Brought in by the last storm, or one from which

The big wind had peeled back the sand grave
To show what was still left: the bleached, chewed-off
Timbers like the ribs of a man or the jaw-bone
Of some extinct beast. Far down the sands its
Broken cage leaned out, casting no shadow
In the veiled light. There was a man sitting beside it
Eating out of a paper, littering the beach
With the bones of a few more fish, while the hulk
Cupped its empty hand high over him. Only he
And I had come to those sands knowing
That they were there. The rest was bones, whatever
Tunes they made. The bones of things; and of men too
And of man's endeavors whose ribs he had set
Between himself and the shapeless tides. Then
I saw how the sand was shifting like water,
That once could walk. Shells were to shut out the sea,
The bones of birds were built for floating
On air and water, and those of fish were devised
For their feeding depths, while a man's bones were
     framed
For what? For knowing the sands are here,
And coming to hear them a long time; for giving
Shapes to the sprawled sea, weight to its winds,
And wrecks to plead for its sands. These things are not
Limitless: we know there is somewhere
An end to them, though every way you look
They extend farther than a man can see.

THE NATIVE

He and his, unwashed all winter,
In that abandoned land in the punished
North, in a gnashing house sunk as a cheek,
Nest together, a bunting bundle crumpled
Like a handkerchief on the croaking
Back-broken bed jacked up in the kitchen; the clock
Soon stops, they just keep the cooker going; all
Kin to begin with then they crawl in under,
     Who covers who they don't care.

He and his, in the settled cozy,
Steam like a kettle, rock-a-bye, the best
Went west long ago, got out from under,
Waved bye-bye to the steep scratched fields and scabby
Pastures: their chapped plaster of newspapers
Still chafes from the walls, and snags of string tattling
Of their rugs trail yet from stair-nails. The rest,
Never the loftiest, left to themselves,
          Descended, descended.

Most that's his, at the best of times,
Looks about to fall: the propped porch lurches
Through a herd of licked machines crutched in their last
Seizures, each as ominously leaning
As the framed ancestors, trapped in their collars,
Beetling out of oval clouds from the black
Tops of the rooms, their unappeasable jowls
By nothing but frayed, faded cords leashed
          To the leaking walls.

But they no more crash
Onto him and his than the cobwebs, or
The gritting rafters, though on the summer-people's
Solid houses the new-nailed shingles open
All over like doors, flap, decamp, the locked
Shutters peel wide to wag like clappers
At the clattering windows, and the cold chimneys
Scatter bricks downwind, like the smoking heads
          Of dandelions.

In his threadbare barn, through
The roof like a snag-toothed graveyard the snow
Cradles and dives onto the pitched backs
Of his cow and plowhorse each thin as hanging
Laundry, and if drifts deep on their spines
So that one beast or other, almost every winter
Lets its knees stiffly down and freezes hard
To the barn floor; but his summer employers
          Always buy him others,

For there is no one else
Handy in summer, there in winter,

And he and his can dream at pleasure,
It is said, of houses burning, and do so
All through the cold, till the spooled snakes sleeping under
The stone dairy-floor stir with the turned year,
Waken, and sliding loose in their winter skins
Like air rising through thin ice, feed themselves forth
      To inherit the earth.

THE DRUNK IN THE FURNACE

      For a good decade
The furnace stood in the naked gully, fireless
And vacant as any hat. Then when it was
No more to them than a hulking black fossil
To erode unnoticed with the rest of the junk-hill
By the poisonous creek, and rapidly to be added
      To their ignorance.

      They were afterwards astonished
To confirm, one morning, a twist of smoke like a pale
Resurrection, staggering out of its chewed hole,
And to remark then other tokens that someone,
Cosily bolted behind the eye-holed iron
Door of the drafty burner, had there established
      His bad castle.

      Where he gets his spirits
It's a mystery. But the stuff keeps him musical:
Hammer-and-anvilling with poker and bottle
To his jugged bellowings, till the last groaning clang
As he collapses onto the rioting
Springs of a litter of car-seats ranged on the grates,
      To sleep like an iron pig.

      In their tar-paper church
On a text about stoke-holes that are sated never
Their Reverend lingers. They nod and hate trespassers.
When the furnace wakes, though, all afternoon
Their witless offspring flock like piped rats to its siren

Crescendo, and agape on the crumbling ridge
   Stand in a row and learn.

Robert Mezey

THE LOVEMAKER

I see you in her bed,
Dark, rootless epicene,
Where a lone ghost is laid
And other ghosts convene;

And hear you moan at last
Your pleasure in the deep
Haven of her who kissed
Your blind mouth into sleep.

But the body, once enthralled,
Wakes in the chains it wore,
Dishevelled, stupid, cold,
And famished as before—

And hears its paragon
Breathe in the ghostly air,
Anonymous carrion,
Ravished by despair.

Lovemaker, I have felt
Desire taking my part,
But lacked your constant fault
And something of your art,

Unwilling to bend my knees
To such unmantled pride
As left you in that place,
Restless, unsatisfied.

THE WANDERING JEW

Remember, I pray thee, who ever perished, being innocent? or
where were the righteous cut off?
    Teach me, and I will hold my tongue: and cause me to under-
stand wherein I have erred.

When I was a child and thought as a child, I put
The Sabbath wine and prayer-shawl to my lips.
Warmed by such raiment and the cordial fruit,
I approached the Ark and drew the dark blue drapes.

My temple bears a hollow scar or dent;
I called it then the forceps of His will.
I was a boy then, and obedient:
I read the blessings, and I read them well.

I bound the arm and forehead of my faith
In the four thongs of the phylacteries,
Recalling how, when we were sick to death,
God brought the harsh Egyptians to their knees.

Such were His gifts, the praises of Whose Mercy
Fell on my life like rain and made me green—
What simple years they were! I loved Him fiercely,
Who loved the Jew and smote the Philistine.

Leaving for evening prayers, I felt the breath
Of the hot slums on my cheek and saw each door
Crammed with the vendor of a tired mouth;
The fairies camping in a lightless bar;

A wino sprawled beside a spattered sill,
Blotting his open cheek with a bloody rag;
The legless beggar propped against a wall;
A childish FUCK chalked on the Synagogue.

One great door made the neon ghetto seem.
The dark fell richly on the congregation,
The weeping cantor called to Elohim,
And I wept also, brimming with sweet emotion.

2

I cannot now remember when I left
That House and its habitual old men,
Swaying before the Ark. I was adrift,
And much in need of something I had seen.

At morning and at evening, in my mind,
A girl in vague silk over nothing on
Smiled with her eyes, and with her meaning hand
Undid the sash of that translucent gown

And touched herself at length; her touch was sure.
It was not long, I ached for her, and acted,
And found one like her, although not as pure.
I liked the real as well as I expected.

I made the rounds, was married and unmarried,
And either way, I seldom slept alone—
But there beside the sticky headboard tarried
Always a Presence that would not be gone.

Not long after, leaving a girl one night,
I thought of Him and what He had intended
And saw His anger in a traffic light.
But suddenly I laughed, and it was ended.

And the next night, obedient to my nature,
My head was filled with dew as we leaned to kiss:
Why should I leave my Egypt, seeing that creatures
Suffered and perished in the wilderness?

I sucked for milk and honey at her tongue,
I strained against her, though we moved alone;
And still I heard a voiceless questioning,
When I awoke beside her, chilled, at dawn.

I lay unmoving in the small blue light—
What were the years then but the merest ash
Sprayed by a breath? And what half-buried thought
Fastened its pincers in my naked flesh?

Rabbis, I came, pounding with reddened knuckles
On the closed Ark, demanding whether the Lord
Lived in this vacuum of the Tabernacle,
Or had departed, leaving only His word—

3

For years I ate the radish of affliction,
Until my belly sickened at its tang;
The sparks flew upward, and my old affection
Sagged with my argument of right and wrong.

The workless swarmed on the stone hills of the city,
Armed children sacked each drowsy neighborhood,
And I, who had not thought them worth my pity,
Saw beast and angel mingling in their blood.

Women and long desire taught me love;
Ignorance and illusion taught me pain.
However much I learned, it was enough
To learn it was both common and my own.

Tasting my bondage in the lives of others,
I found it bitter, but my constant food;
If all the starved and homeless were my brothers,
How could I find their father in my God?

I was at rest until a dream of death
Jammed the idling mechanism of my heart;
Nightly now, nomads with broken teeth
Come muttering brokenly of a black report.

Reeking with gas, they hint what ancient fame,
What mad privation made them what they are,
The dead and dying— I am one of them—
Dark-blooded aliens tagged with David's star.

A flock of people prey to every horror,
Scattered by thirty centuries of war,
The sport of Christian duke and Hauptsturmfuehrer—
Is this the covenant we were chosen for?

Sometimes, at noon, the dull sun seems to me
A jahrzeit candle for the millions gone,
—As if that far, indifferent fire could be
Memorial to the black, disrupted bone!

Tempted and fallen, the Lord God is brooding
Over the ashes where Job sat in pain.
And yet his tribe is ashes, and unbidden,
Its blood cries out to God, and cries again.

I speak of those that lived by rope and spade,
Of those that dug a pit for friend and brother,
And those that lay down, naked, in its shade—
There, at last, the prisoners rest together.

I speak it in the anguish of the spirit:
What is man, I ask, and what am I?
I am but one of many to inherit
The barren mountain and the empty sky.

It is a modern habit of the mind
To look at flesh and tear its clothes away,
That makes consoling speech a figment of wind
And rescue seem like something in a play.

The nights are darker than they used to be.
A squalid ghost has come to share my room—
And every night I bring it home with me,
If one can call dissatisfaction home.

All week long, I have read in the Pentateuch
Of how I have not lived, and my bare body
Wrestled with every virtue it forsook.
If there is Judgement, I will not be ready.

The book I read last night will be my last;
I have come too far lacking a metaphysic.
Live, says the Law— I sit here doing my best,
Relishing meat, listening to music.

Vassar Miller

THE TREE OF SILENCE

Upon the branches of our silence hang our words,
Half-ripened fruit.
Gone are the months of summer, gone
Beyond pursuit.
Let us leave, though pinched and wan,
The windfalls wither
Under the tree whose shade affords
No shelter either.

For when was language ever food for human yearning!
Sun-gilded rain
Mocking the sheen of golden peach,
Words only drain
Hearts of strength; let mortal speech
Make time and way
For life, the long and lonely learning
How to pray.

RECEIVING COMMUNION

The world of stars and space being His bauble,
    He gives me, not a toy
    which were I to destroy
would be no waste that caused Him any trouble,
rather, into my fingers cramped and crooked
    entrusts His body real
    as spitted on a nail
as are my own hands piteous, naked—
because He has no creaking heart's mill grind
    His wheat, nor heart's belief
    play oven; for His loaf

cannot be beaten out or baked by hand—
when He, against the mind's backlash,
    would as a splinter list
    here on my turbulent dust
preventing so all fantasy of flesh.

"THOUGH HE SLAY ME"

Still tell me no, my God, and tell me no
Till I repeat the syllable for a song,
Or hold it when my mouth is cracked like clay
Cold for a pebble underneath my tongue;
Or to my comfort as my father's stir
In sleep once solaced my child's heart that knew
Although he did not waken he was near,
Still tell me no, my God, still tell me no
And, opening thus the wound that will never heal
Save torn once more, as Jacob's in his thigh,
Chafed by the hand that dealt it, was made whole,
Still tell me no, my God, still tell me no
Until I hear in it only the hush
Between Good Friday's dusk and Easter Day,
The lullaby that locked his folded lash—
I lulled to a like darkness with Your no,
No, no, still no, the echo of Your yes
Distorted among the crevices and caves
Of the coiled ear which deep in its abyss
Resolves to music all Your negatives.

THE WORSHIPER

Her eyes long hollowed out to pits of shadow,
Her cheeks sucking in darkness, forever making
A face at sorrow, phantom desperado,
Haunting as she is haunted, bent on taking
A stranglehold upon it to cry, "Look!"
That we no more may scoff in answer, "Where?"—
She kneels and, shuddered down into the cloak

Of silence, rears her fragile walls from prayer
And music, candle, creed, and psalter
Where she may tell upon her beads her seven
Most dolorous mysteries. Above her altar
Stern Witnesses who one time crashed to Heaven
Out of their flesh's glory-gutted hull
Turn from her, being also pitiful.

FULFILLMENT

Sitting in the disorder of my silence,
Fingering first this fantasy and that,
Having scant room for practicing the balance
Of prayer, making a labor of delight,
Scrabbling within myself for space to kneel,
I pick up whims more tenuous than hair:
Threads of a hope or fragments of a fear,
When—as a mother gives her child some chore
To do, and, having watched him fret and frown,
Pauses beside him after the long hour
To guide his hand a moment with her own—
From cluttered void God plucks my mind sweat-sodden
Into His hush all of a gracious sudden.

A LESSON IN DETACHMENT

She's learned to hold her gladness lightly,
Remembering when she was a child
Her fingers clenched a bird too tightly,
And its plumage, turned withered leaf,
No longer fluttered wild.

Sharper than bill or claw, her grief
Needled her palm that ached to bleed,
And could not, to assuage the grief
Pulsations of the tiny scrap
Crumpled against her need.

To prison love: a tiny snap
Of iron to be forged a band,
A toy to prove one day a trap
Destined to close without a qualm
Upon itself, her hand.

She bids her clutching five grow calm
Lest in their grip a wing might buckle
Beyond repair, and for her balm
She'll cup no joy now in her palm,
But perch it on her knuckle.

THE QUARRY

What are you, then, my love, my friend, my father,
My anybody-never-mine? Whose aim
Can wing you with a knowledge-bullet, tame
You long enough to term you fur or feather?
Labeled one species, you become another
Before I have pronounced your latest name.
My fingers itching after you, like flame
Melting to frost, you vanish into neither.

Face, mind, heart held in honor for your sake,
Magical creature none can ever snare,
Are but the trails you beat, the arcs you make,
Shy animal the color of the air,
Who are the air itself, the breath ashake
Among the leaves—the bird no longer there.

Howard Moss

UNDERWOOD

From the thin slats of the Venetian blinds
The sun has plucked a sudden metaphor:
A harp of light, reflected on the floor,
Disorients the chair and desk and door.
Those much too delicate hands still tapping
The Underwood seem now Hindu dancers
Or five or ten young Balinese children
Hopping up and down in a clearing where
The striped light scrapes through bamboo seedlings
And moves from skinny shade to thin veneer
And changes as the harp of light is changing
Its twanging image on the office floor,
Being so remarkably the blinding heir
Of something that is not, and yet is, there.

Once I watched at the water cooler
A face bent over the jet-thin water:
The iris of the bent eye changed its color
As if the water jet had stained it green;
I saw the animal head's slight shudder,
Lifted from the surface of that running stream.
Tall branches then grew green in the hallway,
Arching above a green-ferned pathway;
A screen of green leaves hung in the doorway.
Was that a mirror where I saw the beaked birds,
The sluggish coffin of the alligator,
The monkeys climbing up the sunlit tree trunks?
Or did imagination, in that corridor,
Create, like the harp, its sudden metaphor?

Inside that drawer, among the blotters, folders,
Memos, carbons, pencils, papers,

Is the youngest animal of all awaking
In that coarse nest where he's been sleeping?
If I should reach into that dangerous drawer,
What singular teeth might pierce my skin?
Or if he should leap, should I then kill him,
And watch, where the harp had set its lightness,
The marvelous animal blood go thin?

MOVIES FOR THE HOME

I see the map of summer, lying still,
Its edges under water, blue, fragile.
You cannot hear, of course, from here
The Pacific's portable orchestra—
A kind of shimmery marimba music—
But if you follow all those lines of light,
The nerve-nets of connection, coast to coast,
That screened the days and nights from east to west,
You'll come upon their visions and their sounds:
The dawn's fine print when ink has leaked away,
And a radio turned off still tuned to play
Invisible music. Riding in that car,
I think that where we were is where we are.

The towns the distance fired into being
(By dint of light diagonally drawn
Downward to strike a steeple with a star)
Became fool's gold the closer we came near,
Assembling into lassitudes of palms,
The fresh rot of the wharfs, the hunchbacked hills,
But none of those visions we were driving for.
They drained away, strip cities come and gone,
As if we stayed while we went driving on,
Or they remained where they had never been,
Before us and behind us. They disappeared,
And what at first was flame at last was char.
One wheel turns or another, and there you are.

By supple deviations, twisting on,
The Snake River bent its shapely mail

In moonlight, enlarged and palpable.
The Tetons capped by a display of snow
Refreshed four lakes of summer far below
(Thimblefuls of a barbarian sky);
We dipped our fingers in their sunburnt water
To dribble waterdrops back into blue.
Telegraph wires stitched themselves to trees,
Then dropped away, somewhere in the Rockies.
The pictures pass. We are what we need.
If I remember rightly, we were lost.
We lost the way, being the way we are.

A beautifully painted abstract speed
Lacquered the windshield's cemetery
Of wing and smear so factually there
It seemed the factual was arbitrary
But natural. In those swift ends we saw
The wreckage of ourselves, our wheels in air . . .
Transparent vacancies attack the brain
At one point or another, as if a train
Should smash into a moving mirror of itself
Point-blank high up upon a mountain pass
And the snow, not even disturbed, give back
Its glacial white indifference to the wreck.
And there, where imagination ends, we are.

Where are we? In a country of lakes?
A Switzerland of Self through which we ski,
Dropping down a lighted scoop of valley
That soon transforms itself into the sea?
(And thus we might arrive at the Impossible:
That place where there is nothing left to see.)
Now we are standing on a wooden pier
Watching the Pacific stun itself on rocks;
If the camera stopped, if you could stare
Out far enough, the Orient, over there,
Might have the excitement of intense boredom.
Our house in Berkeley? You turn the corner there,
Go left and down the hill, and there you are.

Alongside water all the afternoon,
The sea so far below we could not fall,

What threatened ending rose from its abyss
To rattle in the tin can of the car?
Was it the blue that flaked away to cloud,
The green that flew away on either side,
The white-lined serpent of the road ahead,
Intense as distance in its silences,
That colored what we thought until we thought:
The color of the distance is the color bled
Out of the time it takes to get us there?
The pictures pass. We are the way we were.
Being here and there is what we are.

By going forward we were coming back.
When the film rewinds, you'll see what I mean.
In the woods, that lipsticked drinking cup,
Stuck in the drying margins of the stream,
Turns up again in the desert coming up
Quite soon in malignant iodine and green.
Now we are looking at an estuary
Whose waters gently poach an evening star
Whose spidery edges are collapsing down
As far as the eye can see, but just so far.
I wonder if you can go as far as far
And still not see things as they really are,
Only as they were, if that is where you are.

LOCAL PLACES

The song you sang you will not sing again,
Floating in the spring to all your local places,
Lured by archaic senses to the wood
To watch the frog jump from the mossy rock,
To listen to the stream's small talk at dark,
Or to feel the springy pine-floor where you walk—
If your green secrecies were such as these,
The mystery is now in other trees.

If, in the desert, where the cactus dryly,
Leniently allows its classic bloom
To perfume aridness, you searched for water,

And saw, at night, the scalp of sand begin
To ripple like the sea, as though the moon
Had tides to time those waves of light's illusion,
The rock that spilled so softly from your hand
Is now ten thousand other grains of sand.

If you lay down beside the breathing ocean,
Whose lung is never still, whose motion pulls
A night-net over sleep, you knew the way
It lulled the dreamer toward his vision, how
Drowned mariners turned over in its slough,
Green-eyed among the weeds. You see it now
A less than visionary sea, and feel
Only its blue surfaces were ever real.

Or if you were born to naked flatness
Of rock, or rock that twisted up in mountains,
The jagged risers stonily ascending,
And bent down once to see the mica's tight,
Flat scales of silver, layered in the granite,
And kept one scale to be your jewel at night,
Another sliver now breaks light; its gleam
Is similar to yours, yet not the same.

Once history has used your single name,
Your face is one time will not see again.
Into such a din is every singer born,
The general music mutes the single horn.
The lights in the small houses, one by one,
Go out, foundations topple slowly down—
The tree, the sand, the water, and the stone,
What songs they sing they always sing again.

HORROR MOVIE

Dr. Unlikely, we love you so,
You who made the double-headed rabbits grow
From a single hare. Mutation's friend,
Who could have prophecied the end
When the Spider Woman deftly snared the fly

And the monsters strangled in a monstrous kiss
And somebody hissed, "You'll hang for this!"?

Dear Dracula, sleeping on your native soil,
(Any other kind makes him spoil),
How we clapped when you broke the French door
    down
And surprised the bride in the overwrought bed.
Perfectly dressed for lunar research,
Your evening cape added much,
Though the bride, inexplicably dressed in furs,
Was a study in jaded jugulars.

Poor, tortured Leopard Man, you changed your spots
In the debauched village of the Pin-Head Tots;
How we wrung our hands, how we wept
When the eighteenth murder proved inept,
And, caught in the Phosphorous Cave of Sea,
Dangling the last of synthetic flesh,
You said, "There's something wrong with me."

The Wolf Man knew when he prowled at dawn
Beginnings spin a web where endings spawn.
The bat who lived on shaving cream,
A household pet of Dr. Dream,
Unfortunately, maddened by the bedlam,
Turned on the Doc, bit the hand that fed him.

And you, Dr. X, who killed by moonlight,
We loved your scream in the laboratory
When the panel slid and the night was starry
And you threw the inventor in the crocodile pit
(An obscure point: Did he deserve it?)
And you took the gold to Transylvania
Where no one guessed how insane you were.

We thank you for the moral and the mood,
Dear Dr. Cliché, Nurse Platitude.
When we meet again by the Overturned Grave,
Near the Sunken City of the Twisted Mind,
(In The Son of the Son of Frankenstein),

Make the blood flow, make the motive muddy:
There's a little death in every body.

WATER ISLAND

To the Memory of a friend, Drowned off Water Island,
April, 1960

Finally, from your house there is no view;
The bay's blind mirror shattered over you
And Patchogue took your body like a log
The wind rolled up to shore. The senseless drowned
Have faces nobody would care to see,
But water loves those gradual erasures
Of flesh and shoreline, greenery and glass,
And you belonged to water, it to you,
Having built, on a hillock, above the bay,
Your house, the bay giving you reason to,
Where now, if seasons still are running straight,
The horseshoe crabs clank armor night and day,
Their couplings far more ancient than the eyes
That watched them from your porch. I saw one once
Whose back was a history of how we live;
Grown onto every inch of plate, except
Where the hinges let it move, were living things,
Barnacles, mussels, water weeds—and one
Blue bit of polished glass, glued there by time:
The origins of art. It carried them
With pride, it seemed, as if endurance only
Matters in the end. Or so I thought.

Skimming traffic lights, starboard and port,
Steer through planted poles that mark the way,
And other lights, across the bay, faint stars
Lining the border of Long Island's shore,
Come on at night, they still come on at night,
Though who can see them now I do not know.
Wild roses, at your back porch, break their blood,
And bud to test surprises of sea air,
And the birds fly over, gliding down to feed
At the two feeding stations you set out with seed,

Or splash themselves in a big bowl of rain
You used to fill with water. Going across
That night, too fast, too dark, no one will know,
Maybe you heard, the last you'll ever hear,
The cry of the savage and endemic gull
Which shakes the blood and always brings to mind
The thought that death, the scavenger, is blind,
Blunders and is stupid, and the end
Comes with ironies so fine the seed
Falters in the marsh and the heron stops
Hunting in the weeds below your landing stairs,
Standing in a stillness that now is yours.

Robert Pack

RESURRECTION

On the taut shore, the bald skull,
Bleached, abandoned, more regular than stone,
Glistens, a little cast-away sun
Among planetary pebbles, galaxies of sand.
Dragged out again, again to drown,
By choked water, wheezing waves,
The outflung aged angel gulls
Gossip its descent; cliffs moulder,
Smoldering the anger of the drugged earth's age,
While the skull's sockets suck the foam,
Windows for eels to swim like sight away,
With the crooked teeth laughing seaweed,
Sighing from the ribs of the deep sea-dunes.

Beyond bird-rubbed air, a skeleton,
From denial of its burned-out blood,
Rises erect in the moonlight like a soul;
Like shaped clouds clustered in, see
There is the furled skull, and there to the south,
Outstretched, float delicate finger-bones;

To the north, the cupped right palm
Catches feathers fallen from angel-wings.
Thigh-bones, knee-bones, ankle-bones, toes, dangle
Eastward, all parts are there, jointed,
All held intact, prayerful, and pure.

He rises swiftly now, rises
To the west, as if summoned, as if
Called forth and dreaming himself unencumbered
Up through space, without
A tongue, voiceless, with no lips.
The sea sparkles with the sperm
Of his rejected light.

PARABLE

Within the introspection of my dying
I reversed myself in the darkness of indecision
Because of all that hate:
The anger of birds—their shrill philosophy,
The fish uncaring and cold in their own blood,
And the animals who would not talk with me,
And I wiped the honey from my jaw with the paw
Of my hand, and I said to the quarrelsome birds: beware,
For the fox will find your nest and devour your eggs;
And I said to the meditative fish: beware,
For the carefree otter will spear you in the foam,
And to the arty beaver, the snobbish deer,
And the arrogant porcupine, I said: beware
The season when the leaves and flowers bloom dry
And the bark of the tree is acid to your tongue,
But they did not reply,
And I reversed myself in the darkness of indecision.
This was the first warning, the elemental cry,
The hate; and I started back from where I came
Where waters fountained once in happiness
And the mothering season cradled me secure,
But now the trees were clothed in funereal light,
The ground seemed sinking now beneath my feet,

And insects heckled me out of the grass.
This was the second warning, the change,
The strangeness; and I reversed myself
Within the introspection of my dying.
And the first warning and the second warning sounded
In my ears like leaves, like waves, like crumbling crags,
And I turned to the heedless animals and said:
It is not bad to feel you are alone,
But bad that no one's company consoles;
It is not bad to feel that you are lost,
But bad to think there is no place to go
Beyond the darkness of your indecision.
And this third warning I told the animals,
But they did not reply.
Within the darkness of my indecision,
Within the introspection of my dying,
I stopped still as I could and did not move,
And the animals came forth and licked my hands.

DESCENDING

It is all falling away, the days fall faster now;
There float the first two dried and curling leaves,
Gathered by a wind into the emptiness
That only we are able to imagine,
The emptiness of ourselves and of our falling.
And having shaped the sorrows of my breath
Into the sorrow of autumnal elegy,
Why do I turn so suddenly it shakes my eyes,
Only to discover my own surprise
And the road narrowing over the hill behind me?

And have I known you in no other way
Beyond the little cruelties that turned your lip
And told me I was not a god,
Beyond the urgency whose dreams betray—
Of immemorial lovers rotting in their mutual grave,
Whom no autumnal elegy can save,
Touching bone fingertip to fingertip?
It is all falling away, the emptiness

That held us reaching, always the same,
And the touch by which we turned apart;
And now, emptied even of blame,
There is only our falling and the leaves
Curled in the wind, curling past the maple tree,
Falling and scattering like choices that we made
That quivered with revealed surprise
As the road narrowed over the hill behind me.

Conceived in the spaceless womb,
Moving through emptiness thereafter,
What can I find but terror in the laughing
Stars, knowing the trout cannot know
Of a drowning world, nor the mole,
His warm belly brushing through a hole,
Know that he desecrates a grave?
And the hawk, in his brave circling,
Will he never lift his eyes to see the sun?
And we, what more could we have done,
Before we kept in dispossession
The kisses that no mortal lips can keep
And the embrace that does not fall away
Into the passiveness of sleep?

Descending past the garden where the dead crow
Jangles on a stick; descending past
The graveyard where the bluebird prinks
In uncontemplative delight; down past the orchard
Where the cherry trees are hung with silver cups
To frighten off the bobolinks;
Down through the meadow where the summer went,
The pastoral melancholy and the scythe's lament,
Only the falling sustains me, only the falling
Seems steady now, open as it is, and near,
Almost to touch, as the consummation that I fear
No man and woman can achieve,
And perfect as the paradise whose gates—
Closing behind the hill of the road
That narrows behind me—beckon me back.

THE BOAT

I dressed my father in his little clothes,
Blue sailor suit, brass buttons on his coat.
He asked me where the running water goes.

"Down to the sea," I said. "Set it afloat!"
Beside the stream he bent and raised the sail,
Uncurled the string and launched the painted boat.

White birds, flown like flags, wrenched his eyes pale.
He leaped on the tight deck and took the wind.
I watched the ship foam lurching in the gale,

And cried, "Come back, you don't know what you'll find!"
He steered. The ship grew, reddening the sky.
Water throbbed backward, blind stumbling after blind.

The rusty storm diminished in his eye,
And down he looked at me. A harbor rose.
I asked, "What happens, father, when you die?"

He told where all the running water goes,
And dressed me gently in my little clothes.

IN A FIELD

Here, in a field
Of devil's paintbrushes,
The circle of far trees
Tightens, and near bushes
Hump like ruins
When the moon floats loosely
Past the desolation
The owl's cry winds.
Here, as if
In first astonishment,

We, the last lovers,
Have rung from the ruins
The whip-poor-will's
Thrust of melody.
You have fallen asleep,
Breathing as the wind breathes
Among the wetted thistle,
The scented vine,
And, listening, I move
My body toward you,
When a small convulsion
Shakes your hand,
The moonlight flashes
On your teeth.
I am afraid to kiss you.
Never have I wished more
Not to die.

CHOPPING FIRE-WOOD

Up from my belly, up from my back,
The good swinging blood floods in my arms,
Locks my elbows flat; my fingers grip
Against the grim smack of the axe
As the thud, the wood's recoil
And clap, echoes out, out
Into the quick wide weather
Of the unfailing, far-flung afternoon.

Cheeks puffed with not quite yet spent
Breath, the little nut of left air
Grows in an instant in my lungs
Into an oak, into my raised axe,
My strength's good anger; it grows,
Fruited out, into my thought's words
That cry, "again, again," into
A bugle-call of first joys. Yes,
Here I am, my axe, my tree of breath,
Flames in my hair, my hands, flames
In my back and in my belly's hearth.

And there is the piled wood,
And the defied wind,
And the boulders behind the apple trees
Gone grey in the drop of the sun,
And the stopped song of the fed birds,
And the ice, the mirror of ice,
The sky in the mirror, and the afternoon
Over.

    Inside,
My fire-place, my wife, my books;
Inside, without fear,
The drowsiness.

Ronald Perry

STILL-LIFE

Oranges in a wooden bowl,
Orange and Moorish drape, like
A study in the contradictions
Of color.
      The palest fruit
Turns long and lush as any
Odalisque, and the drape burns
Into a bush, Grandfather,
Under the swift, blue incursions
Of your terrible brush. Or,
A tree turns to stone
After your touch.
        In your liquid world,
The sun floats through the window,
As delicate as any bobbing boat
Fishing for shrimp in the harbor. Or,
The sun sinks, and the trees
Open like umbrellas, to disclose
An incandescent opulence

Of bitter rose and gold
As the trees open and close,
Close and open,
And the blue hands of the leaves
Blaze with birds.

Still your slick pen delivers
The world—as, below Oran
And the burning Cape, touch
Is an experience, like
These few pungences
Of scent and color
On a yellow afternoon
At the other end of summer.

Yellow, and an intimation
Of red. (Perspectives alter.)

Now oranges are worlds that all
Your boats can circle, sleek
Damosels of the gliding harbor
Beyond the headland, where
The sun spills on your lids
Like yellow water in a river
Somewhere in the turning sea.

The problem of evil escapes
The mind. Lyrics
From your stone fingers drop
In African intervals, as
The sun spills its profusion
On the walks and few villages,
Like the achievement
Of an antique design.

Now the waterlights glow
Unseen in a thin distance,
And the solitary gulls wheel
And cry, gliding beyond the harbor,
Beyond the headland, where
The sun sets like a sonata,
With the rustling of red violins

In a dark window, transparencies
Of air, and the cry of gulls,
And the formal sun setting
Over and over.
                    The world
Is a shifting world
Of little air and color
In your hands. But you are
Aware of your limitations:

Next winter, the oranges
Will bloom on another hill.

THE SHELLPICKER

This lady, curled like a shell
In her work of love, picks
And pokes at everything. All
The long tide's wilderness
Is grief she touches to tell
How the blazing fish fall
Incredibly down, and the press
Of fathoms under the shell
Pours color up, or locks
The world in a diving bell
As water-shaped and delicate
And full of sound as a shell.
She knows the mysterious, deep
Music that the creatures tell
In rainbows, but in her sleep
The salt sea-weed is all
She catches in her net
Of hands. The fire fish fall
Up to drown, as tenuous
And insubstantial as the coral
Strikes its flower, or the sun
Prints the loveliest shell
With fire, or furious, hacks
Out long lightnings to tell

Its weaving watery shape
Up the fantastic waves. Tall
As any creature in her sleep,
Her hands feed on the shell.
For love she is undone,
And deep as the drowned bell
At death dives to a miracle,
The long sun in her sleep
Becomes a wilderness to tell
The perfect secret of her shape—
This lady, curled like a shell.

PROLOGUE FOR A BESTIARY

The emerald cages a jungle.
At jewel-heart the jaguar
And the doe wait by the water.

Roots snare in the sun's tangle,
Tangling in the buried wood
Where the sun spills blood
On the leaves, and herons feed
In a house of vines, creepers,
Sad lianas woven in whispers.

By the water, intricately dead,
The ghosts of birds are sailing.

Everywhere the sun is falling,
But in another, and remoter
World than this, as green
As the garden before Eden.

Now the wind walks on the water,
And the shapes that began
As shadows in the child's hand
Are ghosts no longer: bestiaries
Of the sudden thumb, fistsful
Of birds and blue animals.

In the jewel, evenings, elegies
Are spoken for the dead child
In the wood, and the wild
Beasts that he made on the wall
In the nursery before sleep:

The sun sails up in the shape
Of a bird, the elephants are tall
As trees, all the beasts at ease
In their skins have eyes
That speak, and minnows swim
Through the drinking trees
Like boats on a river of leaves.

The child sleeps. Roots bury him
Deep, as green with beasts
The jungle on his body feasts.

Among the vines, the parrot claws
The air with his green noise.

By the water the jaguar cries,
Announcing ruin in his delicate jaws,
Altering perspective—until
The world curls like a shell,
And all summer long, as he dreams
In the jewel, the jungle
Interprets the fable:

The secret of the animals' names
Discloses centuries of leaves,
Where nothing moves or grieves
But the legends in his thumbs,
Where no bird flies but a ghost,
And the emerald crumbles into dust.

Donald Petersen

TRUE TO A DREAM

And the curtains, the lamp,
The rose-papered wall,
The familiar cramp
Of books in the rack,
Would fade; he would fall
Through a slumbrous abyss
To a great zodiac
Where the lions hiss,
Where the master swings
A nine-tailed whip
Or the bluebird sings
In a private arbor
Or a wonderful ship
Has the sky for a harbor

And when it was past
All that he saw
Was darkness and vast
Confusions of vapor,
And rubbed his eyes raw.
And when he awoke,
The book-laden shelf
And the old rose-paper
Appeared the same
And he fancied himself
Cut off at a stroke,
In a trice undone,
For as quick as it came
The show passed on.

And the persons he met
Were brave but sad.

One paused by the bed
But could not talk.
Another one had
A limp in his walk.
There was a lone
Boy on a crutch.
An heir to a throne
Was locked out of touch.
And the princess was pining
As princesses must
And everything shining
Began to rust.

And hour after hour,
Yet always true,
To the one highest tower
The boy withdrew.
And true to a dream
That opens and closes,
He ruled supreme,
Suppressing the roses
That mounted the wall,
Until in a bold,
Deliberate choice
He relinquished his hold
At the faraway call
Of a downstairs voice.

SONNET IN AUTUMN

When the flesh of summer piecemeal mars the lawn,
And the big white house sits smokily among
The skeletal branches, and comer Jack has stung
A few late crabs and the hummingbird is gone;
When milkweed shakes her heavy pod at the sun
That shows a paling grin, and the backward worm
Is backward slid and the mole is stuck for a term
In his hole—when dun earth and raw sky are one—
What mind of mine will comprehend the wind
That elbows through the naked trellises,

That irks the testy leaves and leaves them pinned
In pinetrees, fences, stalks, and crevices,
That jams the stolid chimneys with its sound,
That hales the acorns to the brindled ground?

NARCISSUS

In memoriam R. S.

I

Was it his face that so unsettled him?
(For it was beautiful and childly wise.)
One day he watched a water spider skim
Across a pool. His image met his eyes,
And changing as the water's surface changed,
It filled him with a terrible delight.
He knew that all his life had been arranged
By some unwished-for providence. He might
Go on pretending that he didn't know,
But people in their drawing rooms would show
Him as a thing of some refinement, sought
For taste or wit or common sense alone,
While in their privacy they railed and fought
Like stray dogs yapping at a bloody bone.

II

Take any subway to the nearest place—
He's standing like a statue in the crowd.
And schoolgirls titter when they see his face
Dejected, overserious, soft and proud.
They edge about him in the evening press,
Lovely as sparks struck from electric rails.
In him they sense a kind of tenderness
At which the heart despairs. The current fails.
The lights go out. He ponders for a spell,
Wound in the deepest catacombs of hell
Where one awaits the springing of a door
To loose a ravenous, half-human beast
On his bent form. The lights come on once more.
And all at once the monster is released.

III

Day-long upon the baked or windy street
The pavement seemed to bristle with the eyes
Of swarms of women he would never meet
And fawning men who followed him like flies.
If night was kind to him it made his face,
Beneath its glow, an amber-lighted bronze,
And gave his form a more than human grace.
At evening in the park, beside the ponds,
He walked among the statues, who were dumb,
Who could not hear his step or tell him from
Those solid citizens, the sculptured dead.
But from the benches of the fenced-in park
The eyes peered out at him and made him dread
The will to live that terrorized the dark.

IV

Had he foreseen, since that first fatal day,
The nature and the passion of his fall?
The sunlight beats the panes but will not stay.
He shuts his eyes and feels the bedroom wall
Fill up with shadow till his life seems trapped
As in some narrow, subterranean flaw
In which he lies awake, his nerves unsnapped,
Alive and throbbing. Did he know the law
That ties a man in knots but leaves him whole,
Giving the flesh in marriage to a soul
That shrieks, "I will escape your dirty fates
By putting on the rectitude of stone,"
Then drinks the blood, grows dumb, and suffocates,
Submissive to the flesh it claimed to own?

V

Must all of life's perfections come to rot
Eventually in some unhallowed place?
In bashful belles the rarest beauty spot
Glows but a day, blood ranging in the face,
At last relinquished to an old gravure:
While in a lonely grave the grave worm goes
At what was called the soul's investiture,
Peeling the lips, the brows, the grecian nose,

And stripping every smoothly shaven limb.
One night he dreamed a woman followed him,
Calling him softly by his childhood name.
He turned, and in an ecstasy of fright
Went scampering down the streets till she became
Less than a whisper dying through the night.

VI

Why should paternal Heaven wish to keep
This image that a mirror cannot hold?
Better to lose oneself in a quartz sleep
Than bear the indignity of growing old.
And what if sculptors cut him from the quartz
And set him up before the general eye?
Why, then a more serene existence starts,
Locked in the stone, descended from the sky,
Ascended from the windings of the earth.
By the still pool he had his second birth,
Studying his imagery in fateful springs;
He leaned more closely, arching his thin spine;
Kissing his face, he shivered it in rings.
And the dream passed in broken water-shine.

VII

Where does the form go when it disappears?
Into a pool whose depth no man may tell;
Into a wellspring's throat, the pit of years;
Into the always churning floods of hell.
It goes to join the spun world at the source
(All form being changed to movement there below),
Tumbling from cave to cave until its force
Speaks in the blossoms of the flowers that blow.
Maiden, beside what fountain do you dare
To pick this flower and flaunt it in your hair?
Here lies the virgin boy bound in his bed
With no fair love, no marriageable heart;
By day the world pursued him and he fled
To its dark night where the clear waters start.

Sylvia Plath

THE COLOSSUS

I shall never get you put together entirely,
Pieced, glued, and properly jointed.
Mule-bray, pig-grunt and bawdy cackles
Proceed from your great lips.
It's worse than a barnyard.

Perhaps you consider yourself an oracle,
Mouthpiece of the dead, or of some god or other.
Thirty years now I have laboured
To dredge the silt from your throat.
I am none the wiser.

Scaling little ladders with gluepots and pails of lysol
I crawl like an ant in mourning
Over the weedy acres of your brow
To mend the immense skull-plates and clear
The bald, white tumuli of your eyes.

A blue sky out of the Oresteia
Arches above us. O father, all by yourself
You are pithy and historical as the Roman Forum.
I open my lunch on a hill of black cypress.
Your fluted bones and acanthine hair are littered

In their old anarchy to the horizon-line.
It would take more than a lightning-stroke
To create such a ruin.
Nights, I squat in the cornucopia
Of your left ear, out of the wind,

Counting the red stars and those of plum-colour.
The sun rises under the pillar of your tongue.

My hours are married to shadow.
No longer do I listen for the scrape of a keel
On the blank stones of the landing.

SNAKECHARMER

As the gods began one world, and man another,
So the snakecharmer begins a snaky sphere
With moon-eye, mouth-pipe. He pipes. Pipes green.
    Pipes water.

Pipes water green until green waters waver
With reedy lengths and necks and undulatings.
And as his notes twine green, the green river

Shapes its images around his songs.
He pipes a place to stand on, but no rocks,
No floor: a wave of flickering grass tongues

Supports his foot. He pipes a world of snakes,
Of sways and coilings, from the snake-rooted bottom
Of his mind. And now nothing but snakes

Is visible. The snake-scales have become
Leaf, become eyelid; snake-bodies, bough, breast
Of tree and human. And he within this snakedom

Rules the writhings which make manifest
His snakehood and his might with pliant tunes
From his thin pipe. Out of this green nest

As out of Eden's navel twist the lines
Of snaky generations: let there be snakes!
And snakes there were, are, will be—till yawns

Consume this piper and he tires of music
And pipes the world back to the simple fabric
Of snake-warp, snake-weft. Pipes the cloth of snakes

To a melting of green waters, till no snake
Shows its head, and those green waters back to
Water, to green, to nothing like a snake.
Puts up his pipe, and lids his moony eye.

BLACK ROOK IN RAINY WEATHER

On the stiff twig up there
Hunches a wet black rook
Arranging and rearranging its feathers in the rain.
I do not expect miracle
Or an accident

To set the sight on fire
In my eye, nor seek
Any more in the desultory weather some design,
But let spotted leaves fall as they fall,
Without ceremony, or portent.

Although, I admit, I desire,
Occasionally, some backtalk
From the mute sky, I can't honestly complain:
A certain minor light may still
Leap incandescent

Out of kitchen table or chair
As if a celestial burning took
Possession of the most obtuse objects now and then—
Thus hallowing an interval
Otherwise inconsequent

By bestowing largesse, honour,
One might say love. At any rate, I now walk
Wary (for it could happen
Even in this dull, ruinous landscape); sceptical,
Yet politic; ignorant

Of whatever angel may choose to flare
Suddenly at my elbow. I only know that a rook
Ordering its black feathers can so shine

As to seize my senses, haul
My eyelids up, and grant

A brief respite from fear
Of total neutrality. With luck,
Trekking stubborn through this season
Of fatigue, I shall
Patch together a content

Of sorts. Miracles occur,
If you care to call those spasmodic
Tricks of radiance miracles. The wait's begun again,
The long wait for the angel,
For that rare, random descent.

MUSHROOMS

Overnight, very
Whitely, discreetly,
Very quietly

Our toes, our noses
Take hold on the loam,
Acquire the air.

Nobody sees us,
Stops us, betrays us;
The small grains make room.

Soft fists insist on
Heaving the needles,
The leafy bedding,

Even the paving.
Our hammers, our rams,
Earless and eyeless,

Perfectly voiceless,
Widen the crannies,
Shoulder through holes. We

Diet on water,
On crumbs of shadow,
Bland-mannered, asking

Little or nothing.
So many of us!
So many of us!

We are shelves, we are
Tables, we are meek,
We are edible,

Nudgers and shovers
In spite of ourselves.
Our kind multiplies:

We shall by morning
Inherit the earth.
Our foot's in the door.

BLUE MOLES

1

They're out of the dark's ragbag, these two
Moles dead in the pebbled rut,
Shapeless as flung gloves, a few feet apart—
Blue suede a dog or fox has chewed.
One, by himself, seemed pitiable enough,
Little victim unearthed by some large creature
From his orbit under the elm root.
The second carcase makes a duel of the affair:
Blind twins bitten by bad nature.

The sky's far dome is sane and clear.
Leaves, undoing their yellow caves
Between the road and the lake water,
Bare no sinister spaces. Already
The moles look neutral as the stones.
Their corkscrew noses, their white hands

Uplifted, stiffen in a family pose.
Difficult to imagine how fury struck—
Dissolved now, smoke of an old war.

2

Nightly the battle-shouts start up
In the ear of the veteran, and again
I enter the soft pelt of the mole.
Light's death to them: they shrivel in it.
They move through their mute rooms while I sleep,
Palming the earth aside, grubbers
After the fat children of root and rock.
By day, only the topsoil heaves.
Down there one is alone.

Outsize hands prepare a path,
They go before: opening the veins,
Delving for the appendages
Of beetles, sweetbreads, shards—to be eaten
Over and over. And still the heaven
Of final surfeit is just as far
From the door as ever. What happens between us
Happens in darkness, vanishes
Easy and often as each breath.

THE GHOST'S LEAVETAKING

Enter the chilly no-man's land of about
Five o'clock in the morning, the no-colour void
Where the waking head rubbishes out the draggled lot
Of sulphurous dreamscapes and obscure lunar conundrums
Which seemed, when dreamed, to mean so profoundly
     much,

Gets ready to face the ready-made creation
Of chairs and bureaus and sleep-twisted sheets.
This is the kingdom of the fading apparition,
The oracular ghost who dwindles on pin-legs
To a knot of laundry, with a classic bunch of sheets

Upraised, as a hand, emblematic of farewell.
At this joint between two worlds and two entirely
Incompatible modes of time, the raw material
Of our meat-and-potato thoughts assumes the nimbus
Of ambrosial revelation. And so departs.

Chair and bureau are the hieroglyphs
Of some godly utterance wakened heads ignore:
So these posed sheets, before they thin to nothing,
Speak in sign language of a lost otherworld,
A world we lose by merely waking up.

Trailing its telltale tatters only at the outermost
Fringe of mundane vision, this ghost goes
Hand aloft, goodbye, goodbye, not down
Into the rocky gizzard of the earth,
But toward a region where our thick atmosphere

Diminishes, and God knows what is there.
A point of exclamation marks that sky
In ringing orange like a stellar carrot.
Its round period, displaced and green,
Suspends beside it the first point, the starting

Point of Eden, next the new moon's curve.
Go, ghost of our mother and father, ghost of us,
And ghost of our dreams' children, in those sheets
Which signify our origin and end,
To the cloud-cuckoo land of colour wheels

And pristine alphabets and cows that moo
And moo as they jump over moons as new
As that crisp cusp toward which you voyage now.
Hail and farewell. Hello, goodbye. O keeper
Of the profane grail, the dreaming skull.

David Ray

X-RAY

Strangely
　　my mother's sad eyes
　　　　did not show up
　　　　　　on the X-ray
though I had long since
　　swallowed
　　　　all her sorrows
and they should have been
　　　　right there—
　　　　　　where the pain IS

nor my father's
　　　　old loves
　　　　　　which should have been
　　　　　　　　THERE
　　cavorting
heedless of fluoroscopic
　　　　　　　　voyeurs

nor was the little boy
　　　　loveless and snotnosed
who'd been entombed
　　　　for sure
　　　　　　there
　　　　years ago
in sight,

Perhaps he hid
　　　　behind the spleen
　　　　　　behind the ribs
Oh he is out of hiding now
　　　　and is drumming drumming
　　　　　　drumming my heart.

ON THE POET'S LEER

Certain poets
   have written good poems
      surely
   because of their passion
for girls drawing on their coats.
I know at least one who benefited,
seeing how, one night, she drew
on her scarf and the coat held for her,
going out, after a party,
   not only into the cold
   but into all the years
   and all the arms of her years
   and into the snow
   and the time to cover her
But I merely
   mutter
      disconsolate sighs
         and sip
            the evening's last pale glass
               wondering
                  how far the fat-cheeked
                    boy's hands
                      have plowed
                        by now.

ON A FIFTEENTH-CENTURY
FLEMISH ANGEL

The toe sticking out from under the hem
Of that angel's blue skirt
Shows, along with the finger raised
In no-nonsense admonishment,
That you are dealing here
With a down-to-earth angel,
An angel whose wings belong, organic

As a bird's: not like those Greco
Angels, sour-faced and grim with doubt.
The face of this particular red-haired
Angel, with blue wings and ruddy cheeks,
Holding a mace he'd use to crack
Your noggin, tingles from the chill
Of Northern skies; yet those cheeks
Are luminous with the long light
Of stars. His flesh is warmed
By blood that never need be drained.

THE PROBLEMS OF A WRITING TEACHER

Her patience is infinite
For she will keep the coffee warm
Forever if I wish. I have given her
Electricity, though she is only slightly
Indebted to electricity, she with her breasts
Large enough to nurse three
If we did not worry about statistics.

My students think I fail to understand
Their metaphors. To hear them talk
They all want to throw themselves
Off gorges, yet they are happy,
With the nipples of young girls to pinch,
And they can voice distant ambitions
To be completed in their twenty-fourth
Year. Time, O time an endless spool,
Rolls out before them and they slowly
Bend to it. Who knows at what hour
The kitchen will close? The clocks
Are uncertain. Her robe falls open
At the oddest times. Often
It is two in the morning
Before I open my first *Schlitz*.

Who can understand my metaphor?
I will let it drip from the houseroof—
Isn't that what he did, the showoff?

—And let it congeal into ice and then
Melt again and it will mean jumping
Off the gorges, over the wicker railing,
Screaming across the page, Ahhhhhhhh.

Adrienne Rich

AT MAJORITY

When you are old and beautiful
And things most difficult are done,
There will be few who can recall
Your face as it is ravaged now
By youth and its oppressive work.

Your look will hold their wondering looks
Grave as Cordelia's at the last,
Neither with rancor at the past
Nor to upbraid the coming time,
For you will be at peace with time.

But now, a daily warfare takes
Its toll of tenderness in you,
And you must live like captains who
Wait out the hour before the charge—
Fearful, and yet impatient too.

Yet someday this will have an end,
All choices made or choice resigned,
And in your face the literal eye
Trace little of your history,
Nor ever piece the tale entire

Of villages that had to burn
And playthings of the will destroyed
Before you could be safe from time

And gather in your brow and air
The stillness of antiquity.

THE RAVEN

If, antique hateful bird,
flapping through dawn-gagged streets
of metal shopfronts grated down
on pedestrian nerve-ends,

if, as on old film,
my features blurred and grained like cereal,
you find me walking up and down
waiting for my first dream,

don't try to sully my head
with vengeful squirtings. Fly on,
ratfooted cautionary of my dark,
till we meet further along.

You are no dream, old genius.
I smell you, get my teeth on edge,
stand in my sweat—in mercury—
even as you prime your feathers and set sail.

LUCIFER IN THE TRAIN

Riding the black express from heaven to hell
He bit his fingers, watched the countryside,
Vernal and crystalline, forever slide
Beyond his gaze: the long cascades that fell
Ribboned in sunshine from their sparkling height,
The fishers fastened to their pools of green
By silver lines; the birds in sudden flight—
All things the diabolic eye had seen
Since heaven's cockcrow. Imperceptibly
That landscape altered: now in paler air

Tree, hill and rock stood out resigned, severe,
Beside the strangled field, the stream run dry.

Lucifer, we are yours who stiff and mute
Ride out of worlds we shall not see again,
And watch from windows of a smoking train
The ashen prairies of the absolute.
Once out of heaven, to an angel's eye
Where is the bush or cloud without a flaw?
What bird but feeds upon mortality,
Flies to its young with carrion in its claw?
O foundered angel, first and loneliest
To turn this bitter sand beneath your hoe,
Teach us, the newly-landed, what you know;
After our weary transit, find us rest.

THE TOURIST AND THE TOWN

(SAN MINIATO AL MONTE)

Those clarities detached us, gave us form,
Made us like architecture. Now no more
Bemused by local mist, our edges blurred,
We knew where we began and ended. There
We were the campanile and the dome,
Alive and separate in that bell-struck air,
Climate whose light reformed our random line,
Edged our intent and sharpened our desire.

Could it be always so—a week of sunlight,
Walks with a guidebook, picking out our way
Through verbs and ruins, yet finding after all
The promised vista, once!—The light has changed
Before we can make it ours. We have no choice:
We are only tourists under that blue sky,
Reading the posters on the station wall—
Come, take a walking-trip through happiness.

There is a mystery that floats between
The tourist and the town. Imagination

Estranges it from him. He need not suffer
Or die here. It is none of his affair;
Its calm heroic vistas make no claim.
His bargains with disaster have been sealed
In another country. Here he goes untouched,
And this is alienation. Only sometimes
In certain towns he opens certain letters
Forwarded on from bitter origins,
That send him walking, sick and haunted, through
Mysterious and ordinary streets
That are no more than streets to walk and walk—
And then the tourist and the town are one.

To work and suffer is to be at home.
All else is scenery—the Rathaus fountain,
The skaters in the sunset on the lake
At Salzburg, or, emerging after snow,
The singular clear stars at Castellane.
To work and suffer is to come to know
The angles of a room, light in a square,
As convalescents know the face of one
Who has watched beside them. Yours now, every street,
The noonday swarm across the bridge, the bells
Bruising the air above the crowded roofs,
The avenue of chestnut-trees, the road
To the post-office. Once upon a time
All these for you were fiction. Now, made free,
You live among them. Your breath is on this air,
And you are theirs and of their mystery.

DOUBLE MONOLOGUE

To live illusionless, in the abandoned mine-
    shaft of doubt, and still
mime illusions for others? A puzzle
    for the maker who has thought
once too often too coldly.

Since I was more than a child
    trying on a thousand faces

I have wanted one thing: to know
    simply as I know my name
at any given moment, where I stand.

How much expense of time and skill
    which might have set itself
to angelic fabrications! All merely
    to chart one needle in the haymow?
Find yourself and you find the world?

Solemn presumption! Mighty Object
    no one but itself has missed.
What's lost, if you stay lost? Someone
    ignorantly loves you—will that serve?
Shrug that off, and presto!—

the needle drowns in the haydust.
    Think of the whole haystack—
a composition so fortuitous
    it only looks monumental.
There's always a straw twitching somewhere.

Wait out the long chance, and
    your needle too could get nudged up
to the apex of that bristling calm.
    Rusted, possibly. You might not want
to swear it was the Object, after all.

Time wears us old utopians.
    I now no longer think
"truth" is the most beautiful of words.
    Today, when I see "truthful"
written somewhere, it flares

like a white orchid in wet woods,
    rare and grief-delighting, up from the page.
Sometimes, unwittingly even,
    some of us are truthful.
In a random universe, what more

exact and starry consolation?
    Don't think I think

facts serve better than ignorant love.
   Both serve, and still
our need mocks our gear.

NEW YEAR'S EVE IN TROY

Out in the dark beyond my gates
deliberate quiet falls tonight.
Has all that fury spent itself
or simply frozen into sleep?
Enormous, motionless and blind
an image gathers itself up
as if pure cold had breathed on cold
and left this artifact behind,
from all the years of rant and spleen,
failure of champions, loss of heart,
a petrifaction of the night:
And this was what I waited for.

This is the image of a year.
Nineteen-hundred and fifty-nine
comes at me like a gift tonight
lugged by my enemies, the last
tribute or bribe or act of scorn.
This naked equine face
stares across breached wall and tower,
not really bestial nor human,
nothing to arm or rant against,
neither to be refused nor praised.
This year draws up whose belly sings
with some three hundred ruinous days.

THE MIDDLE-AGED

Their faces, safe as an interior
Of Holland tiles and Oriental carpet,
Where the fruit-bowl, always filled, stood in a light
Of placid afternoon—their voices' measure,

Their figures moving in the Sunday garden
To lay the tea outdoors or trim the borders,
Afflicted, haunted us. For to be young
Was always to live in other peoples' houses
Whose peace, if we sought it, had been made by others,
Was ours at second-hand and not for long.
The custom of the house, not ours, the sun
Fading the silver-blue Fortuny curtains,
The reminiscence of a Christmas party
Of fourteen years ago—all memory,
Signs of possession and of being possessed,
We tasted, tense with envy. They were so kind,
Would have given us anything; the bowl of fruit
Was filled for us, there was a room upstairs
We must call ours: but twenty years of living
They could not give. Nor did they ever speak
Of the coarse stain on that polished balustrade,
The crack in the study window, or the letters
Locked in a drawer and the key destroyed.
All to be understood by us, returning
Late, in our own time—how that peace was made,
Upon what terms, with how much left unsaid.

Anne Sexton

THE TRUTH THE DEAD KNOW

*for my mother, born March 1902, died March 1959
and my father, born February 1900, died June 1959*

Gone, I say, and walk from church,
refusing the stiff procession to the grave,
letting the dead ride alone in the hearse.
It is June. I am tired of being brave.

We drive to The Cape. I cultivate
myself where the sun gutters from the sky,
where the sea swings in like an iron gate
and we touch. In another country people die.

My darling, the wind falls in like stones
from the whitehearted water and when we touch
we enter touch entirely. No one's alone.
Men kill for this, or for as much.

And what of the dead? They lie without shoes
in their stone boats. They are more like stone
than the sea would be if it stopped. They refuse
to be blessed, throat, eye, and knucklebone.

THE DIVISION OF PARTS

1.

Mother, my Mary Gray,
once resident of Gloucester
and Essex County,
a photostat of your will
arrived in the mail today.
This is the division of money.
I am one third
of your daughters counting my bounty
or I am a queen alone
in the parlor still,
eating the bread and honey.
It is Good Friday.
Black birds pick at my window sill.

Your coat in my closet,
your bright stones on my hand,
the gaudy fur animals
I do not know how to use,
settle on me like a debt.
A week ago, while the hard March gales
beat on your house,
we sorted your things: obstacles
of letters, family silver,
eyeglasses and shoes.
Like some unseasoned Christmas, its scales
rigged and reset,
I bundled out with gifts I did not choose.

Now the hours of The Cross
rewind. In Boston, the devout
work their cold knees
toward that sweet martyrdom
that Christ planned. My timely loss
is too customary to note; and yet
I planned to suffer
and I cannot. It does not please
my yankee bones to watch
where the dying is done
in its ugly hours. Black birds peck
at my window glass
and Easter will take its ragged son.

The clutter of worship
that you taught me, Mary Gray,
is old. I imitate
a memory of belief
that I do not own. I trip
on your death and Jesus, *my stranger*
floats up over
my Christian home, wearing his straight
thorn tree. I have cast my lot
and am one third thief
of you. Time, that rearranger
of estates, equips
me with your garments, but not with grief.

2.

This winter when
cancer began its ugliness
I grieved with you each day
for three months
and found you in your private nook
of the medicinal palace
for New England Women
and never once
forgot how long it took.

I read to you
from *The New Yorker*, ate suppers
you wouldn't eat, fussed

with your flowers,
joked with your nurses, as if I
were the balm among lepers,
as if I could undo
a life in hours
if I never said goodbye.

But you turned old,
all your fifty-eight years sliding
like masks from your skull;
and at the end
I packed your nightgowns in suitcases,
paid the nurses, came riding
home as if I'd been told
I could pretend
people live in places.

3.

Since then I have pretended ease,
loved with the trickeries of need, but not enough
to shed my daughterhood
or sweeten him as a man.
I drink the five o'clock martinis
and poke at this dry page like a rough
goat. Fool! I fumble my lost childhood
for a mother and lounge in sad stuff
with love to catch and catch as catch can.

And Christ still waits. I have tried
to exorcise the memory of each event
and remain still, a mixed child,
heavy with cloths of you.
Sweet witch, you are my worried guide.
Such dangerous angels walk through Lent.
Their walls creak *Anne! Convert! Convert!*
My desk moves. Its cave murmurs Boo
and I am taken and beguiled.

Or wrong. For all the way I've come
I'll have to go again. Instead, I must convert
to love as reasonable
as Latin, as solid as earthenware:

an equilibrium
I never knew. And Lent will keep its hurt
for someone else. Christ knows enough
staunch guys have hitched on him in trouble,
thinking his sticks were badges to wear.

4.

Spring rusts on its skinny branch
and last summer's lawn
is soggy and brown.
Yesterday is just a number.
All of its winters avalanche
out of sight. What was, is gone.
Mother, last night I slept
in your Bonwit Teller nightgown.
Divided, you climbed into my head.
There in my jabbering dream
I heard my own angry cries
and I cursed you, *Dame*
keep out of my slumber.
My good Dame, you are dead.
And Mother, three stones
slipped from your glittering eyes.

Now it is Friday's noon
and I would still curse
you with my rhyming words
and bring you flapping back, old love,
old circus knitting, god-in-her-moon,
all fairest in my lang syne verse,
the gauzy bride among the children,
the fancy amid the absurd
and awkward, that horn for hounds
that skipper homeward, that museum
keeper of stiff starfish, that blaze
within the pilgrim woman,
a clown mender, a dove's
cheek among the stones,
my Lady of my first words,
this is the division of ways.

And now, while Christ stays
fastened to his Crucifix
so that love may praise
his sacrifice
and not the grotesque metaphor,
you come, a brave ghost, to fix
in my mind without praise
or paradise
to make me your inheritor.

THE FARMER'S WIFE

From the hodge porridge
of their country lust,
their local life in Illinois,
where all their acres look
like a sprouting broom factory,
they name just ten years now
that she has been his habit;
as again tonight he'll say
honey bunch let's go
and she will not say how there
must be more to living
than this brief bright bridge
of the raucous bed or even
the slow braille touch of him
like a heavy god grown light,
that old pantomime of love
that she wants although
it leaves her still alone,
built back again at last,
mind's apart from him, living
her own self in her own words
and hating the sweat of the house
they keep when they finally lie
each in separate dreams
and then how she watches him,
still strong in the blowzy bag

of his usual sleep while
her young years bungle past
their same marriage bed
and she wishes him cripple, or poet,
or even lonely, or sometimes,
better, my lover, dead.

FOR GOD WHILE SLEEPING

Sleeping in fever, I am unfit
to know just who you are:
hung up like a pig on exhibit,
the delicate wrists,
the beard drooling blood and vinegar;
hooked to your own weight,
jolting toward death under your nameplate.

Everyone in this crowd needs a bath.
I am dressed in rags.
The mother wears blue. You grind your teeth
and with each new breath
your jaws gape and your diaper sags.
I am not to blame
for all this. I do not know your name.

Skinny man, you are somebody's fault.
You ride on dark poles—
a wooden bird that a trader built
for some fool who felt
that he could make the flight. Now you roll
in your sleep, seasick
on your own breathing, poor old convict.

Louis Simpson

WALT WHITMAN AT BEAR MOUNTAIN

". . . life which does not give the preference to any other life,
of any previous period, which therefore prefers its own exist-
ence . . ."
                                                —Ortega y Gasset

Neither on horseback nor seated,
But like himself, squarely on two feet,
The poet of death and lilacs
Loafs by the footpath. Even the bronze looks alive
Where it is folded like cloth. And he seems friendly.

"Where is the Mississippi panorama
And the girl who played the piano?
Where are you, Walt?
The Open Road goes to the used-car lot.

"Where is the nation you promised?
These houses built of wood sustain
Colossal snows,
And the light above the street is sick to death.

"As for the people—see how they neglect you!
Only a poet pauses to read the inscription."

"I am here," he answered.
"It seems you have found me out.
Yet, did I not warn you that it was Myself
I advertised? Were my words not sufficiently plain?

"I gave no prescriptions,
And those who have taken my moods for prophecies
Mistake the matter."
Then, vastly amused— "Why do you reproach me?
I freely confess I am wholly disreputable.
Yet I am happy, because you have found me out."

A crocodile in wrinkled metal loafing . . .

Then all the realtors,
Pickpockets, salesmen, and the actors performing
Official scenarios,
Turned a deaf ear, for they had contracted
American dreams.

But the man who keeps a store on a lonely road,
And the housewife who knows she's dumb,
And the earth, are relieved.

All that grave weight of America
Cancelled! Like Greece and Rome.
The future in ruins!
The castles, the prisons, the cathedrals
Unbuilding, and roses
Blossoming from the stones that are not there . . .

The clouds are lifting from the high Sierras,
The Bay mists clearing,
And the angel in the gate, the flowering plum
Dances like Italy, imagining red.

AGAINST THE AGE

Under broad banners and barbarian
Words gather armies, as the liars wish.
And what's the aftermath? A murdered man,
A crying woman, and an empty dish.
Caesar rides cockhorse through triumphant Rome
And falls into a fit when he's at home.

Those banners fade behind that blew before,
The ships are rusting at the harbor wall,
And we will go to Normandy no more.
Clean up the streets and mop the city hall
And then go home. The war continues there
Against a vague and gathering despair.

Our minds are mutilated—*gueules cassées,*
They walk the night with hood and mask and stick,
The government won't let them out by day,
Their ugliness threatens the Republic.
Our minds are like those violated souls
That pass in faceless, threatening patrols.

Landscape and garden, village of the mind—
This is man's only state. Here he survives,
And only in a corner will he find
His happiness, if any. But our lives
Are lies of State, the slogans for today.
That wind is carrying the world away.

THE BIRD

"*Ich wünscht', ich wäre ein Vöglein,*"
Sang Heinrich, "I would fly
Across the sea . . ." so sadly
It made his mother cry.

At night he played his zither,
By day worked in the mine.
His friend was Hans; together
The boys walked by the Rhine.

"Each day we're growing older,"
Hans said, "This is no life.
I wish I were a soldier!"
And snapped his pocket-knife.

War came, and Hans was taken,
But Heinrich did not fight.
"*Ich wünscht', ich wäre ein Vöglein,*"
Sang Heinrich every night.

"Dear Heinrich," said the letter,
"I hope this finds you fine.
The war could not be better,
It's women, song and wine."

A letter came for Heinrich,
The same that he'd sent East
To Hans, his own hand-writing
Returned, and marked *Deceased*.

*

"You'll never be a beauty,"
The doctor said, "You scamp!
We'll give you special duty—
A concentration camp."

And now the truck was nearing
The place. They passed a house;
A radio was blaring
The *Wiener Blut* of Strauss.

The banks were bright with flowers,
The birds sang in the wood;
There was a fence with towers
On which armed sentries stood.

They stopped. The men dismounted;
Heinrich got down—at last!
"That chimney," said the sergeant,
"That's where the Jews are gassed."

*

Each day he sorted clothing,
Skirt, trousers, boot and shoe,
Till he was filled with loathing
For every size of Jew.

"Come in! What is it, Private?"
"Please Sir, that vacancy . . .
I wonder, could I have it?"
"Your papers! Let me see . . .

"You're steady and you're sober . . .
But have you learned to kill?"
Said Heinrich, "No, *Herr Ober-
Leutnant*, but I will!"

"The Reich can use your spirit.
Report to Unit Four.
Here is an arm-band—wear it!
Dismissed! Don't slam the door."

*

"*Ich wünscht', ich wäre ein Vöglein,*"
Sang Heinrich, "I would fly . . ."
They knew that when they heard him
The next day they would die.

They stood in silence praying
At midnight when they heard
The zither softly playing,
The singing of the Bird.

He stared into the fire,
He sipped a glass of wine.
"Ich wünscht'," his voice rose higher,
"Ich wäre ein Vöglein . . ."

A dog howled in its kennel,
He thought of Hans and cried.
The stars looked down from heaven.
That day the children died.

*

"The Russian tanks are coming!"
The wind bore from the East
A cannonade, a drumming
Of small arms that increased.

Heinrich went to Headquarters
He found the Colonel dead
With pictures of his daughters,
A pistol by his head.

He thought, his courage sinking,
"There's always the SS . . ."
He found the Major drinking
In a woman's party dress.

The prisoners were shaking
Their barracks. Heinrich heard
A sound of timber breaking,
A shout, "Where is the Bird?"

*

The Russian was completing
A seven-page report.
He wrote: "We still are beating
The woods . . ." then he stopped short.

A little bird was flitting
Outside from tree to tree.
He turned where he was sitting
And watched it thoughtfully.

He pulled himself together,
And wrote: "We've left no stone
Unturned—but not a feather!
It seems the Bird has flown.

"Description? Half a dozen
Group snapshots, badly blurred;
And which is Emma's cousin
God knows, and which the Bird!

"He could be in the Western
Or in the Eastern Zone.
I'd welcome a suggestion
If anything is known."

*

"*Ich wünscht', ich wäre ein Vöglein,*"
Sings Heinrich, "I would fly
Across the sea," so sadly
It makes his children cry.

MY FATHER IN THE NIGHT
COMMANDING NO

My father in the night commanding No
Has work to do. Smoke issues from his lips;
    He reads in silence.
The frogs are croaking and the streetlamps glow.

And then my mother winds the gramophone;
The Bride of Lammermoor begins to shriek—
    Or reads a story
About a prince, a castle and a dragon.

The moon is glittering above the hill.
I stand before the gateposts of the King—
    So runs the story—
Of Thule, at midnight when the mice are still.

And I have been in Thule! It has come true—
The journey and the danger of the world,
    All that there is
To bear and to enjoy, endure and do.

Landscapes, seascapes . . . where have I been led?
The names of cities—Paris, Venice, Rome—
    Held out their arms.
A feathered god, seductive, went ahead.

Here is my house. Under a red rose tree
A child is swinging; another gravely plays.
    They are not surprised
That I am here; they were expecting me.

And yet my father sits and reads in silence,
My mother sheds a tear, the moon is still,
    And the dark wind
Is murmuring that nothing ever happens.

Beyond his jurisdiction as I move
Do I not prove him wrong? And yet, it's true
   They will not change
There, on the stage of terror and of love.

The actors in that playhouse always sit
In fixed positions—father, mother, child
   With painted eyes.
How sad it is to be a little puppet!

Their heads are wooden. And you once pretended
To understand them! Shake them as you will,
   They cannot speak.
Do what you will, the comedy is ended.

Father, why did you work? Why did you weep,
Mother? Was the story so important?
   "Listen!" the wind
Said to the children, and they fell asleep.

TO THE WESTERN WORLD

A siren sang, and Europe turned away
From the high castle and the shepherd's crook.
Three caravels went sailing to Cathay
On the strange ocean, and the captains shook
Their banners out across the Mexique Bay.

And in our early days we did the same.
Remembering our fathers in their wreck
We crossed the sea from Palos where they came
And saw, enormous to the little deck,
A shore in silence waiting for a name.

The treasures of Cathay were never found.
In this America, this wilderness
Where the axe echoes with a lonely sound,
The generations labor to possess
And grave by grave we civilize the ground.

W. D. Snodgrass

A FLAT ONE

Old Fritz, on this rotating bed
For seven wasted months you lay
Unfit to move, shrunken, gray,
No good to yourself or anyone
But to be babied—changed and bathed and fed.
    At long last, that's all done.

Before each meal, twice every night,
We set pads on your bedsores, shut
Your catheter tube off, then brought
The second canvas-and-black-iron
Bedframe and clamped you in between them, tight,
    Scared, so we could turn

You over. We washed you, covered you,
Cut up each bite of meat you ate;
We watched your lean jaws masticate
As ravenously as your useless food
As thieves at hard labor in their chains chew
    Or insects in the wood.

Such pious sacrifice to give
You all you could demand of pain:
Receive this haddock's body, slain
For you, old tyrant; take this blood
Of a tomato, shed that you might live.
    You had that costly food.

You seem to be all finished, so
We'll plug your old recalcitrant anus
And tie up your discouraged penis
In a great, snow-white bow of gauze.

We wrap you, pin you, and cart you down below,
    Below, below, because

    Your credit has finally run out.
    On our steel table, trussed and carved,
    You'll find this world's hardworking, starved
    Teeth working in your precious skin.
The earth turns, in the end, by turn about
    And opens to take you in.

    Seven months gone down the drain; thank God
    That's through. Throw out the four-by-fours,
    Swabsticks, the thick salve for bedsores,
    Throw out the diaper pads and drug
Containers, pile the bedclothes in a wad,
    And rinse the cider jug

    Half filled with the last urine. Then
    Empty out the cotton cans,
    Autoclave the bowls and spit pans,
    Unhook the pumps and all the red
Tubes—catheter, suction, oxygen;
    Next, wash the empty bed.

    —All this Dark Age machinery
    On which we had tormented you
    To life. Last, gather up the few
    Belongings: snapshots, some odd bills,
Your mail, and half a pack of Luckies we
    Won't light you after meals.

    Old man, these seven months you've lain
    Determined—not that you would live—
    Just to not die. No one would give
    You one chance you could ever wake
From that first night, much less go well again,
    Much less go home and make

    Your living; how could you hope to find
    A place for yourself in all creation?—
    Pain was your only occupation.
    And pain that should content and will

A man to give it up, nerved you to grind
   Your clenched teeth, breathing, till

   Your skin broke down, your calves went flat,
   And your legs lost all sensation. Still,
   You took enough morphine to kill
   A strong man. Finally, nitrogen
Mustard: you could last two months after that;
   It would kill you then.

   Even then you wouldn't quit.
   Old soldier, yet you must have known
   Inside the animal had grown
   Sick of the world, made up its mind
To stop. Your mind ground on its separate
   Way, merciless and blind,

   Into these last weeks when the breath
   Would only come in fits and starts
   That puffed out your sections like the parts
   Of some enormous, damaged bug.
You waited, not for life, not for your death,
   Just for the deadening drug

   That made your life seem bearable.
   You still whispered you would not die.
   Yet in the nights I heard you cry
   Like a whipped child; in fierce old age
You whimpered, tears stood on your gun-metal
   Blue cheeks shaking with rage

   And terror. So much pain would fill
   Your room that when I left I'd pray
   That if I came back the next day
   I'd find you gone. You stayed for me—
Nailed to your own rapacious, stiff self-will.
   You've shook loose, finally.

   They'd say this was a worthwhile job
   Unless they tried it. It is mad
   To throw our good lives after bad;
   Waste time, drugs, and our minds, while strong

Men starve. How many young men did we rob
   To keep you hanging on?

   I can't think we did *you* much good.
   Well, when you died, none of us wept.
   You killed for us, and so we kept
   You; because we need to earn *our* pay.
No. We'd still have to help you try. We would
   Have killed for you today.

MEMENTOS, *i.*

Sorting out letters and piles of my old
   Cancelled checks, old clippings, and yellow note cards
That meant something once, I happened to find
   Your picture. *That* picture. I stopped there cold
Like a man raking piles of dead leaves in his yard
   Who has turned up a severed hand.

Yet, that first second, I was glad: you stand
   Just as you stood—shy, delicate, slender,
In the long gown of green lace netting and daisies
   That you wore to our first dance. The sight of you
      stunned
Us all. Our needs seemed simpler, then;
   And our ideals came easy.

Then through the war and those two long years
   Overseas, the Japanese dead in their shacks
Among dishes, dolls, and lost shoes—I carried
   This glimpse of you, there, to choke down my fear,
Prove it had been, that it might come back.
   That was before we got married.

—Before we drained out one another's force
   With lies, self-denial, unspoken regret
And the sick eyes that blame; before the divorce
   And the treachery. Say it: before we met.
Still, I put back your picture. Someday, in due course,
   I will find that it's still there.

MEMENTOS, ii.

I found them there today
in the third floor closet,
packed away
among our wedding gifts
under the thick deposit
of black coal dust that sifts
down with the months:
that long white satin gown
and the heavy lead-foil crown
that you wore once
when you were Queen of the May,
the goddess of our town.

That brilliant hour
you stood, exquisite, tall,
for the imperious Power
that drives and presses all
seed and the buried roots
to rise from the dead year.
I saw your hair,
the beauty that would fall
to the boy who won you. Today,
I wondered where,
in what dark, your wedding suit
lies packed away.

How proud I was to gain you!
No one could warn
me of the pride or of
the fear my love might stain you
that would turn your face to scorn—
of the fear you could not love
that would tease and whine and haunt you
till all that made me want you
would gall you like a crown
of flowering thorn.

My love hung like a gown
of lead that pulled you down.

I saw you there once, later—
the hair and the eyes dull,
a grayness in the face—
a woman with a daughter
alone in the old place.
Yet the desire remains:
for times when the right boys sought you;
to be courted, like a girl.
I thought of our years; thought you
had had enough of pain;
thought how much grief I'd brought you;
I wished you well again.

George Starbuck

POEMS FROM A FIRST YEAR IN BOSTON

To Jonathan Edwards, d. 1758

I. NEW YEAR: VIEW WEST OVER STORROW

Boston. Lord God, the ocean never to windward,
never the sweet snootful of death a West Coast
wind on its seven-league sea-legs winds its wing-ding
landfalling up by upheaving over you.

                              Wonders.
Streetsful of San Francisco my thirst still wanders.
Head still heavy with harvest of rot winrowed
on beaches, hands with a haul of fishes weed-wound
in jetsam of nets, throat with a rise of white-winged
wallowing sea birds, I dream that city, the once-loved
weight of those seas, and the sea-sucked girl I waylayed
through deserts who sours here, a sick wife.

                                    With land wind.
Nothing but land wind hot with steel, but lint-white
bundles of daily breath hung out over textile
towns, but the sweat sucked from mines, but white smoke-
        stacks
soaring from hospital workyards over grassplots
of pottering dotards. Life. Life, the wind whispers;
crouch to its weight: three thousand miles, three hun-
        dreds-
of-years of life rolled up in a wind, rolled backwards
onto this city's back, Jonathan Edwards.

And never the full sea wind. Lord God, what wonder
kids go skinny and pale as ale down one-way
pavements to pitch pinched pennies onto the subway's
eyes, his cast-iron eyes.

                            Jonathan Edwards,
funny old crank of Social History lectures,
firm believer in hell and witches, who knows whether
you of all witnesses wouldn't watch this wayward
city with most love?

                            Jonathan, while prim Winter
bustles with steam and batting bundling the wind-torn
birth of your death's two-hundredth year—while internes,
sober as bloody judges, clean the downtown
haul of the mercy-fleet—while rearing and sounding
through panicked traffic the sacred scows came horns-
        down
and huge with woe—while heavy-headed thousands
of bells nod off to sleep like practiced husbands
propped in high corners of their lady Boston's
white-laid and darkened room—while worst- and best-
        born,
Beacon and Charlestown, clench, giving this stubborn
year nineteen hundred fifty-eight its birth-bath
of blood, I turn to you as to a sabbath—
turn, as the drugged dawn deadens, to the solace
of your staid rage.

                            At least no wretch went soulless
when you had damned him Man. Nor would you sell us

that Freedom-to-end-Freedoms that the self-sold
crow about: Freedom from Guilt, they name it, shiftless
for any other shrift. Yachtsmen, their footloose
legatees fitting reefers into faultless
features with febrile wrists, protest: some leftist
restlessness threatens them in brittle leaflets;
some angry boy, some undiscovered artist
has put soot whiskers on their public statues.
They wring their strange left hands that every-whichways
scatter the khakied corpses onto elsewhere's
turbulent waters to save oil. The world-wise
rage at the world—

　　　　　　　　　where you, Jonathan Edwards,
wise to the same sad racket, bore some inward
wisdom, some inward rage. There and there only,
letting this city sicken me and own me,
knowing the grief there is, taking it on me,
may I hope (having not your Christ for bondsman)
to earn these hearts, their paradise, this Boston.

　　　II. OUTBREAK OF SPRING

Stirring porchpots up with green-fingered witchcraft,
insinuating cats in proper outskirts,
hag Spring in a wink blacks the prim white magic
of winter-wimpled Boston's every matesick
splinter of spinster landscape.

　　　　　　　　　Under the matchstick
march of her bridgework, melting, old lady Mystic
twitches her sequins coyly, but the calls
of her small tugs entice no geese. Canals
take freight; the roads throw up stiff hands, and the
　　　Charles
arches. Spring's ón us: a life raft wakes the waters
of Walden like a butt-slap.

　　　　　　　　　And yet she loiters.
Where is song while the lark in winter quarters
lolls? What's to solace Scollay's hashhouse floaters

and sing them to their dolls? and yet—
                                   strange musics,
migrant melodies of exotic ozarks,
twitter and throb where the bubble-throated jukebox
lurks iridescent by these lurid newsracks.
Browser leafing here, withhold your wisecracks:
tonight, in public, straight from overseas,
her garish chiaroscuro turned to please
you and her other newsstand devotees,
the quarter-lit Diana takes her ease.

So watch your pockets, cats, hang onto your hearts,
for when you've drunk her glitter till it hurts—
Curtain.

Winds frisk you to the bone.

                        Full-feasted
Spring, like an ill bird, settles to the masthead
of here and there an elm. The streets are misted.
A Boston rain, archaic and monastic,
cobbles the blacktop waters, brings mosaic
to dusty windshields; to the waking, music.

III. SURFEIT AND HOT SLEEP

Heavy on branch, on tight green knuckles heaves
the Spring. Cumulus, thick as broodhens, thieves
green from the earthy bark like worms, like leaves,
like dollars from up sleeves.

                        Outbreak of billfolds,
bellbottoms, burleycue babes. Musical billboards
join the parade. And deep in bars the railbirds
listen: "They selling something?" "Can't tell, traffic."
On corners cats bounce once or twice: "Hey frantic."
"Yeah." and they stop. Flared forward like an intake
the lips lurch on. DISASTER OUTLET, NATICK
BEHEMOTH BARGAINS MONSTER DEALS TITANIC
the soundtruck reads; but what it says is "Mine.
You're my obsession. No I can't resign

possession. I'm confessin' that you're mine
mine mine mine mine click." Da Capo. Move on.

Slowly the moon, that shifty chaperone,
performs her preconcerted wink, but none
are quite prepared. Hag Spring's had it: she's made
her bed of faggots and goes up in jade
flame like the tough old bird she is. Green, green
upon green, hips the store windows—I mean
it's summer now, that lolloping large mother,
comes puttering about some spell or other
among her brats the beasts.

                    But back streets trammel
her traipse with tracks and snood her up in metal;
she smiles from Fenway's temple walls too madly
to matter much, and though admission's free,
few worship, fewer dance, and none with glee.

What then? Her bouncing boy—that honeyed wonder's
hernia'd ruiner Love—has aged no tenderer:
portly he paces the parks, poking under
odd scraps of news his forcible reminder
what buds had best be at. They mull it over.
Rest, Mr. Edwards, not a Boston voter
calls him paisan: save your grave pocket veto;
for if they still make time in Waltham's drugstores,
if ladies see new light on Beacon's backstairs,
the fault's not Venus's, it's not the Dog Star's;
if Cupid's in, he's not the deepest prankster;
for spring and fall and all, the hapless hustler
cries her undoubted wound in rouge past picture
palaces; winter long her helter-skelter
sisters go squealing to the marriage-smelter:
the tin-pan Moon, the Moon's to blame!

                          for throngs
follow the bouncing ball and sing along,
"Moon, salivary Moon, won't you please be
around, Moon, silv'ry dollar Moon so's we
can go to town, Moon: ain' no one aroun'
to get us high, O, Dionysian Moon,

like to die . . ." Moon. Lubricious spinster. Crone.
A pox!—

       Powder with stardust. And the bride's
the broad's the broodmare's Moon at a cloud's side
poses, while slowly the light is hers. She glides,
golden, an apple of eyes, and so cold, only
heart at its heaviest can join the lonely
circle in emptiness that is her dance.
Yet she is Love, our Love, that frantic cadence.
Listen:

       O Love, Love, but I had such dreams!
The wood was thick but knived with light, and streams
from a warm spring tangled about my feet.
Behind me the single pair of hooves beat
and shaggy hands played in the splash of my heels.
"Sister!" I cried, "Diana . . ." and the squeals
of the magpie bushes, ricochet of stones
struck from his hooves like sparks, impertinence
of woodmice in the leaves, and all sound, stopped.
Far and treeless away the gray plain steeped
to blackness. I leapt far—but slow, through heavy
moonlight, so slow in a long falling the very
land seemed to cringe from me, and that blue moon
—Earth—to reach out for me—(O Love be bone,
be burning flesh, be weight and heat and breath,
bear me beneath your bodysweight of earth
to earth) I woke and dreamed I was alone.

Crying. Poor creatures tying across the torn
spilt-milk grin of a sheet their sweating knot—
while at the westward window see with what
aplomb the round haunch of the Moon hangs through,
and far back in the dark she truckles to,
stoppling her champagne giggles, what dark crew . . .

    IV. AUTUMN: PROGRESS REPORT

Becalmed in old Back Bay's dead water sulk
the square four-storey barges, hulk to hulk.

These increments, so brusquely set aside
by the busy longshore muscle of the tide,
nurse the cut glint of chandelier and cup
like geodes: here Cathay lies silted up,
where tides of trade once moved: old weather eyes
look from the mansard portholes sans surmise.
Sans tooth, sans claw, late blood-competitors
hold in the faces of inheritors
a tight precarious old man's embrace.

WHADDAYA DO FOR ACTION IN THIS PLACE?

Taxicabs scuttle by on the wet streets.
I weave with two sweet ladies out of the Ritz,
stare at the Garden pond.
                    Old pioneer,
Jonathan Edwards, did you stop off here
where marsh birds skittered, and a longboat put
its weed-grown bones to pasture at the foot
of Beacon, close on Charles Street? And see then,
already sick with glut, this hill of men?
And even there, see God? And in this marsh,
and in the wood beyond, grace of a harsh
God? And in these crabbed streets, unto the mid-
mire of them, God? Old Soul, you said you did.

It's still the same congested spit of land—
Dry Heaven's devil's-island, where the banned
gods of the blood's regime still play at court
in the stripped palatial prisons of the heart.
Poor pagan spooks, so gently spoken of
in Boston—brainwashed beggar-ghosts of love
so painfully, as if we knew such gods,
trying our neoclassical façades—

Prayer without praise. Glut in the atrium.
Jonathan, praise *is* said where the heart's drum
carries from camp to camp through jungles of
the entwined dark flesh, and the beat of love,
forcing that forest, overflows the sky.

Vegetal flesh, huge-bosomed, fills the eye
on Washington Street. Portly drummers fall,
their clotted hearts into their hands, on Wall,
unsounded and unsung. You had your grand
God at your heart; you trembled in his hand;
you magnified his universe, his voice
cupped in your ear by farthest space: "Rejoice
that you know not!" And knew, curled like God's spit
in dust, his meanest Incarnation: it
can be State Street and Monday Noon: it may
be a shape to damn: passersby might say
Satan the Tempter put that quaking on
to bend your hand toward his halt heart, alone
of all those godly—
               God what else but flout
a Kingdom we can never know, cast out
with all our flesh and blood before our birth?
What else but turn to this hard island, earth,
and dig for its downed gods? God I could laugh,
so many pray; and yet—
                I have seen half
the sculpted heads of Boston make the face
of one caged lion of a man their place
of weary battle: every day again
he must survive them all—the lettered men,
the men of means, the men of parts and shares—
and if he seeks God's peace instead of theirs,
God rest him for it: though I no more can
stomach your God than you my faith in man,
I too must worship blindly, Jonathan.

David Wagoner

THE MAN FROM THE TOP OF THE MIND

From immaculate construction to half death,
See him: the light bulb screwed into his head,
The vacuum tube of his sex, the electric eye.
What lifts his foot? What does he do for breath?

His nickel steel, oily from neck to wrist,
Glistens as though by sunlight where he stands.
Nerves bought by the inch and muscles on a wheel
Spring in the triple-jointed hooks of his hands.

As plug to socket, or flange upon a beam,
Two become one; yet what is he to us?
We cry, "Come, marry the bottom of our minds.
Grant us the strength of your impervium."

But clad in a seamless skin, he turns aside
To do the tricks ordained by his transistors—
His face impassive, his arms raised from the dead,
His switch thrown one way into animus.

Reach for him now, and he will flicker with light,
Divide preposterous numbers by unknowns,
Bump through our mazes like a genius rat,
Or trace his concentric echoes to the moon.

Then, though we beg him, "Love us, hold us fast,"
He will stalk out of focus in the air,
Make gestures in an elemental mist,
And falter there—as we will falter here

And turns in rage upon our horrible shapes—
When the automaton pretends to dream
Those nightmares, trailing shreds of his netherworld,
Who must be slaughtered backward into time.

A WARNING TO MY LOVE

Born in my mouth, the naked beast leaned out
And bit the world at random for its meat.

Then, coveting all, it ate reflected light,
Drank shape and darkness from a richer throat,

And shuffled itself apart. O love, from Thing,
It turned into a man, lofted my tongue,

And cried blue language at the enemy:
All who were washed with sweeter milk than I.

Lusting, its flesh grew backward through my own,
Possessed it, leaped, and caught another skin,

Pierced it and crowed, strutted and beat my breast,
Then sprawled and tried the half-sleep of the lost,

And lies there yet, its seven sins at my lips,
Less dead than deadly. Waiting for you, perhaps.

THE FEAST

Maimed and enormous in the air,
The bird fell down to us and died.
Its eyelids were like cleats of fire,
And fire was pouring from its side.

Beneath the forest and the ash
We stood and watched it. Beak to breast,
It floundered like a dying fish,
Beating its wings upon the dust.

What vague imbalance in our hearts
Leaned us together then? The frost

Came feathered from a sky of quartz;
Huge winter was our holy ghost.

O for light's sake, we turned to see
Waterglass forming on a stone;
A hag laughed under every tree;
The trees came slowly toppling down,

And all of the staring eyes were false.
Our jaws unhinged themselves, grew great,
And then we knelt like animals
To the body of this death, and ate.

THE EMERGENCY MAKER

"Still alive—" the message ran,
Tapped on a broken rail—
"The air is somewhere else, the shaft
Is blacker than the coal.
Lower a light and break the rock
That plugged this bloody hole."
But I, who had tossed the dynamite,
Had better things to do
Than juggle stones from here to there
Or bring the dark to day.
Go shovel yourself and hold your nose:
The diggers have to die.

"We'll starve in a week—" the radio said,
Fading in salty weather—
"We've eaten kelp and canvas shoes,
Played at father and mother,
And now we've run out of things to do
To seaweed and each other."
But I, who had drained their compass oil,
Had better fish to fry
Than those I'd caught in a wet canoe
Or over my father's knee.
Go down to the sea and drink your fill:
The lubbers have to die.

"For God's sake—" said the heliograph
High on the mountaintop—
"We're frozen quick on a narrow ledge.
If you want us down, come up.
The avalanche slopes above our heads
Like a nose over a lip."
But I, who had cut their ropes in half,
Gone tumbling on the scree,
Stuffed the crevasse with edelweiss,
And pointed the wrong way,
Said, *Pull up your boots and take the air:*
We climbers have to die.

NEWS FROM THE COURT

Summoned by love and heat and God knows what,
On the plush-filled stairway, raising his plushy feet,
(Silent, his lips as purple as his robes),
The King climbs to the Queen by candlelight.

Before his knees have knocked at the outer door,
Before his voice has lifted like a latch,
Before the ring-led fingers of the King
Have found bed-curtains flapping at a touch,

The news is trumped abroad through corridors
To the streets and sticks, earholes and buttresses,
From cup to spigot, rake to gutterstone,
And along the chancel through the bishop's nose:

Will it be prince, or princess, or still-birth?
What's the most regal answer to a bite?
How many fathoms deep is mother of pearl?
If the watchman says, "Ahem," how goes the night?

But secret in state, themselves conspirators,
Ageless Regina and the First of Shades
(The King, without the knavery of his lords,
The Queen, without lip-service from her maids)

Perform once more their ceremonious love
For love, for time, for rage they have never lost:
He riding on her field of the cloth of gold,
She striking again the history of his breast,

And the royal couple lie in a chronicle—
Despite the clucks and pennysheets in the town—
Strewn through each other like their images:
The orb, the scepter, and the whirling crown.

BIOGRAPHICAL NOTES

KINGSLEY AMIS: born in London, 1922. His four novels include *Lucky Jim* and *Take a Girl Like You*. He has published three books of verse of which the most recent is *A Case of Samples*. A critical survey of science fiction was called *New Maps of Hell*. He is teaching at Cambridge.

GENE BARO: born in New York City, 1924. His *Northwind and Other Poems* was published by Scribner's in Volume VI of *Poets of Today*. He teaches at Bennington.

PHILIP BOOTH: born in Hanover, New Hampshire, 1925. He teaches at Syracuse University and has published reviews, poems, and essays in a wide range of magazines. His first collection of poems, *Letter from a Distant Land,* was a Lamont Poetry Selection. He is most recently the author of *The Islanders*.

ARTHUR BOYARS: born in London, 1925. He attended Wadham College, Oxford, and edited *Mandrake* from 1946 to 1957. A group of his poems was published in the Fantasy Poets pamphlet series. At present Mr. Boyars is reviewing books and music for English journals and for the Third Programme.

GEORGE MACKAY BROWN: born in the Orkney Islands, 1927. A collection of his poems, *Loaves and Fishes,* was published in 1959.

JANE COOPER: born in Atlantic City, New Jersey, 1924. She has published poems in *The New Yorker, New World Writing, Poetry, Harper's, Midland,* and in *Best Poems of 1957*. She spent the winter of 1960-61 in Rome on a Guggenheim Fellowship and now teaches at Sarah Lawrence College.

HENRI COULETTE: born in Los Angeles, 1927. He has published poems in *The New Yorker, Hudson Review, Paris Review,* and *Mademoiselle,* among other magazines, is Associate Editor of *Midland,* and teaches at Los Angeles State College.

DONALD DAVIE: born in the north of England, 1922. He attended Cambridge University, and has taught at Trinity College, Dublin, the University of California at Santa Barbara, and Cambridge. His critical books include *Purity of Diction in English Verse*, and he has published three books of poems in England. In the United States, the Wesleyan University Press recently issued his *Poems: New and Selected*.

JAMES DICKEY: born in Atlanta, Georgia, 1923. He has taught at Rice University and the University of Florida, has worked in advertising, and has been awarded a Guggenheim Fellowship. *The Suspect in Poetry*, a volume of criticism, will be published soon, and a second book of poems, *Drowning with Others*, was published in 1962. His first book of verse, *Into the Stone*, was published by Scribner's in Volume VII of *Poets of Today*. He has published poems in numerous periodicals, has been awarded the Union League and Vachel Lindsay prizes given by *Poetry*, and has received a Longview Foundation award.

DONALD FINKEL: born in New York City, 1929. He has published in various periodicals and anthologies, and a book of his poems, *The Clothing's New Emperor*, was published by Scribner's in Volume VI of *Poets of Today*. He teaches at Washington University in St. Louis.

JOHN FULLER: born in England, 1937. He is the son of the poet Roy Fuller. He attended St. Paul's School and New College, Oxford, where he was graduated in 1960 and is now engaged on research into the work of John Gay. He was editor of *Oxford Poetry 1960* and *Isis*. At Oxford in 1960 he won the Newdigate Prize for English Verse. A volume of his poems, *Fairground Music*, was published in 1961.

S. S. GARDONS: born in Red Creek, Texas, 1929. Works as a gas station attendant in Fort Worth. He has published in *Hudson Review*.

THOM GUNN: born in England, 1929. He has lived in Paris, Rome, Berlin, and San Antonio, but for the last seven years has remained in or near San Francisco most of the time. He is now teaching at the University of California in Berkeley. He was graduated from Cambridge University in 1953. His third book of poems, *My Sad Captains*, appeared in 1961.

DONALD HALL: born in New Haven, Connecticut, 1928. Two volumes of his poems, *Exiles and Marriages* and *The Dark Houses*, and one volume of prose, *String Too Short to Be Saved*, have been published. He teaches at the University of Michigan.

MICHAEL HAMBURGER: born in Germany, 1924. Educated in Berlin, Edinburgh, London, and Oxford. At present he is Reader in German at the University of Reading. He has published three books of poems, a critical book called *Reason and Energy*, and several books of translations. In collaboration with Christopher Middleton, he has recently edited and translated *Modern German Poetry: 1910-1960.*

ANTHONY HECHT: born in New York City, 1923. He has published two books of poems, *A Summoning of Stones* and *The Seven Deadly Sins*, and now occupies himself with writing and teaching.

GEOFFREY HILL: born in Worcestershire, 1932. He attended Bromsgrove County High School and Keble College, Oxford. He was visiting lecturer in English at the University of Michigan in 1959-60. At present he is Lecturer in English Literature, University of Leeds. His first book of poems, *For the Unfallen*, appeared in 1959.

DAVID HOLBROOK: born in Norfolk, 1923. He was educated at the City of Norwich School and at Downing College, Cambridge. He is now tutor at Bassingbourn Village College, Cambridge. His publications include *Children's Games, English for Maturity*, and a number of anthologies. His first book of poems, *Imaginings*, was Poetry Book Society choice for spring 1961.

JOHN HOLLANDER: born in New York City, 1929. He has published *A Crackling of Thorns*, and another volume of his poems, *Movie Going*, was published in 1962. A critical study, *The Upturning of the Sky*, has also appeared, and he has edited two selections of poems. He now teaches at Yale University and acts as Editorial Associate for *Poetry* and *Partisan Review.*

ROBERT HUFF: born in Evanston, Illinois, 1924. He has published in many periodicals and a volume of his poems, *Colonel Johnson's Ride and Other Poems*, has appeared. At present he is poet in residence at the University of Delaware.

TED HUGHES: born in Yorkshire, 1930. He took his B.A. at Cambridge. He has published two books of verse, *The Hawk in the Rain* (1957) and *Lupercal* (1960). His children's verses, *Meet My Folks!*, are his most recent publication. He was a Guggenheim Fellow in 1959-60, and won both the Somerset Maugham travel award and the Hawthornden Prize in 1960. He was married to the late Sylvia Plath.

ELIZABETH JENNINGS: born in Lincolnshire, 1926. Attended Oxford University. Her first book, *Poems*, won an Arts Council prize, and her second, *A Way of Looking*, won the Somerset

Maugham award in 1956. *A Sense of the World* appeared in 1956 and *Song for a Birth or a Death* in 1961. She has also published several anthologies and some literary criticism.

DONALD JUSTICE: born in Miami, Florida, 1925. He has published *The Summer Anniversaries* and now teaches at the State University of Iowa.

X. J. KENNEDY: born in Dover, New Jersey, 1929. His book of poems, *Nude Descending a Staircase*, was the Lamont Poetry Selection for 1961. He teaches at the University of Michigan.

GALWAY KINNELL: born in Pawtucket, Rhode Island, 1927. He has published a book of poems, *What a Kingdom It Was*, and a number of translations.

CAROLYN KIZER: born in Spokane, Washington, 1925. A volume of her poems, *The Ungrateful Garden*, was published recently. She describes her present occupation as "the practice of poetry."

MELVIN WALKER LA FOLLETTE: born in Evansville, Indiana, 1930. He has contributed to various anthologies, his poems have appeared in a number of periodicals, and a book of his poems, *The Clever Body*, has been published. In 1954 he received the New Poets of the Midwest Award and he was named James Phelan Scholar in Literature, University of California, for 1956-7. He teaches English and Creative Writing at San Jose State College in California.

PHILIP LARKIN: born in Coventry, 1922. He has published two novels and two books of poems, of which the most recent is *The Less Deceived* (1955). He is librarian of the University of Hull.

LAURENCE LERNER: born in Capetown, South Africa, 1925. Attended the Universities of Capetown and Cambridge. He taught at the University College of Ghana from 1949 to 1953 and has been at the Queen's University, Belfast, since 1953. The year 1960-61 he spent in the United States, attached first to Earlham College and then to the University of Connecticut. His publications include a novel, a book of criticism, and *Domestic Interior and Other Poems* (1959).

DENISE LEVERTOV: born in London, 1923. Since 1948 she has lived in the United States. Her books are *The Double Image*, *Here and Now*, *Overland to the Islands*, *With Eyes at the Back of Our Heads*, and *The Jacob's Ladder*.

PETER LEVI, S.J.: born in Middlesex, 1931. He became a Jesuit in the autumn of 1948, and attended Oxford University for four years. For three years he was a schoolmaster in Lancashire, and at present he is reading theology. He has written two books of poems, published in 1960 and 1961.

PHILIP LEVINE: born in Detroit, Michigan, 1928. He teaches English at Fresno State College in California, and has published poems in many magazines.

JOHN LOGAN: born in Red Oak, Iowa, 1923. He has published two volumes of poetry, *Cycle for Mother Cabrini* and *Ghosts of the Heart,* as well as short stories and criticism. He teaches at the University of Notre Dame.

EDWARD LUCIE-SMITH: born in Jamaica, 1933. He attended the King's School, Canterbury, and Merton College, Oxford. He works as a copywriter in a London advertising agency, writes art criticism, and broadcasts for the BBC. He has published his first book of poems, *A Tropical Childhood.*

GEORGE MACBETH: born in the mining village of Shotts, Scotland, 1932. He was educated at King Edward II School, Sheffield, and New College, Oxford. He works as a BBC Talks producer and is responsible for "New Comment," a weekly review of the arts on the Third Programme. He has published one book of poems, *A Form of Words* (1954).

JAMES MERRILL: born in New York City, 1926. He has published two books of poems, *First Poems* and *The Country of a Thousand Years of Peace,* and a novel, *The Seraglio.*

W. S. MERWIN: born in New York City, 1927. He has published four books of poems, *A Mask for Janus, The Dancing Bears, Green with Beasts,* and *The Drunk in the Furnace,* as well as various translations.

ROBERT MEZEY: born in Philadelphia, 1935. His book of poems, *The Lovemaker,* was a Lamont Poetry Selection. He teaches at Memphis State University.

JAMES MICHIE: born near London, 1927. Is chief editor of an English publishing house. He has published one book of verse, *Possible Laughter,* and has translated the Odes of Horace. He attended Trinity College, Oxford.

CHRISTOPHER MIDDLETON: born in Truro, England, 1926. He studied modern languages at Merton College, Oxford, and has translated considerably from the German, With Michael Hamburger he edited *Modern German Poetry: 1910-1960.* Five of the Herman Moon poems have been performed in Basel and Berlin in a setting for vocal quartet by Hans Vogt, with whom

Mr. Middleton is now working on an opera. He teaches at London University, and took leave in 1961 to teach at the University of Texas. A collection of his poems, *Torse 3*, appeared in 1962.

VASSAR MILLER: born in Houston, Texas, 1924. Her books are *Adam's Footprint* and *Wage War on Silence*.

DOM MORAES: born in India, 1938. He attended Jesus College, Oxford, and won the Hawthornden Prize with *A Beginning*, his first book of poems, which appeared in 1957. *Poems* was published in 1960 and was a choice of the Poetry Book Society.

HOWARD MOSS: born in New York City, 1922. He is poetry editor of *The New Yorker*. His books of poems are *The Wound & the Weather*, *The Toy Fair*, *A Swimmer in the Air*, and *A Winter Come, a Summer Gone*. His play, *The Folding Green*, was produced by the Poets' Theatre, Cambridge, Massachusetts, and he has edited a book on Keats.

ROBERT PACK: born in New York City, 1929. He has published two volumes of poetry, *The Irony of Joy* and *A Stranger's Privilege*, as well as a book on Wallace Stevens. A volume of poetry, *Guarded by Women*, will be published in 1962. He teaches at Barnard College.

RONALD PERRY: born in Miami, Florida, 1932. At present he is working in advertising and public relations in Nassau. He has published two books of poems, *The Fire Nursery* and *The Rock Harbor*.

DONALD PETERSEN: born in Minneapolis, Minnesota, 1928. He has published poems in numerous magazines, has been on the editorial staff of *The Western Review*, and teaches in the State University of New York.

SYLVIA PLATH: born in Boston, October 27, 1932, died in England, February 11, 1963. Was married to Ted Hughes. Her book of poems, *The Colossus*, was published in England and in the United States in 1962.

DAVID RAY: born in Sapulpa, Oklahoma, 1932. He is the editor of *The Chicago Review Anthology* and has published poems in various magazines. He teaches at Cornell University.

PETER REDGROVE: born in London, 1932. He has published two volumes of poetry, *The Collector and Other Poems* and *The Nature of Cold Weather*. He has been employed as a chemist and a copywriter, and is at present teaching at Buffalo. He was educated at Queen's College, Cambridge, and was a founder of the Cambridge literary review *Delta*.

ALASTAIR REID: born in Scotland, 1926. He served in the Royal

Navy during the war and afterward spent some time in the United States, where he taught at Sarah Lawrence College. He now lives in Spain, where he is a correspondent for *The New Yorker*. Two books of his poems have been published, *To Lighten My House* and *Oddments, Inklings, Omens, Moments*. He also translates extensively from Spanish and has written a number of books for children.

ADRIENNE RICH: born in Baltimore, 1929. Her books are *A Change of World* and *The Diamond Cutters*.

ANNE SEXTON: born in Newton, Massachusetts, 1928. She was elected to The Society of Scholars at The Radcliffe Institute for Independent Study for the year 1961-62. Her first book of poems is *To Bedlam and Part Way Back*, and her poems have appeared in periodicals as well as in anthologies.

JON SILKIN: born in London, 1930. He held the Gregory Fellow-ship in Poetry at Leeds University from 1958 to 1960, and is now reading English at Leeds. He has published three books of poems, of which the most recent is *The Re-ordering of the Stones* (1961).

LOUIS SIMPSON: born in 1923, Jamaica, British West Indies. He teaches at the University of California at Berkeley. He has published short stories and criticism, as well as three books of poems: *The Arrivistes, Good News of Death*, and *A Dream of Governors*. His first novel, *Riverside Drive*, was published in 1962.

BURNS SINGER: born in New York, 1928. He was educated in Scotland and studied zoology at the University of Glasgow. His publications include *Living Silver*, an impression of the British fishing industry, *Still and All*, a book of poems, and, in collaboration with Jerzy Peterkiewicz, *Five Centuries of Polish Poetry*.

IAIN CRICHTON SMITH: born in the Outer Hebrides, 1928. He has written and published poems and short stories in Gaelic as well as in English. His second book of English poems, *Thistles and Roses*, appeared in 1961. He is a schoolteacher.

W. D. SNODGRASS: born in Wilkinsburg, Pennsylvania, 1926. He has published a book of poems, *Heart's Needle*, and his poems have appeared in a number of magazines. He teaches at Wayne State University.

GEORGE STARBUCK: born in Columbus, Ohio, 1931. He is now a Fellow of the American Academy in Rome. He has published a book of poems, *Bone Thoughts*, and has made a record for the Yale Series of Recorded Poets.

ANTHONY THWAITE: born in England, 1930. He spent part of the war in the United States. He is a features producer for the BBC and has published a book of literary criticism, two anthologies, and a book of poems called *Home Truths* (1957).

CHARLES TOMLINSON: born in Stoke-on-Trent, Staffordshire, 1927. He was educated at Queen's College, Cambridge, and the University of London. The Hand and Flower Press brought out his first pamphlet of poems, *Relations and Contraries* in 1951, and the Fantasy Press brought out *The Necklace* in 1955, but his first widespread publication was in the United States. *Seeing Is Believing* appeared in New York in 1958 and in England in 1960. Mr. Tomlinson lectures at Bristol University.

DAVID WAGONER: born in Massillon, Ohio, 1926. He has published two books of poems, *Dry Sun, Dry Wind* and *A Place to Stand*, and three novels, *The Man in the Middle, Money Money Money*, and *Rock*. He teaches at the University of Washington.

JOHN WAIN: born in Staffordshire, 1925. He graduated from Oxford University and for a time taught English at Reading, but he has been a free-lance writer since 1955. He has edited several books and has published one book of literary criticism, five novels, a book of short stories, and three books of verse. His most recent poems are included in *Weep before God* (1961).